Total Revolution

Studies in Comparative Politics

PETER H. MERKL, SERIES EDITOR

Total Revolution

A Comparative Study of
Germany under Hitler
the Soviet Union under Stalin
and
China under Mao

C. W. CASSINELLI

CLIO BOOKS
SANTA BARBARA, CALIFORNIA   OXFORD, ENGLAND

Library of Congress Cataloging in Publication Data
Cassinelli, C W
    Total revolution.
    (Studies in international and comparative politics: no. 10)
    Includes bibliographical references and index.
    1. Revolutions—history. 2. Germany—Politics and government—1933–1945. 3. Russia—Politics and government—1936–1953. 4. China—politics and government—1949–   I. Title. II. Series.
    D445.C34   301.6'333   76-10302
    ISBN-0-87436-227-X
    ISBN-0-87436-228-8 pbk.

First Printing
Composed, printed, and bound in the United States of America

American Bibliographical Center—Clio Press, Inc.
2040 Alameda Padre Serra
Santa Barbara, California

European Bibliographical Center—Clio Press
Woodside House
Hinksey Hill
Oxford OX5BE England

Contents

The antagonism between the proletariat and the bourgeoisie is a struggle of class against class, a struggle which carried to its highest expression is a total revolution.

KARL MARX

I
Introduction

1

1

Revolutionary Change

Three great social movements have shaken the normal world of the twentieth century, movements departing so far from precedent that they often have surpassed the understanding of ordinary people, yet so closely related to ordinary society that they have caught the imagination of many of its intellectuals and political activists. In Hitler's Third Reich, in Stalin's Soviet Union, and in the China of Mao Tse-tung, there have occurred political regimes that, each in its own way and at its own time and place, have attempted to transcend the past and the present and to create a new kind of society and a new type of human being. In making these attempts, they have directly and deliberately challenged the purposes and the procedures of the rest of humankind.

The cataclysmic and traumatic policies of National Socialism and Soviet and Chinese Communism have been based on two shared presuppositions: first, that total social change is possible and, second, that it can be brought about when total power is possessed by those who desire it. I have chosen the expression "total revolution" to refer to movements subscribing to these principles and acting in accordance with them.

Each of the three movements investigated in the present work is in itself a subject of great interest, and hopefully the text that follows will provide a better understanding of their specific policies and methods. The principal purpose behind the separate analyses of the three, nonetheless, is to reveal as concretely as possible the characteristics they have had in common. The most important of these characteristics, the one that underlies and accounts for the others, is a system of theoretical ideas or an "ideology." The ingredients of this ideology are not unique to

3

the study of total revolution: similar ideas have been stated more elegantly by the philosophers than by the revolutionaries and analyzed more thoroughly by the historians than they will be here. The universe of ideas, however, is not where the total revolutionary has had his devastating impact, and his ideology will be examined in this study as it has operated in the practical world of human action and interaction.

The ideology of total revolution differs sharply from the standard beliefs of common sense and the basic assumptions of natural and social science. Its central tenet is that the apparently disorderly and refractory conditions and circumstances of human life can be shaped according to plan by anyone fanatically determined to master them and to tolerate no opposition in so doing. The power of the human will can triumph over all odds, and indeed a true understanding of the physical world, of society, and of human nature itself can be had only by those who dare to exercise this power. Since this approach to reality by and large ignores the hard facts of the normal person's world, the thought of the total revolutionary can proceed deductively, and it consequently displays an extraordinary comprehensiveness and internal consistency. Much of the seeming irrationality of the revolutionary regimes under consideration results from their rejection of the inductive method of reasoning typical of the dominant culture of the twentieth century. An analysis of their ideologies must be careful not to read into them epistemological presuppositions and principles of reasoning that are not their own. Although the ideologies may appear bizarre at first acquaintance, upon reflection they can be seen to make perfect sense. Since this sense is not that of the nonrevolutionary, the policies pursued and methods adopted by totally revolutionary regimes for the most part fall outside the generalizations devised by modern social science to account for the goals and processes of normal social systems.

The ideology of total revolution contains a precise concept of what constitutes a social revolution based upon a similarly exact concept of what constitutes a society. Every society is seen as an integrated whole of ideas, institutions, and behavior, whose interdependence is such that a significant change in any single element produces a general instability that can be resolved only by commensurate changes in all the others. Society, in other words, is a thoroughly comprehensive phenomenon, embracing and supported by every aspect of human experience. A social revolution, therefore, is a complete change in institutions, social systems, principles of science and technology, standards of esthetics and morality, and presuppositions of knowledge and understanding, a process that brings into being a brand-new society, and with it a brand-new kind of human being. According to the total revolutionary, humankind throughout its history has experienced a number of such revolutionary changes from one type of society and human being to another, and his own revolution will be only the most recent in this series.

The National Socialists and the Communists derived this theory of revolution from the great social development that took place in Western Europe in the eighteenth and nineteenth centuries, the transformation that they and others have called the "bourgeois revolution." During this period, there occurred a number of changes in basic beliefs and institutions, all founded on the unprecedented propositions that physical nature was subject to human control, that all the members of society were politically equal, that governors should represent the governed and be chosen through elections, and that economic production was to be organized through "capitalism." These changes culminated in a new society—called "bourgeois" society by the revolutionaries and in the present study—that has remained the dominant form in the constitutional democracies of Western Europe and North America. The ideas and practices of the new bourgeois society were quite different from those of the society it replaced, a society called "feudalism" by the Communists, the "old regime" by many historians, and "traditional society" in the present work. According to the total revolutionary, his own revolution is to match the bourgeois revolution in scope and intensity, and the ideas and practices of his new society will be as novel and even outlandish to the bourgeois mind as were "liberty, equality, and fraternity" and the election of governmental officials to the ideology of traditional society.

The revolution of the total revolutionary, however, will differ from the bourgeois revolution, and from all other social revolutions preceding it, because it is to be brought into being "from above" rather than "from below." This means that instead of somehow developing out of the society that preceded it and being supported by sections of the old society's population, the new society of the total revolutionary will be created solely by his own actions. This belief has been a sharp departure from the normal view of what is possible in human affairs, and consequently it has contributed significantly both to the total revolutionary's colossal impact upon the twentieth century and to the failure of many nonrevolutionaries to understand what he has been doing.

Social revolutions in the past were piecemeal affairs, with specific changes occurring here and there, earlier and later, in such a disconnected way that satisfactory theories of how they originated and developed have never been devised. Even when, as during the French Revolution, the replacement of a society's old political system by a new one was rapid and reasonably complete, the revolution of the past continued until comparable changes took place in the society's ideas, attitudes, and other social systems, and these changes were usually a long time in coming. Social revolutions of the past have come "from below," originating in the old societies when innovations in technology, religious beliefs, concepts of community, or ways of doing business created inconsistencies within them. The full course of this kind of revolution was the long-term resolution of inconsistency as the other elements of the old society gradually came into line with the new element.

Hitler and the Communist leaders knew that the bourgeois revolution had originated and developed in these ways, but they intended their own revolutions to follow another course. Total revolution is to take place when a group of dedicated revolutionaries seizes control of a society's political system and then uses this power as the base for the planned transfiguration of all aspects of the society, not necessarily simultaneously and immediately, but within a generation or so. Since total revolution does not arise from the society it is to replace, it does not depend upon recently emerging social forces that create an inconsistency to provide the impetus for social change. It thus does not depend upon sources of social power outside the revolutionary movement itself, and its changes are autonomous. Total revolution has nothing resembling "popular support" from any social stratum seeking basic innovations. It is rootless, another characteristic often confusing to those who have approached it from the viewpoint of the bourgeois experience.

The ideology of the total revolutionary, although explicitly and radically departing from the systems of factual and ethical beliefs predominant in the Western world since the French and American revolutions, is nevertheless grounded in these beliefs. Each of its principal ideas is a distorted derivation of a basic principle of the science or the representative democracy integral to contemporary bourgeois society. In this sense, the total revolution of the three great regimes here studied is a child of its times, and it becomes more understandable when perceived as such. This perception, in turn, should make it easier to comprehend other, lesser revolutionary regimes of various times and places, and also to appreciate important strains of "antiestablishment" thought currently present in the Western bourgeois democracies.

The ideologies of National Socialism, Bolshevism, and Chinese Communism are not, of course, identical. Although they share the characteristics outlined above, each has its own peculiarities, and these will be brought out as each is examined in its turn. These differences, however, can best be understood when interpreted as variations on a number of standard themes, variations deriving from the particular geographical, demographic, and cultural environments within which the separate movements have operated. For an understanding of revolution in the twentieth century, the themes are more important than the variations.

The total revolutionary aspires to complete control of the society he wants to change, but his performance falls short of his aspirations. Certain facts of the domestic and international status quo prove notably stubborn, and he is obliged to temper his revolutionary drive and to come to terms with them. A number of the policies of his regime, in consequence, resemble those of bourgeois and traditional governments. This normal behavior occurs in the performance of certain routine social services, in the failure to interfere with a number of elementary human relationships, and in the utilization of some standard procedures of interstate relations. Its principal theoretical significance is that it represents a compromising of the ideology of total revolution, and thus it indicates the force of the nonrevolutionary world. The tension that arises from the conflict of the normal and the revolutionary produces inconsistencies of behavior that outsiders sometimes have misunderstood.

The constant pressure of the ordinary world on the total revolutionary's program of action is the key factor in his chances for a successful realization of his revolution. Although it is extremely difficult to judge the impact of great social movements while they are still in process, the experience thus far of the interaction between the revolutionary's ambitions and the recalcitrant environment of his experiments allows for some tentative judgment of his lasting effect. The limited available evidence suggests that, when he is not destroyed (as was Hitler) by involvement in the terribly practical business of warfare, the total revolutionary's impact is more negative than positive. Of the three regimes under consideration, only that of Stalin has demonstrated some longevity, and it appears to have been more successful in eliminating traditional and bourgeois institutions and attitudes than in replacing them with the new systems and beliefs implied by Stalinism.

The influence of the normal world is greatest upon the total revolutionary during the time he is seeking to gain the control of state power that his venture requires. His "rise to power" occurs in a context over which he has little control, in contrast to the situation after he has "seized power," and hence one of the most interesting questions about the National Socialists and the Communists concerns the nature of the social conditions that gave these movements their opportunities. Any reasonable answers to this question also will suggest answers to the questions of why the twentieth century has experienced total revolution and of whether other such revolutions are likely to occur in the future.

Each of the following studies of the Third Reich, the Soviet Union, and the People's Republic of China will be divided into four chapters covering, respectively, the ideology of the movement as expressed principally by its leader, the social conditions that prevailed when the movement captured state power and how the leader took advantage of them, the changes that the revolutionary movement made and attempted to make in its society once it had become a regime, and the methods that it invented in order to carry out its revolutionary policies.

The three instances of total revolution under consideration cannot possibly be understood in the absence of careful analyses of the ideologies of their leaders. The exceptionally well integrated systems of beliefs of Hitler, Stalin, and Mao give in a most unambiguous way the purposes and the justifications of the great efforts made by their regimes to change their societies and their people. These leaders, in addition, have almost absolutely dominated, in both ideas and actions, their respective regimes, a situation required by the difficulties of bringing about total change in an unavoidably unfavorable setting. The total revolutionary believes, correctly it will be shown, that, without the unification of ideological correctness and social power, his revolution surely will fail.

Although both Hitler and Mao have been coterminous with their revolutions, Soviet Communism has had a number of leaders. A study of total revolution, however, need be concerned with the Soviet Union only during the period when fundamental changes were being made, and this was the period of Lenin and Stalin. Since Stalin's death, many of his innovations have been retained, but, save for a brief and unsuccessful interlude under Khrushchev, they have not been extended or intensified. The ideology of revolutionary Soviet Communism is Stalinism, a set of beliefs including the elements of Leninism that account for the course of the Bolshevik Revolution while it was under Lenin's control.

The second topic, an examination of the history of the capture of state power in Germany, Russia, and China by the total revolutionaries, will concentrate on the social conditions conducive to the success of movements that, by their own reckoning, have no real popular support, and on the methods the movements used to exploit these conditions. The three countries were, in general terms, experiencing breakdowns of their political and other social systems or erosions of their formerly dominant belief systems. Similar developments have taken place at other times in the past, but these specific disintegrations resulted from the penetration of a number of scientific, rational, pragmatic, and political assumptions and practices of bourgeois culture into societies incapable of fully absorbing them. The total revolutionaries, recognizing that "the times were ripe" for postbourgeois revolutions, were able to exploit these disintegrations and take the societies in directions in which they otherwise would not have gone.

The leaders of the three revolutionary movements have seen their captures of state power as integral parts of their comprehensive drives for total change; in other words, they have drawn no sharp distinctions between what they did prior to capturing power and what they later achieved by using this power. Each leader, moreover, has had his own theory of how he was able to gain power by taking advantage of an environment that offered him no positive support. In this area of analysis, the outside observer once again must be careful not to presume that the revolutionary always has followed normal theoretical principles and utilized normal empirical concepts. Concepts such as "classes" and "masses," for example, are often deliberately unscientific in the sense that they have no correspondence to what the bourgeois mind perceives as the facts.

The third part of each study will cover what the total revolutionaries have attempted to accomplish and what they have succeeded in accomplishing once they attained state power. Although there are significant differences among the new orders they have sought, all three orders have been variations of what can be called "mass society," an egalitarian arrangement based upon an extremely comprehensive community. This goal of the new society has led them to adopt gigantic and convulsive policies—such as the Final Solution, the First Five-Year Plan, and the Great Proletarian Cultural Revolution—and the intent and results of these policies are the most important raw data of the phenomenon of total revolution. The utopian visions and odd theories of knowledge of National Socialism and the two Communisms are of little interest in themselves, for similar ideas have been proposed by many obscure and impotent scribblers. Nor does the significance of these total revolutionaries lie in their control of great social power, for both traditional and bourgeois governments also have had great power. Total revolution is remarkable because it has followed policies that have catastrophically affected the lives of hundreds of millions of people who have come under its dominance.

There has been a strong tendency for nonrevolutionaries to interpret these policies as implications of standard bourgeois ideology and thus to conclude that the total revolutionary has done only what anyone else would have done under the circumstances. This severe discounting of total revolution's break with precedent has encouraged the persistent view that Hitler, Stalin, and Mao have been "nationalists" who have sought the "development" of their countries. The present studies of the Third Reich, the Soviet Union, and the People's Republic will show that, on the contrary, these revolutionary regimes fully and explicitly rejected both of these bourgeois concepts. They discarded the bourgeois idea of the nation, a political community based upon the presumed sharing of political interest by all people interrelated by means of a capitalist-type economic system, in favor of a concept of community based on "race" or "class," a community they have seen as providing genuine "togetherness" in contrast to the specious solidarity of the communities it will replace. Similarly, the total revolutionary has understood the concept of economic development—the growth in efficiency and productivity of the system of economic production, and the ability of the system of economic distribution constantly to raise the material standards of living of the entire population—as an integral part of bourgeois culture. Hence he has rejected it in favor of a productive process that encourages or at least does not impede everyone's appreciation of his interdependence with everyone else and a distributive process that provides a decent, modest, and fixed level of material existence in order to avoid the social divisiveness he associates with "consumerism."

The three examinations of the policies of the total revolutionaries contain fairly long accounts of the ways their regimes have dealt with science, art, and history. Although few people are affected, at least in the short term, by efforts to bring about revolutionary changes in intellectual affairs, this very fact allows the revolutionaries to follow the logic of their ideologies in an unusually pure fashion in these areas of human endeavor. Also included in the sections on policy will be brief estimates of the costs in terms of human lives of the three revolutions. Although these estimates are unavoidably crude and although they indicate only one part of the price humanity has had to pay for the self-determined innovations of total revolution, they do show that it has been an extremely serious matter, both for its protagonists and for those who (usually inadvertently) have opposed it.

The fourth and final part of each study will examine the methods adopted by the regimes to put their fundamental innovations into effect. To carry out "from above" a complete transformation of society requires an enormous amount of social power, and to obtain it the total revolutionary has contrived a novel arrangement that has succeeded in collecting an unprecedented amount of such power and concentrating it in the hands of a single person. This arrangement scrupulously avoids organizing power by means of its rational allocation and regularized exercise, the utilization of expertise and hierarchy, and the fixing of authority and responsibility—practices the total revolutionary recognizes as bourgeois and refers to as "bureaucracy." In contrast to bureaucracy, total revolution maintains a fluid, nonstructured accumulation of power, kept meaningful and operative by the ability of the single person, the revolutionary "leader," to have it constantly and entirely at his discretion. Since the leader also has full control over the ideology that defines the revolution, totally revolutionary regimes manifest an unprecedented blending of means and ends, of power and policy; indeed, the exercise of the leader's power often becomes indistinguishable from the pursuit of his policy. This merging of power and policy is, in revolutionary ideology, an aspect of the famous "unity of theory and practice." Because the Stalinist period in the Soviet Union was the time when a single leader possessed the great concentration of power necessary to pursue great innovative policies, it was also the truly revolutionary period. Upon Stalin's death, his peculiar arrangement of power through quasi hierarchies probably contributed to the failure of any of his successors to create for himself a near monopoly of power comparable to Stalin's. No real revolutionary change has been possible in the Soviet Union since 1953.

People who are not revolutionaries understandably have tried to discern in the revolutionary regimes the structures and processes of their own societies. Perhaps the clearest example of this tendency is the persistent contention that the revolutionary regimes are dominated by single "parties," a view that rests upon the implicit assumption that the only way to create, preserve, and exercise power is to structure or organize it, and that ignores the revolutionary's own commitment to "movement." The search for "political support" and "political opposition" in the relationships among the regime's functionaries is another example of presuming that the total revolutionary, like everyone else, is bound to the method of adjusting specific interests in the pursuit of consensual goals.

Despite the success of the leaders of total revolution in building and using their "movements," their power still must exist in a real world not entirely of their making. They thus cannot avoid using many techniques of social control typical not only of emperors and kings but of presidents and prime ministers as well, and they cannot dispense completely with standard organizational structures. They cannot, in short, remain entirely free of bureaucracy. To concentrate on the bureaucratic aspects of revolutionary regimes, however, to search for normal methods and identifiable agencies, is to miss the dynamics of total change and to discover only very great inefficiency in the conduct of the normal social affairs that remain under even a totally revolutionary regime.

Although the total revolutionaries have intended to transcend the normal world of the twentieth century, in the long run it may defeat them. National Socialism was only a brief (although intense) episode in the history of the German people, and Communism may turn out to be not all that much more permanent. As National Socialism appears quite inadvertently to have contributed to the success of the present German Federal Republic, Stalinism and Maoism in retrospect may be seen as methods of preparing the Russians and Chinese, if not for bourgeois democracy, then for some other type of stable society quite different from the perfect communist community. No matter what the future brings, however, during his time of power the total revolutionary has made a strenuous, expensive, and even perversely heroic effort to break with the past and bring forth an antihistoric order. This effort is the subject of the present work, as the text will try to explain what three great revolutionary leaders have sought, why they have sought it, and how they expected to accomplish it.

II
Hitler's Third Reich

I go the way that Providence
dictates with the assurance
of a sleepwalker.
ADOLF HITLER

2
The Weltanschauung

From the discursive formulation of his ideas in *Mein Kampf* in 1924, through his cataclysmic racial and military policies of the 1940s, to his reflections just prior to his suicide, the political career of Adolf Hitler manifests a remarkable consistency. His ideas, as he always insisted, constituted a genuine *Weltanschauung,* and they formed the basis for his later organization of power and the uses to which he put this power. The ideas, the power, and the policies can be understood only as parts of an integrated whole—a program to create a completely new and antihistoric social order based on the revolutionary principle of race.

Hitler's world view included a theory of knowledge, a theory of the history of social change, a theory of education—all of which comprised his commitment to revolution—and a concept of what his own specific revolution was to accomplish. Despite the disjointed nature of his written and spoken words, he always believed he was both concrete and consistent, and it is not difficult to show that again he was correct. A number of his closest associates spelled out some of the implications of his world view, particularly Heinrich Himmler, who was given the practical task of creating a "new breed of man," but the rationale of the Third Reich is found principally in Hitler himself.

Hitler firmly believed that human life has an essence that can be grasped, not by the methods of bourgeois science, which only serve to rationalize bourgeois society, but by the ability to cut through the obfuscations of ideas and the complexities of reality, an ability that is basically unanalyz-

15

able but that he described as the power of the "terrible simplifier." As he said, "There are truths which are so perfectly commonplace that for this very reason the every-day world does not see them."[1] He considered himself to be one of this rare breed of simplifiers, and in addition he credited himself with an unusual capacity for consistency. He was proud of the way he followed, with "ice-cold logic," the implications of his commonplace truths, and in the process he exhibited his famous contempt for what lesser men regard as facts. He fanatically followed his premises—that the times were ripe for revolution, that he could make a revolution, and that the revolution was to be racist—and he saw this fanaticism not only as his own greatest source of strength but as the kind of power given to a man only once in a millennium.

One of these perfectly obvious truths about human history is that it is rigorously determined. In *Mein Kampf* Hitler wrote, "Man must realize that a fundamental law of necessity reigns throughout the whole realm of Nature, and that his existence is subject to the law of eternal struggle and strife," and later in his talks with Hermann Rauschning he used the phrases, "the iron law of our historical development," "the iron necessity of creating a new social order," "the march of history," "the inexorable logic of fact," and "the inner logic of events."[2]

The concept of simplification as the key to true understanding and the principle of historical determinism are by no means foreign to human experience. As the average man frequently believes that there must be a simple explanation to the mysteries of existence, so also does he often see his own life as beyond his control, especially when he reflects on his past. Lacking Hitler's ice-cold logic, however, the average man will acknowledge the existence of chance and grant that during his life he has had certain free choices. Hitler denied these possibilities, and he supported his position by a determinist theology and a behaviorist psychology.

Hitler saw history, nature, and God as virtually identical. Although the political unity of the German-speaking people was weakened by differences in religious confession, religion was no longer a determining factor in their mundane lives, and hence Hitler, unlike the Bolsheviks, did not experience religious belief as an impediment to his effort to reeducate the Germans politically. Since God was an abstraction, it was not difficult for Hitler to incorporate "God" or "Providence" into his own metaphysics. As Martin Bormann shows, this incorporation was little more than an exercise in definition: "The force of natural law . . . we call the Almighty or God. . . . The more accurately we recognize and observe the laws of nature and of life, the more we adhere to them, so much the more do we conform to the will of the Almighty."[3] Hitler identified God with the "dominion of natural laws throughout the whole universe," and he contrasted his "strong, heroic belief in God in Nature, God in our own people, in our destiny, in our blood" with the "Jewish Christ-creed with its effeminate pity-ethics."[4] He was determined, once the churches were no longer useful in maintaining wartime morale, to destroy completely the influence of Christianity, and he had no intention of replacing it with any paganism or mysticism.[5]

Hitler's identification of God with the iron laws of nature, another of his rigorous but not implausible oversimplifications, implies the rejection of all the other qualities usually attributed to the concept of God, and it is associated with his belief that the whole "idealist" or "spiritual" sphere of human life is no more than a fiction. He was a rigid "materialist" or "behaviorist,"[6] who considered the concept of a non-material human existence a dangerous myth designed to prevent man's realization of his true nature through overt and concrete action. This position was not merely a routine denial of a human soul that requires nurturing but an attack upon all abstract mental activity.

If overt human behavior is the only reality and if this reality is subject to an iron law of necessity, it may be asked why anyone should desire to act, and especially how initiative in the form of revolutionary political leadership is meaningful and even possible. Determinism and materialism for Hitler, however, did not imply a mechanistic, fatalistic human universe. He held that creative action could occur because the human will had virtually unlimited power to initiate action that could transcend the constraints of the present and issue in the unpredictable but historically necessary future. Only by means of this kind of action, moreover, could man gain true knowledge: knowing, that is, was identical with doing.

Hitler's theory of willpower amounted to the raising of the commonsense belief in the efficacy of pure determination to the status of an unqualifiable premise. From this premise he inferred that the failure to solve any problem had nothing to do with difficulties inherent in the problem but resulted solely from the incompetence or ill will of the person charged with solving it (which may explain why he has been called a paranoid). The truth, moreover, was what he wanted it to be, and thus he had an "unbelievable capacity to tell falsehoods" and a "total innocence of promises and assertions made only a moment before."[7] This belief in willpower underlies his remarkable indifference to what ordinary people accept as facts:

> We National Socialists, as the supporters of a new world-concept, must never take up our stand on the celebrated "basis of facts." . . . If we did, we would no longer be the supporters of a great new idea, but the slaves of the existing life.[8]

The preparation of young National Socialist revolutionaries, he asserted, must at all costs avoid intellectual training and concentrate upon the teaching of self-command.[9]

Since man possesses the ability to will, he is not inevitably doomed to blind conformity to the laws of nature, as are all lesser forms of life. He indeed can improve his adaptation to these laws because he can understand them, not by observation and reflection, but by active participation in the march of history. By an act of will—a uniquely human action but one as far as possible divorced from the epistemological assumption that human beings can detach themselves from their environment and thereby observe and understand it—this participation can occur, and it both contributes to the unfolding of history's grand design and provides the participant with his only true understanding of this design. Thinking, said Hitler, exists only in giving or executing orders, and only the man who acts becomes conscious of the real world.[10] Said Himmler to his SS, "There is no task that exists for its own sake." National Socialism did not subscribe to "action for the sake of action," nor to its companion, "power for the sake of power."

Hitler held that his theories of reality and knowledge provided the foundations for a "true science," in contrast both to religious dogmatism and to the so-called science of contemporary society. Unlike this latter "Liberal-Jewish" science, his own approach gave true objectivity because it could be tested by the results of its application and because it focused on the "world of living essence" instead of deliberately obscuring this essence through meaningless abstractions. His description of himself as one of that extremely rare breed who are both practical politicians and political philosophers expressed his unbounded confidence in his theory of knowledge through action; his claim to an unparalleled understanding of his period of history was identical with his claim to an unrivaled ability to control human affairs.

His well-known contempt for experts and theoreticians is an extension of this basic theory of knowledge. "I regard," he said, "everything that comes from a theoretician as null and void," and (as Rauschning put it) he treated experts as "mere hacks, as brush-cleaners and color-grinders, to use the terms of his own trade."[11] In practical affairs of apparently great complexity, such as economic and military matters, the thing to do is to act. The complexity, indeed, is not inherent in the situation but created by the experts, and it will vanish once action is taken.

Hitler's scorn of expertise was equaled by his disdain for "bureaucracy," the use of rational, hierarchical organization as a tool of administration, and he waged an "everlasting struggle" against its "idiocy."[12] Bureaucracy combined the obfuscation of the expert with a routinization and caution that completely stifled initiative. As will be shown in Chapter

5, the way the policy of the Third Reich was implemented was a precise correlate of Hitler's belief in the identity of knowing and doing.

Since history follows necessary and unchangeable laws and since these laws can be fully understood, taking appropriate action guarantees that the actor will always be "historically correct." Hitler's assertion that he represented the "wave of the future" and his belief in the "mathematical certainty" of his eventual victory both before and after 1933 (no matter how badly things were going at the moment) were consequently only logical tautologies. When he said, "I go the way that Providence dictates with the assurance of a sleepwalker," he was not manifesting fantasy, emotion, or hysteria, but expressing a truism of his world view. Tautologies and truisms, we must admit, are the simplest and most commonplace truths of all.

The National Socialist movement of convinced revolutionaries and assorted fellow travelers was held together only by the presence of Hitler, who dominated it by his unyielding willpower and perfect self-assuredness. In addition to this practical need for strong leadership, the world view of National Socialism implied that the movement, both before and after 1933, have this structure. Since an infallible understanding of human affairs is obtainable only through action and since action depends upon will, there must be a concentration of willpower that can enjoy perfect freedom of application. Because such unrestricted power can be found only in the person of a single dominant leader, the "leadership principle" *(Führerprinzip)*, the historically unprecedented autocracy of the revolutionary leader, is implied by the basic theories of infallibility and inevitability. The costs of this autocracy—the leader's ignorance of details and the subordinate's lack of initiative—are dismissed as "factual" irrelevancies.

Another of Hitler's perfectly commonplace truths about human history is that its essence is conflict and struggle and the triumph of strength over weakness. The elevation of conflict to the leading principle of social life was a natural concomitant of the theories of action and will. The concept of the human being as an activist appears to imply something "against which" he acts, physical nature, other animals, and finally other people; and willpower seems meaningful only to overcome obstacles, such as the deliberate or unconscious opposition of others. Underlying this reasoning, of course, is the theory that the only reality in human affairs is overt behavior.

With typical simplicity and ice-cold logic, Hitler saw human conflict in its crudest physical sense as the engine of all significant social change and all genuine social progress. If action is the way by which people conform to the inexorable laws of nature, then the victor in any conflict is necessarily raising humankind to a higher stage of development. As Himmler explained to the SS:

> The law of nature is just this: What is hard is good; what is vigorous is good; whatever wins through in the battle of life, physically, purposefully and spiritually, that is what is good—always taking the long view.[13]

When discussing his analysis of human history as struggle, Hitler often referred to the presumed "struggle for existence" and "survival of the fittest" among the various species of animals. This was an argument by a crude analogy, for (as he was aware) Liberal-Jewish science does not admit the division of human beings into species, but he was not especially concerned with support from this source. He believed that, in order to create his own revolution, in order to raise humankind to a new level through conflict and struggle, his movement needed a heightened sense of the grounds of its struggle; and his projection of what he called the natural struggle among animal species and the natural hostility of (for example) cats and mice into the relationships among men was designed to help create a consciousness of the need for the most intense struggle. He was not saying that some kind of Darwinism applies to human affairs, but that for the sake of human progress it should be made to apply. From this it follows that there should be some part of mankind against which the struggle can proceed, and thus occurs the National Socialist concept of the "objective enemy," the opponent of revolution who exists as a result of logic and not by virtue of anything that he has done, said, or thought. As long as Hitler's new order was to persist—he fancied a thousand years—it would depend upon an objective enemy.

This specious analogy with nature also was used to support the proposition that only the healthy survive in the endless struggle constituting human history. Health was principally a matter of physical robustness, for physical vigor and endurance are essential to the action that is the only meaningful human endeavor. Intellectual capacity was, of course, considered counterrevolutionary, and Himmler used physical examinations to screen his SS candidates as a normal modern society might use intelligence tests.

Finally, the analogy with lower species suggested that the group always takes precedence over the individual. The fact that many individual animals die without affecting the persistence of their species was used to support the argument that the "purest idealism" and the "profoundest wisdom" dictate the "subordination of the individual's interest and life to the community." Indeed, any individual who, in critical times, when the species is in danger, "tries, either actively or passively, to exclude himself from the activities of the community, must be destroyed."[14]

The absolute necessity of the solidarity of the group was a critical element in Hitler's theory of society. The past accomplishments of humankind do seem to have depended upon cooperation, and one can argue that people have progressed as they have improved their ability to work with one another. For Hitler, however, these considerations led to the inescapable conclusion that the truly human group was the perfectly solid community completely free from any aspects of individualism. His concept of *Volk* expressed this kind of community, and by the *Volksgeist* he meant the collective consciousness possessed by such a community. The perfect community is clearly the group best fitted for struggle and action, because its power is not wasted in the opposition of individual interests. The power of such a community can be used by a leader who understands the *Volksgeist*, and the results will be beyond contemporary imagination.

Although no true community has yet existed, mankind has the potential to create one and needs only the proper leadership and education. Hitler presumed, moreover, that ordinary people desired this kind of solidarity, and hence he always maintained that his policies only followed the "will and outlook of the people."[15] He probably believed that this subconscious popular longing for true community resulted from an inherent human need for both power and social equality. In any event, his vision of the new and antihistoric society was strongly influenced by his personal experience of the trenches of World War I, where (he insisted) true social equality had once briefly existed.

Hitler saw his problem as the creation of a new community of human beings possessing the power and the will to initiate an irresistible struggle and thus, according to the iron law of history, to bring humankind to a new level of development. His solution was to introduce the concept of race. As he said to Rauschning,

> I know perfectly well, just as well as all these tremendously clever intellectuals, that in the scientific sense there is no such thing as race. . . . [But] I as a politician need a conception which enables the order which has hitherto existed on historic bases to be abolished and an entirely new and anti-historic order enforced and given an intellectual base.

He compared his concept of race with that of nation:

> The "nation" is a political expedient of democracy and Liberalism. We have to get rid of this false conception and set in its place the conception of race, which has not yet been politically used up. The new order cannot be conceived in terms of the national boundaries of the peoples with an historic past, but in terms of race that transcends those boundaries.

The concept of race "disposes of the old order and makes possible new associations"; as the French Revolution used the concept of nation, so the National Socialist revolution would use the concept of race to recast the world.[16]

For Hitler, race was not a physical or biological matter, but a phenomenon of consciousness. Like a nation, a race can be based upon distinctive physical and cultural characteristics, but its essence is a sense of mutual identification among its members. Like a nation, a race exists when a number of people come to believe they have a common and distinct existence and destiny and consequently to develop racial consciousness. Although National Socialism did not invent the concept of race, Hitler's design was to create the first politically significant race in history.

If Hitler had been more of a theoretician, he no doubt would have argued that the nation was an advance over previous human associations because by bringing people together it made possible the release of great stores of energy and the accomplishment of many great things. The idea of the nation, however, had created its own contradictions. Its implication of equality among nations stunted further movement and progress, and its implication of equality among individuals led to a futile attempt to unite people of sharply differing physical and cultural traits. The concept of race, on the other hand, relied upon these latter differences, which it defined as unbridgeable, and therefore it suggested not mutual tolerance but unmitigated struggle. Race consequently involved a higher stage of consciousness, for it would introduce a new dynamism into human history; it was to be the logical successor to the "politically used-up" concept of nation.

The political task of National Socialism was to create races among mankind by a great effort in education; the ordinary person feels that the "brotherhood of man" is a myth, but this feeling must be developed into a conviction. Hitler thus sought to construct a group of people who believed in their own fundamental similarity and in their absolute difference from other people, and who were to be convinced that they were engaged in a life-and-death struggle with these outsiders.

> I set the Aryan and the Jew over against each other; and if I call one of them a human being I must call the other something else. The two are as widely separated as man and beast.[17]

Once these people form the new community based on true racial consciousness, they will be indomitable and their ability to act in conformity with the logic of history will be guaranteed. The community will be a "master race," because its triumph is inevitable. As Hitler summarized his concept of race:

. . . we shall not discuss the growth of a new upper class. We shall create
it. . . . Whoever proclaims his allegiance to *me* is, by this very proclamation
and by the *manner* in which it is made, one of the chosen.[18]

The consciousness of separateness and superiority that defined the
master race was to be obtained in part by calling attention to the most
obvious physical differences among human beings. Hitler and Himmler
believed that large size, blond hair, and blue eyes were distinctive
enough to serve as perceived indicators of racial similarities and differences. (Differences in skin pigmentation, those most suggestive of the
concept of race, were not readily available to National Socialism, although of course Hitler maintained that nonwhite people were innately
inferior.) When he said that mankind's division into races was one of the
truths so perfectly commonplace that it was usually ignored,[19] he meant
that everyone recognizes that people are aware of physical differences
but that few have realized the political potential of this awareness.

Physical characteristics, however, can be misleading. For example,
"there are plenty of Jews with blue eyes and blond hair, and not a few of
them have the appearance which strikingly supports the idea of the Ger-
manization of their kind," but, continued Hitler, their bad blood makes
this impossible.[20] Again, although Himmler believed that a man with
the proper physical characteristics was very likely to do well in the SS,
he acknowledged that possessing them was no guarantee of success.[21]
Physical particularity, in short, is something to which a revolutionary
can refer when he is trying to create a new political community, just as
the nationalist once referred to a distinctive language and the socialist
to a distinctive occupation. None of these common traits, however, is
ever sufficient to create the desired self-awareness, although Himmler,
in particular, considered physical appearances to be extremely useful.

Hitler and other National Socialists repeatedly spoke of "blood" as
uniting a race and dividing it from other races, even though the possession of Aryan blood could be determined only by reference to a person's
behavior. This manner of speaking was an effort to utilize the popular
belief in the importance of blood relationship as a means of educating
people in the new racial thinking. A more accurate concept, better
suggesting the possession of racial consciousness or the ability to achieve
it, was that of "soul," which was often substituted for "blood" as the
essence of a race. The soul, like the will, can be discovered only by
inference from overt behavior, and racial consciousness is basically an act
of will that creates an unprecedented political community. Hitler could
have argued that those who made the nation the dominant political concept of its time did not let the "facts" of social and political divisions
stand in their way.

In order to create the revolutionary racial community, Hitler "set the Aryan and the Jew over against each other." His notorious anti-Semitism was thus an integral part of his revolutionary efforts, for he believed that he could establish racial consciousness only by casting a specific group of people in the role of outsiders and that he could get his chosen people to believe in their own inherent superiority only by designating a specific group as innately inferior. The Jew became the objective enemy of the Aryan, but the two groups could be defined only in terms of their concrete interactions.

Since a race occurs only when a group of people is conscious of its own identity as a race, a Jew could not be defined in terms of his physical or cultural characteristics, and revolutionary anti-Semitism could not be a simple prejudice against people with the characteristics (whatever they may have been) associated with Jewry. Hitler was not an anti-Semite in the usual sense, which he called "cultural anti-Semitism"; his anti-Semitism was "racial," that is, he viewed the Jews as a race and intended to treat them as an inferior race. He proclaimed that they had a racial consciousness of their own, dismissing out of hand any "facts" to the contrary, and that they, too, sought world domination, but for evil purposes. He attributed to this group (which he was trying to create) every characteristic he considered counterrevolutionary: although the Jews seek to rule the world, they are without a conception of community and thus can only destroy; they are the force behind bourgeois democracy, liberalism, capitalism, international finance, socialism, communism, artistic modernism, and miscegenation. The Jews, in short, always disrupt the natural order.[22]

Hitler's decision to become a racial anti-Semite was a matter of political expediency. He needed some group to set off against the Aryans, and the cultural Jews provided the best raw material for a subrace available to him. According to his own account of his political education, the situation in the pre-1914 Austro-Hungarian Empire convinced him that a political community on national lines could not be constructed from people of such cultural diversity, and thus that political integration in Europe had to be based on a new principle. The traditional Jews from the backwaters of the empire were so different from the Viennese that he could not imagine a community that incorporated them, and he saw the modern Jews as leading the attempt to create from such impossible material a national community based upon the stultifying principle of human equality. He thus was predisposed to convert the cultural anti-Semitism prevalent enough in Central Europe into racial feeling and the cultural Jews into a subhuman species. He persisted in cultural anti-Semitism even though it probably weakened the support given him by non-Jewish Germans, he tolerated its vulgar manifestations by men like Julius Streicher (which he probably considered in bad taste), and he himself expressed it frequently and intemperately—all in order to prepare the ground for the racial anti-Semitism implied by his political theory.[23]

A racial Jew for Hitler thus was someone who was innately inferior, and the only way his inferiority could be established was to treat him as inferior, to behave toward him as if he were beyond the pale of humanity, for once he was so treated he indeed became more of a beast than a man. That which is real is only that which is done. Hence Hitler and Göring could say that a person was a Jew only if they declared he was a Jew, and Himmler could be puzzled why anyone would consider it criminal to have witnessed the death of a race that was unfit to live.

Nonetheless, the people chosen for the demonstration in racial inferiority came principally (but not exclusively) from the body of cultural Jewry. As Hitler said, "Once the principle of race has been established by the exposure of the particular case of the Jews, the rest is easy."[24] This "exposure" culminated in the Final Solution, the deliberate killing of five million or more people identifiable as cultural Jews.

Racial inferiority was significant only to the extent that it helped create racial superiority. The logical counterpart of the subrace called the "Jews" was the superrace called the "Aryans," a group that demonstrated its status as a "master race" by its triumph over first the Jews and later other inferior races. The principal raw material for this master race was the body of cultural Germans, supplemented by other northern Europeans called "Nordics" or "Germanics." All of these people, but especially the Germans proper, had to be purged of their sense of national identity and infused with racism. The most effective method for making Aryans out of Germanics was to involve them in master-race behavior, either through direct participation in the killing of cultural Jews, including their fellow nationals, or through acquiescence in this mass homicide.[25] This was a difficult task, but, said Hitler,

> All those who cut themselves off from our movement, who cling to the old order, die away and are doomed. But those who listen to the immemorial message of man, who devote themselves to our eternal movement, are called to a new humanity.[26]

For Hitler the essence of a true revolution was thorough and unceasing education. In the past, many revolutions have failed because "their leaders have not realized that the essential thing is not the assumption of power, but the education of men"; a true revolutionary movement must "continuously educate the people in the spirit . . . of its mission."[27] Although all members of the group that was to become the new community were to be educated, the process of transformation was to begin with a select minority, an elite vanguard of the revolution whose structure and practices transcend the understanding of the as yet only potentially revolutionary masses, for, said Hitler, "Understanding in its passive form will be found with the majority of mankind, which is indolent and faint-hearted. Membership requires an active mind, which is found only in a minority of mankind."[28] The SS was to be this vanguard, and Hitler's confidence in National Socialism's power to educate—to create "a new type of man, a race of rulers, a breed of viceroys"—was unbounded: "our spirit is so strong, and the power of our magnificent movement to transform souls so elemental, that men are remodeled against their will." This new model was to be a "free man," one who is "master of life and death, of human fear and superstition, who has learned to control his body, his muscles and his nerves but remains at the same time impervious to the temptations of the mind and of sciences alleged to be free." "The will to create mankind anew" would produce a "new variety of man . . . a mutation," who would bring with him a new social order and indeed a new world order.[29]

Himmler's SS men were subjected to a rigorous racial education. His first priority was to imbue them with the highest possible sense of community: "We must be honest, decent, loyal, and comradely to members of our own blood and to nobody else."[30] The watchword of the SS, *Meine Ehre heisst Treue,* indicates that loyalty *(Treue)* to the order encompasses everything that is morally meaningful *(Ehre,* "honor"). Although the SS man was to have nothing but contempt for everyone outside his order, he was subject to severe penalties for abusing any outsider for his personal benefit; for example, an SS man could be put to death for stealing the possessions of a Jew awaiting liquidation. The true revolutionary had to avoid the sins as well as the virtues of normal society, and above all he had to be selfless.

SS candidates were recruited according to a common physical appearance in order to facilitate their identification with one another and their sense of distance from outsiders. Final admission to the order, however, depended upon the individual's response to its demands and, as Himmler said, to "repeated tests both physical and mental, both of the character and the soul"; the "most severe selection procedure," he said, was the struggle for life and death itself.[31] Men thus tested might well have offspring who possessed "good blood," and so Himmler encouraged them to procreate, but he intended that a considerable proportion of future SS men would not be the sons of SS men.

The most severe test for this new variety of man came in the "struggle for life and death" against the inmates of the concentration and extermination camps. Standing guard over the "slave-like souls" in the concentration camps, said Himmler, "will be the best indoctrination on inferior beings and the inferior races." He accepted the Final Solution to the "Jewish problem" as the next stage in the education of his men, although he was well aware of how difficult it was to see "a thousand corpses lying side by side." Even before the Final Solution, he had noted how difficult it was for his men to learn to view outsiders as beyond the pale of humanity.[32] He realized, however, that his program of education had transformed the racial issue from "a negative concept based upon matter-of-fact anti-semitism" into "an organizational task for building up the SS," and thus "for the first time, the racial question . . . had become the focal point, going far beyond the negative concept underlying the natural hatred of Jews."[33] Himmler responded to the distaste and later horror involved in creating a race of subhumans by urging his men to be brave in the performance of their duty and by sympathizing with the extremely heavy burdens that this duty imposed upon them.

The Final Solution to the "Jewish problem"—that is, to the problem of how to use the Jews to maximum advantage in the creation of racial consciousness—was not necessarily the prototype of the "unheard-of education" Himmler envisioned for the postwar period.[34] Although this new program of education, no matter what its form, would undoubtedly have been strikingly inconsistent with liberal values, it might have involved reducing "non-Germanics" to an animallike existence rather than killing them outright.

According to Himmler, the SS man is not interested in daily problems but thinks in terms of centuries; he must feel the future to be part of his being.[35] As Hannah Arendt has said, the strength of such an elite order was in its "ability immediately to dissolve every statement of fact into a declaration of purpose."[36] The ideology of the SS man was not a doctrine, for the identification of understanding and action precluded any set of logically related propositions about reality. The result of this orientation was not "action for the sake of action," but action for the sake of history. The "active mind" that Hitler sought was a mind that saw the world as it willed the world, and such minds in the SS came close to dooming all who were cut off from the movement and close to making themselves into a new humanity.

Hitler was not fully consistent regarding the geographical scope of his racial new order. At times he maintained that his revolution had universal applicability; at other times, and particularly later in his career, he spoke as if his movement were to be restricted to Europe between the Atlantic Ocean and the Ural Mountains.[37] Recruitment for the SS was undertaken in every occupied country (including Poland), but little was done to organize the movement elsewhere. Hitler's final position was probably that he would establish racism in one continent, thus creating a society with such strength that other areas of the world would either be absorbed into it or perish from senility.

The National Socialist revolution could not be restricted to Germany proper nor to the area inhabited by cultural Germans because Hitler had to break physically, as well as psychologically, out of the confines of the nation-state. He also needed large numbers of people to provide the raw material for his lower races, and hence he required physical control of areas beyond those filled by the raw material for his master race. Eastern Europe was his natural field of social experimentation.

Eastern Europe had other appealing features. German prejudices against the Slavs (similar to Hitler's own) could be used to support the creation of racial differences. The chaotic political situation in the east, and especially the absence of viable national communities, provided an excellent opportunity for introducing the new principle of race. And, finally, Hitler realized that the Bolsheviks, in their part of this area, had utilized these very political weaknesses to establish a "new order" as radical as the one he himself envisioned and therefore necessarily were his implacable enemies.

"What we are building," said Hitler, "is the Germanic Reich, or simply the Reich. . . ." His accounts of its basic principles were extremely abstract: it was to be the "sovereign embodiment of the self-preservation instinct," a "mighty weapon in the service of the great eternal fight for life," and the "expression of a common will for the conservation of life."[38] His more detailed descriptions in his informal conversations were fanciful and without theoretical importance, and Himmler contemplated a few romantic arrangements, such as special living conditions and areas for his elite order, but none of these implied anything about the form of the future Reich. This form could not in strict logic be described with any precision because its features could be determined only after it had been established. Only one thing could be said about it with certainty, that it would be antihistoric.

There is in Hitler a strong emphasis on fluidity, unpredictability, and constant change: "We are motion itself, we are eternal revolution"; "There is no permanency, only eternal change"; the revolution "has no fixed aim"; and National Socialism "is never consummated."[39] A master race, moreover, must continuously prove itself in the "struggle for life and death" and natural selection depends upon "a free play of forces." This strand of Hitler's thought has suggested to some observers that he had in mind not so much a "new order" as a condition of "permanent revolution," a condition of complete unpredictability and thus total insecurity. His emphasis on fluidity, however, does not imply that he envisioned the Reich as orderless, but only that the ruling race, which would have its own principles of cohesion, must have complete freedom to experiment both with its internal nature and especially with its environment. Only thus could history be made and understood. The Reich was conceived as a permanent arrangement—no new revolutions were expected for a millennium—but in theory no one could predict just what this arrangement would be and how it would evolve.

Notes

1. *Mein Kampf* (New York: Stackpole Sons, 1939), p. 277.
2. *Mein Kampf,* p. 240; Hermann Rauschning, *The Voice of Destruction* (New York: G. P. Putnam's Sons, 1940), pp. 39, 40, 107.
3. "Relationship of National Socialism and Christianity," in *Nazi Conspiracy and Aggression* (Washington, D. C.: U. S. Government Printing Office, 1946), 6:1037–38.
4. *Hitler's Secret Conversations, 1941–1944* (New York: Farrar, Straus & Young, 1953), p. 5; Rauschning, p. 49.
5. Alan Bullock, *Hitler* (London: Odhasus Press, 1952), p. 256; Colin Cross, *Adolf Hitler* (London: Hodder & Stoughton, 1973), p. 226.
6. H. R. Trevor-Roper, Introduction to *Hitler's Secret Conversations,* p. xxviii; Bullock, p. 356.
7. Rauschning, pp. 22, 135, 200.
8. *Mein Kampf,* p. 381.
9. *Mein Kampf,* v. 2, ch. 2.
10. Rauschning, p. 224; *Hitler's Secret Conversations,* p. 184.
11. *Hitler's Secret Conversations,* p. 181; Rauschning, p. 184.
12. Albert Speer, *Inside the Third Reich* (New York: Macmillan, 1970), p. 297.
13. *Nazi Conspiracy and Aggression,* 4:565.
14. *Hitler's Secret Conversations,* pp. 116, 421; *Mein Kampf,* p. 291.
15. Norman H. Baynes, ed., *The Speeches of Adolf Hitler* (London: Oxford University Press, 1942), 1:118.
16. *The Voice of Destruction,* p. 232. Compare one of his last recorded statements (13 February 1945): "We use the term Jewish race as a matter of convenience, for in reality and from the genetic point of view there is no such thing as the Jewish race." The Jewish race is a community; it is "first and foremost an abstract race of the mind." It is not a matter of religion nor of physical characteristics. François Genoud, ed., *The Testament of Adolf Hitler* (London: Cassell, 1961), pp. 55–56.
17. *The Voice of Destruction,* p. 241.
18. *The Voice of Destruction,* p. 40.
19. *Mein Kampf,* p. 277.
20. *Hitler's Secret Conversations,* p. 384.

21. *Nazi Conspiracy and Aggression,* 4:617–18.
22. Speech of 12 April 1922, in Baynes, p. 17; Alan Bullock, "The Political Ideas of Adolf Hitler," in Maurice Baumont et al., eds., *The Third Reich* (New York: Frederick A. Praeger, 1955), p. 377; *Hitler's Secret Conversations,* p. 255.
23. That he was not a cultural anti-Semite is shown by his giving German or half-Jewish status to 340 "first-rate Jews." Hannah Arendt, *Eichmann in Jerusalem* (New York: Viking Press, 1963), p. 118.
24. *The Voice of Destruction,* p. 236.
25. See Waldemar Gurian, "Antisemitism in Modern Germany," in Koppel S. Pinson, ed., *Essays on Antisemitism* (New York: Conference on Jewish Relations, 1946), p. 258.
26. *The Voice of Destruction,* p. 246.
27. Quoted by Bullock, "The Political Ideas of Adolf Hitler," p. 373.
28. *Mein Kampf,* p. 562.
29. *Hitler's Secret Conversations,* p. 16; *The Voice of Destruction,* pp. 131, 43, 245–46, 39, 70.
30. *Nazi Conspiracy and Aggression,* 4:559.
31. *Nazi Conspiracy and Aggression,* 4:564–65, 617–18.
32. *Nazi Conspiracy and Aggression,* 4:557, 563.
33. Quoted by Hannah Arendt, *The Origins of Totalitarianism,* 2d ed. (Cleveland: World Publishing Co., 1958), p. 386.
34. *Nazi Conspiracy and Aggression,* 4:555.
35. *Nazi Conspiracy and Aggression,* 4:571, 626.
36. *The Origins of Totalitarianism,* p. 385.
37. *Mein Kampf,* p. 371; *The Voice of Destruction,* p. 253; *Hitler's Secret Conversations,* p. 397. In a statement of 13 February 1945, he credited the Japanese and Chinese with "racial pride" and said that he had never regarded them "as being inferior to ourselves." Genoud, p. 53.
38. *Hitler's Secret Conversations,* p. 327; *Mein Kampf,* p. 386.
39. *The Voice of Destruction,* pp. 175, 187, 189.

3
The Time of Struggle

Hitler's first step in constructing his Reich was to capture governmental power in Germany, potentially the strongest state on the European continent and the political entity recognized as legitimate by most of the people who were to be made into a master race. After the failure of the Munich Putsch in November 1923, Hitler insisted that National Socialism come to power in Germany by fully "legal" means. In retrospect it can be seen that "coming to power legally" meant the constitutional investiture of Hitler in the highest office available to him under the Weimar Republic, and except for his indirect reliance upon the threat of organized violence posed by the SA prior to January 1933, leading President Hindenburg and his advisers to fear civil war if Hitler were denied the chancellorship, he did what he had set out to do. After becoming chancellor, he rapidly and illegally dismantled the Weimar Republic and suppressed its supporters and others who did or might oppose him. Even then, however, he tried to retain a facade of legality in order to suggest that the Third Reich was somehow a natural successor to Weimar, and his policies of destruction and suppression met with remarkably feeble resistance.

The decision to seek power legally was not merely a response to the failure of the Putsch, and Hitler's persistence in following the legal course was not a result of his weakness. Despite many pressures from his own movement to use its considerable physical strength for a coup, he insisted that the "inner logic of events" demanded that he come to power by legal means.[1] He saw the "time of struggle"—the period prior to January 1933—as an integral part of his total revolution and the logic of

31

this struggle, consequently, as part of the larger logic of creating a new and antihistoric order.

An explanation of Hitler's capture of German state power therefore requires answers to three questions: first, why did he believe that history had decreed that he come to power according to the rules of the bourgeois-democratic Weimar Republic, thus assuring the success of this initial stage of his revolution; second, how was he able to take advantage of these rules and build a mass movement and a large electoral following; and, third, was there any connection between his perception of the situation and the reasons for his actual success?

By 1932 there were 800,000 or 900,000 Germans formally associated with the National Socialist movement, as members of the NSDAP (National Socialist German Worker's Party) proper or of one of its associated groups. They were typically self-employed artisans and tradesmen, lowest-grade civil servants including schoolteachers, white-collar employees, and later manual workers, with a strong contingent of professionals in the higher echelons. The movement had been organized prior to the demoralizing impact of the Great Depression, and it depended to a surprising degree upon the voluntary efforts of these activists, who more often than not formed local groups that were organizationally and financially self-sustaining.[2]

The best-known activists were in the paramilitary formation of the SA, the "storm troopers." The SA included the "old fighters," the so-called front generation of World War I who had never been reintegrated into society, and also a large number of people in their twenties who rejected the society of the Weimar Republic on more idealistic grounds.[3] There is no evidence that either the cynicism of the one group or the idealism of the other encompassed the Hitlerian racial new order. According to Rauschning, the SA tended to be "scornful of Hitler as a visionary and a crank" and (to the extent they were aware of it) to dismiss his racial doctrine as "Adolf's bunkum."[4]

Although the SA provided not only the physical force that gave Hitler such an advantage over his enemies and rivals but also the core of his all-important propaganda apparatus,[5] he had an equally low opinion of them. Such antisocial types could never be taught the principles of the racial community; once he had used them to gain power, he purged their leadership and ignored their aspirations.

The activists of the National Socialist movement included a high proportion of young people who were attracted by its "antiestablishment" posture. The "establishment" in this case was the bourgeois-democratic Weimar Republic, which had the reputation—carefully cultivated by the National Socialists—of being "leftist" and even socialist. National Socialist student organizations and the Hitler Youth were very popular, but they added little to Hitler's drive for power.[6] Their membership was excellent raw material for a superrace, but there is no evidence that much of it understood what Hitler had in mind for the youth of Germany.

Most of the movement's activists were people of normal views and hopes who were profoundly disturbed by what had happened to Germany and to themselves since 1914 and who saw National Socialism as a vehicle for accomplishing concrete reforms. Undoubtedly, many of them were motivated by their desire to preserve or enhance their own material wealth and social status, which they perceived as threatened by the growth of large-scale economic and governmental organization and by the "socialism" of the Weimar Republic. Yet such selfish motives do not fully account for the commitment to give Hitler active support, rather than, say, just to vote for his party. Theodore Abel's "life histories" of 600 activists indicate that most of them believed they were working to correct specific public ills, such as Germany's international humiliation, its economic misfortunes, the threat of communism, the influence of social and clerical reaction, the decay of morals, and the divisions among the German people. These pre-1933 activists may well have been anti-Semitic, but their anti-Semitism was surely no more than cultural.

The people upon whom Hitler relied during his time of struggle were ideologically concerned with Germany's regaining its rightful place in the normal international system and with the unification and regeneration of the German people. This ideology was inconsistent with Hitler's vision. Prior to 1933 he rejected the theory that the NSDAP was a model for the new social order; it was to be no more than a means to power.[7] After 1933, he turned to an entirely new group to lead the next stage of the revolution.

The impressive numbers, structure, and vigor of the NSDAP served Hitler's goal of attaining power "legally" by obtaining for him a substantial electoral following under the competitive conditions of the Weimar system. Although he fell far short of an "electoral mandate," his support at the polls was large enough to allow his legal investiture as chancellor, and the motives of the people who supported him are thus a significant part of the explanation of his ultimate success.

The NSDAP's best electoral performance prior to January 1933 occurred in the first Reichstag election of 1932, on July 31. It won 230 seats (of a total of 608) and received 13,779,000 votes, or 37.3 percent of the votes cast and (with a turnout of 84 percent) 31.3 percent of the votes that could have been cast. Although fewer than one-third of those eligible voted for Hitler on the occasion of his most successful mass appeal, few revolutionaries have done better in electoral competition.

The motives of the approximately thirteen million nonactivists who voted National Socialist cannot, of course, be determined with any precision, but some concrete evidence exists, and the historians who have examined this period are in broad agreement regarding the type of people in Hitler's electorate.

In the parliamentary election of 1928, the NSDAP received 2.6 percent of the votes cast; by 1932 Hitler had increased his vote fourteenfold. In 1928, a number of parties that appealed to what are customarily called the "lower middle classes," especially those outside the large cities, polled 27.5 percent of the popular vote, but in July 1932 they polled only 5.2 percent. The Center (Roman Catholic) Party increased its vote during this period by 1.3 percent (from 15.4 percent to 16.7 percent); the Conservatives (DNVP) lost 8.3 percent (14.2 percent to 5.9 percent); and the Socialists and Communists together lost 4.5 percent (from 40.4 percent to 35.9 percent). Much of the NSDAP's new support came from newly eligible voters and from those who had not voted prior to 1932, but massive shifts in voting also clearly occurred. The most obvious shift was to the NSDAP from the "lower-middle-class" parties,[8] which had been opposed to big business, big labor, and bureaucratic and centralized government, and strongly critical of the "divisiveness," "atheism," and "internationalism" of the Socialists and Communists.[9]

Although the National Socialists attracted voters from all social strata, the consensus of historians corresponds to the suggestion of the electoral data that the bulk of these voters were "lower-middle-class." Whether the motives of these voters were typically those of this group—whether they saw Hitler as the champion of the small businessman and small farmer, as one who favored decentralization and local autonomy, as a nationalist opposed to exacerbating economic and status divisions among Germans, and as one who held that religious issues had no place in politics—cannot be determined. It seems reasonable to see both "middle classes" and peasantry as feeling threatened by bigness,[10] and it is difficult to imagine other motives, since (as Hitler would have put it) the masses cannot be idealists. The likelihood of this modest view of National Socialism by its electors gets some support from William Sheridan Allen's study of the growth of National Socialism in the town of Thalburg in Central Germany.[11] Once the NSDAP had become respectable by gaining the support of some of the town's "best people," it became increasingly popular with the middle groups, who responded favorably to its ostensible patriotism, attitude toward religion, and respect for the values of traditional Germany, especially military values. Most importantly, the "middle classes" came to see the National Socialists as the only alternative to the Socialists, who were perceived as determined to divide Germany along "class" lines and according to religious attitudes.

It is also impossible to judge accurately the place of anti-Semitism in the electoral campaigns of the NSDAP. The most reasonable conclusion is that the average voter did not take Hitler's anti-Semitism seriously—as reported by Abel and Allen—or that it repelled him. Anti-Semitism was strongest among the general population where there were Jews in obvious positions of power—the Bavarian peasant, for example, was anti-Semitic in response to the prominence of Jewish cattle dealers—but, save for such exceptions, there were very few Jews in the countryside and small towns where the National Socialist vote was highest. The average voter was probably little influenced by Hitler's anti-Semitism, and it probably resulted in a net loss of votes for the NSDAP.[12]

The motives of the thirteen million electors of 1932 cannot be described with any confidence, but these electors seem to have been supporting quite unexceptional policies. Whatever they were doing, they no doubt were voting, in Bracher's words, against the existing state and not for the barely defined National Socialist state.[13] The question now is why their negativism and normal expectations served to aid Hitler, who was most positive in his determination to found an extraordinary new social order based upon the revolutionary principle of race.

The people who supported Hitler rejected both the "German political tradition," best represented by conservative parties such as the German National People's Party (DNVP), and the principles of representative democracy exemplified by the Weimar Republic. Their action is partly accounted for by the series of calamities experienced by the Germans from the beginning of World War I until the last days of Weimar. The familiar list of the military defeat, the harsh and humiliating terms of the Treaty of Versailles, the drastic inflation of the early 1920s, and the severe depression of the late 1920s and early 1930s—all of these were traumatic experiences prompting many Germans to despair of their present circumstances and to be tolerant of those who promoted new schemes and solutions. Yet, as Hitler himself recognized, although his fortunes were improved by hard times, this sense of despair did not fully account for the eventual triumph of the specific forces and policies of National Socialism. The traumas were, in other words, experienced by a particular people in a particular social context.

By 1914 Germany was both highly "developed" economically, possessing a highly productive and technologically sophisticated industry, and "underdeveloped" politically, with many of the forms of representative democracy but little of its spirit. The prevailing values were traditional, anti-individualistic, and autocratic; social power was in the hands of the upper status and economic groups, and the rest of the population was regularly deferential to the standards and directives of their betters. This political underdevelopment can be traced to two critical features of Germany's immediate past. The first is the relatively late political unification of the cultural Germans, who thus by 1914 had had little time to develop their national consciousness and to gain the sense of self-confidence required by bourgeois democracy. The second is the method by which the German economy was modernized, the deliberately rapid importation of advanced technology sponsored by an autocratic government and effected by very large private and governmental organizations. This operation "from above" did not challenge, as economic development had done elsewhere, the presumption that the traditional ruling group knows best. It will be recalled that even Germany's great programs of social welfare were bestowed upon the populace by its wise and benevolent rulers.[14]

World War I demonstrated the ineffectiveness of the Second Empire's autocratic political system by showing that, in modern warfare, society's "better elements" cannot take care of the average person, who must be called upon to defend himself. The "better elements" in Germany, moreover, used the emergency of war to justify the maintenance of their privileged positions and in so doing they "mortgaged the future by making it dependent upon victory."[15] When they were discredited by defeat, the larger part of the German people had been modernized enough by their economic environment to expect some kind of "popular" government, but there were no indigenous varieties with which anyone had had any experience. The establishment of the Weimar Republic—another operation "from above"—was not opposed, but it singularly failed to elicit any enthusiasm from the general citizenry.

During the life of the Weimar Republic, the Germans had a strong tendency to blame the government for everything that they were unhappy about, including things, such as the loss of the war, that occurred prior to the Republic's birth. Their unfamiliarity with their new government undoubtedly encouraged this focusing of blame, but the question remains why a democratic system, even an unfamiliar one, was rejected in favor of the completely unknown autocratic system that Hitler was promising.

Despite Hitler's repudiation of the values of the former rulers of Germany, his support has often been attributed to the German people's mistrust of democracy and desire for a strong government that would take care of them. This description, however, does not fit Hitler's following. His electors were small businessmen, white-collar workers, independent farmers, and the like; these people surely did not consider themselves complete political incompetents. The activists in the National Socialist movement were political volunteers whose enthusiasm has often been noted but whose political sophistication has usually been ignored. Only people who considered mass political participation possible, reasonable, and desirable, and who possessed the modern skills of organization, could have initiated and sustained such a mass movement. It seems reasonable to conclude that Hitler's supporters were not "antidemocratic" but only "not willing to support forever a regime that seemed incapable of solving economic crises or of restoring Germany to a pre-eminent position in the international realm."[16] Disaffection was not with the idea of popular government but with the specific institutions of the Weimar Republic, especially with the confusion and lack of responsibility associated with its fragmented party system and cabinet instability. The rejection was not of popular participation but of that type of participation embodied in the representative or parliamentary government of the Weimar Republic.

The need to create a true community among the German people, to merge social and economic and religious differences into a new *Volksgemeinschaft,* was a constant and emphatic theme of Hitler's propaganda during the time of struggle. He created this concept of community by deliberately combining the two ideals of nationalism and socialism, ideals for which (as he said) men "were ready if necessary even to die."[17] The patriotic middle economic and status sectors responded to Hitler's nationalist line because its "socialist" aspect emphasized its egalitarianism, but they tended to see the conservatives such as the DNVP, who also claimed to represent German tradition, as aristocrats who denied the political equality of the German people.[18] The Communists obviously failed the test of national unity—indeed they were a threat to the German community—and the Socialists were seen as a similarly divisive force. It is extremely improbable that any large numbers of Hitler's supporters were anticipating anything resembling a "tribal community of blood and soil." Most of them saw in the *Volksgemeinschaft* a promise of a new community characterized by the consensus of a politically homogeneous people. Electors and activists alike perceived the NSDAP as seeking a unified German nation of upper, middle, and working strata.

The second important theme in Hitler's pre-1933 propaganda was his unremitting attack upon the Weimar Republic and his promise to institute a completely new order that included a political system based on his own dictatorship. Since the middle groups obviously could not have seen the new order as an antihistoric racial society, the message they received was that the Weimar government, which after all was to blame for most of their specific misfortunes, was to be dismantled. Because neither the Second Empire nor the Republic had resolved the problem of bringing the Germans together in a single, self-confident national community, many people were willing to experiment with a new form of government, a form they were assured would be "popular government." They were modern and democratic in their commitment to a community of political equals, but most naive in their failure to realize (as Hitler did) that a new form of government implied a new form of society, that political equality as they understood it was incompatible with the autocracy that National Socialism was promising. Had the Weimar Republic been a little luckier and a little more clever, the German "middle classes" might have had time to acquire the political sophistication that would have made the Third Reich impossible.

Under the extremely unsettled conditions of the Weimar Republic, the appeal of strong leadership and discipline was very great. Although the NSDAP was vague about what it was going to do, it made perfectly clear that it could and would act vigorously. Its propaganda, demonstrations, and campaigning gave the impression of an indomitable activism and an unlimited optimism. Many citizens saw Hitler as a strong man, another Bismarck, who had come in a time of troubles. To accept his calls for duty and obedience and against happiness and individual profit was not necessarily more "antidemocratic" than responding to similar calls in established democracies during emergencies such as war. This appreciation of strength and order was not the sheeplike response of premodern man, nor the desire of millions of sadomasochists to punish themselves, nor the urge of mass man to destroy hypocritical reality. It was a naive belief that there existed a political shortcut to a German national community and thus to domestic self-confidence and international respect.

"At critical periods in history," said Hitler, "all the tinsel falls away and the great rhythm of life alone rules the hour."[19] Needless to say, he believed that the period following World War I was critical and tinsel-free and thus ripe for revolution. His own revolution was to culminate in the establishment of a racial new order, but it was to begin with his formation of a mass movement and his capture of German state power. He saw his revolutionary response to the possibilities of the times as a continuous whole: the "inner logic of events" demanded that he follow the course to governmental power described above, just as it demanded that he found the SS and conquer Eastern Europe. He said that "our struggle against Versailles" (a nationalist enterprise) and "our struggle for a new world order" (a racist enterprise) "are one and the same."[20]

Hitler's early decision to come to power "legally" may have been influenced by the failure of the Munich Putsch, but it was far from a rationalization of practical necessity. He had understood the weakness of national consciousness as a principle of political order in continental Europe and he had recognized the fragility of the German national community; he concluded that these conditions would allow him to substitute racial consciousness for national consciousness and to transform the Germans into a master race. In order to effect these changes, he had to proceed according to the rules of a political system he despised and publicly condemned, because only thus could he prove that bourgeois democracy had destroyed itself, that the German people had utilized its mechanisms—the election of deputies and the parliamentary confirmation of governments—to commit themselves to his own revolutionary program.

In choosing the legal way to power, Hitler forced himself to seek the support of the Weimar electorate. Although competitive elections were not among his favorite political devices, he considered himself a great mobilizer of the "masses," a man who could rule them because he always took their vital laws into consideration.[21] Although the average man did not have the "active mind" required of a true revolutionary, he could be educated by a revolutionary vanguard. The electoral system of the Weimar Republic provided Hitler with a convenient forum for his preliminary effort at popular education, and he designed his electoral propaganda to present certain elements of his revolutionary belief system in an approximate, transitional form. The true racial community was presented as a *Volksgemeinschaft* for all social strata of Germans; the creation of a new, antihistoric order, as the replacement of the Weimar Republic and the regaining of Germany's "rightful place in the world"; the rejection of universal human equality, as "nationalism"; the destruction of traditional German society, as "socialism"; and the dependence of revolution upon the will of one man, as the need for discipline and firm leadership. All this propaganda gained votes and membership for the NSDAP.

On the other hand, anti-Semitism, the core of Hitler's program of education, repelled many people who might otherwise have voted for him. Nonetheless, although he badly needed to increase his electorate,[22] he pursued it, because cultural anti-Semitism, including the attribution of all the world's ills to a universal Jewish conspiracy, was the first essential step in his vast program to educate men in the spirit of his revolutionary mission. Anti-Semitism had the positive effect of moving people toward thinking in racial terms and the negative effect of undermining the bourgeois concept of the rights of man. Even though many of his supporters objected to his anti-Semitism, his persistent expression of it meant that when, for other reasons, they joined his movement or voted for his candidates, they were indirectly approving his position on the "Jewish question." Indeed, every citizen of the Weimar Republic, by accepting the "legality" of Hitler's capture of the government, associated himself with all of National Socialism's policies. Only by following the "legal" road to power could Hitler have accomplished such education.

Hitler did not believe that the German people supported his specific plan for revolution or supported him as the initiator of a brand-new order they did not understand (or care to understand); he did not, moreover, attribute support of either kind to the 30 percent of the eligible voters who backed him in 1932, nor even to the main body of the activists in his movement. He would have objected, however, to the charge that he was tricking these people by seeking and obtaining their support under false pretenses. Since the average man was incapable of revolutionary consciousness, it would have been nonsense to expect him to appreciate a sophisticated revolutionary world view. On the other hand, the average man had revolutionary potential, and thus he could respond to properly phrased appeals adjusted to his level of comprehension and containing the first elements in an educational program that logically culminated in full-scale racism. Put briefly and bluntly, Hitler's theory of his rise to power contained two propositions: first, that the German people were unconsciously ready for a revolutionary change and he alone had the ability to take advantage of this situation; and, second, that, despite liberal bourgeois propaganda to the contrary, the average man was at heart a racist and needed only Hitler's special program of gradual education in order to become conscious of and confirmed in his racism.

To become chancellor of the Weimar Republic, Hitler followed a specific plan based on a general theory of social change, and he attributed the plan's success to the theory's correctness. Whether he really did achieve power according to his plan, and, if he did, whether his triumph can actually be accounted for by his theory, must now be determined.

The literature on National Socialism contains three general types of explanation of the movement's prepower success relevant to the present problem. The first maintains that Hitler was the natural outgrowth of the German past, that he brought the mainstreams of German thought and the German traditions of political and social life to their logical conclusions. This explanation, in addition to completely discounting all evidence of liberal and humanistic ideas and of democratic practices and commitments in German history, makes the fatal error of interpreting

National Socialism, not as the totally revolutionary force that it was, but as an autocratic movement concerned principally with maintaining order and discipline. This type of theory, in short, has carefully chosen its evidence in order to find causes for something that did not exist.

Another way in which National Socialism has been linked with the German past does not assume that the Third Reich was an autocracy devoted to stability; it maintains only that the people who supported Hitler before 1933 did so because they believed he would establish an orderly society in which their aspirations for economic and social security would be satisfied. This argument belongs to the second general type of explanation of Hitler's pre-1933 success, a type that completely divorces his ultimate goals from the reasons why he obtained his popular support. His triumph becomes a masterly exercise in hoodwinking the German people, and it came about by virtue of his consummate skill as a propagandist, organizer, and fisherman in the troubled waters of military defeat, national humiliation, and economic misery.

This second type of explanation has some merit in its emphasis on the fact that those people who supported Hitler were not motivated by a desire to bring about a new society based on the principle of race. It must be remembered, however, that they supported him because they sought the social equality and the political community dear to the middle sectors, not because they perceived him as a restorer or guarantor of the so-called German political tradition.

The argument that the Germans did not, in effect, know what they were doing implies that Hitler also was mistaken in his analysis of the political situation and in his calculated response to it. Since it does not appear reasonable to account for great social events, and especially great directed political movements, solely in terms of chance and accident, the third general type of explanation of Hitler's capture of power—namely, that the German people consciously and deliberately chose revolution—gains some credibility.

Theories of this third type are concerned with the presumed general phenomenon of the "revolt of the masses" or the "revolution of nihilism." It is argued that in the German case Hitler's activists and possibly also his voters, although they did not fully understand the concept of the racial new order, were aware that it implied the complete destruction of all existing social forms, ideals, and conventions. This nihilism, the argument continues, had been caused by the disintegrative forces of urban industrial life, an erosion of respect for authority accompanying political democratization, an arrogance attendant upon the weakening of religion, and a revulsion against the hypocrisy of the bourgeois principle that the public interest is served by the pursuit of individual interest.[23] The German people, according to this account, were suffering from the presumed illnesses of modernity, rather than (as above) from the repressions of an ironbound tradition.

The strength of this type of theory is that it can rely upon the intense and widespread rejection of both the Weimar Republic and the traditionalism associated with the Second Empire, and it also has some resemblance to Hitler's own contention that the German people were "ready for revolution." Even if it is assumed, however, that those who supported National Socialism wanted completely to destroy all aspects of normal society—and there is no evidence whatever that any great numbers had this desire—the theory in question does not explain why they exhibited this nihilistic urge. The German environment was not of the type that produces the rootlessness and anomie the theory presupposes.

Germany's problem was not that it was too modern, but that it was not modern enough. The Germans were groping for a bourgeois national community and a political system to represent this community; they were not suffering from overexposure to advanced democratic, capitalist society. And Hitler, it will be recalled, did not say that the German people were without normal aspirations, but only that revolutionary leadership could deflect them from these aspirations.

In accounting for Hitler's successful struggle for German state power, it must always be remembered that the German people did not rise as one and unanimously demand that he govern them according to the principles of National Socialism. In the second Reichstag election of 1932 (in November), slightly more than 4 percent of all people casting ballots deserted the NSDAP, and there was a small movement back to the parties of the Weimar Republic. At his best showing, in the July election of 1932, fewer than one-third of Germany's citizens gave Hitler the small amount of commitment involved in voting for his candidates. Nonetheless, he did achieve power more or less legally and by means of "mobilizing" a substantial segment of the population.

Only a very few people supported Hitler in the knowledge that he intended to destroy all aspects of normal society and to initiate the racial new order, and he was perfectly aware of this situation. His belief in his ability to take into account the vital laws of the masses did not imply that the "masses" comprehended everything he was trying to tell them. His claim, which proved correct, was only that at a particular point in time a large number of people were unconsciously willing to support a complete social revolution, but in his theory of his rise to power he did not state precisely at what time they possessed this inclination. According to the preceding analysis of German social and political conditions in the post–World War I period, the "tinsel fell away" at the critical time when

Germany was in the midst of a transition from one set of beliefs and institutions to another. The collapse of the Second Empire and the Germans' temporary inability to create a national community and to devise a popular government left them in a kind of social limbo; the specific disasters that Germany suffered at this time enhanced and prolonged but did not create the revolutionary potential of the situation. Implicit in Hitler's theory is the proposition that, during such a period, a significant number of people can be persuaded to commit themselves to innovations that exceed their expectations and probably even their imaginations.

This theory of popular revolutionary potential has a corollary to the effect that such potential can be used only by a man who recognizes the arrival of a critical period and who knows how to respond to it. In concrete terms, Hitler's triumph depended upon certain personal qualities he alone possessed, a statement supported by almost all outside observers, by everyone who participated in the movement before 1933, and by Hitler himself. Although other leading National Socialists may have realized that the times were ripe for revolution, their revolution could not have been consummated without Hitler's unique persistence and power of will.

The second part of Hitler's own theory of his rise to power, that the average man was unconsciously racist and could be made overtly racist by the proper education, is concerned less with why people supported him than with why his anti-Semitic propaganda (and later his anti-Semitic policies) did not lead people to reject him. It thus is less relevant to his success in his "legal" path to power than to his accomplishments once he no longer depended upon the bourgeois-democratic device of the free expression of popular opinion. In any event, clearly no one but Hitler would have persisted in anti-Semitism during the Weimar period when conventional wisdom strongly suggested that it was impeding the desperate effort of the NSDAP to increase its votes. No one but Hitler, moreover, had the foresight to conduct racist education in the context and according to the rules of bourgeois society.

The Germans had lost their old way of life; although they had envisioned a new one, they had not yet discovered how to implement it. Those who responded to this basic uncertainty by supporting Hitler were not opting for total revolution, but a total revolutionary was able to take advantage of their inability to see the contradiction between their political goals and his political methods. Hitler's theory of his own rise to power did not apply to as many people as he claimed it did, but with respect to his critical minority it was essentially correct.

Notes

1. Hermann Rauschning, *The Voice of Destruction* (New York: G. P. Putnam's Sons, 1940), p. 107.
2. Theodore Abel, *The Nazi Movement* (New York: Atherton Press, 1966), ch. 4.
3. Karl Dietrich Bracher, *The German Dictatorship* (New York: Frederick A. Praeger, 1970), p. 159.
4. Bracher, pp. 72, 234, 235.
5. Geoffrey Pridham, *Hitler's Rise to Power* (New York: Harper & Row, 1973), p. 203.
6. Pridham, pp. 206, 207.
7. Dietrich Orlow, *The History of the Nazi Party, 1919-1933* (Pittsburgh: University of Pittsburgh Press, 1969), p. 296.
8. Pridham, p. 196; Bracher, p. 183; see S. M. Lipset, *Political Man* (Garden City, N. Y.: Doubleday, 1960), pp. 140-52.
9. Abel, p. 135; Milton Mayer, *They Thought They Were Free* (Chicago: University of Chicago Press, 1955), pp. 101-2.
10. Bracher, p. 180.
11. *The Nazi Seizure of Power: The Experience of a Single German Town, 1930-1935* (Chicago: Quadrangle Books, 1965).
12. Pridham, pp. 237-39, 242.
13. Pridham, p. 159.
14. Ralf Dahrendorf, *Society and Democracy in Germany* (Garden City, N. Y.: Doubleday, 1967), especially ch. 3, entitled "Imperial Germany and the Industrial Revolution," following in title and argument Thorstein Veblen's remarkable work of 1915.
15. James H. McRandle, *The Track of the Wolf* (Evanston, Ill.: Northwestern University Press, 1965), p. 32.
16. McRandle, p. 39; see Dahrendorf, pp. 42-43.
17. Speech of 2 December 1938, in Norman H. Baynes, ed., *The Speeches of Adolf Hitler* (London: Oxford University Press, 1942), 1:91.
18. Abel, p. 129; Bracher, p. 182.
19. Rauschning, p. 280.
20. Rauschning, p. 70.
21. Rauschning, p. 211.
22. Orlow, p. 283.
23. The most forceful expression of this type of argument has been given by Hannah Arendt, *The Origins of Totalitarianism,* 2d ed. (Cleveland: World Publishing Co., 1958).

4
Toward the Racial New Order

As soon as Hitler became chancellor of the Weimar Republic, he began to institute the policies and to devise the mechanisms of power that were to characterize the Third Reich throughout its brief but highly intense existence. The creation of the racial new order required the destruction of existing social structures and values, the construction of the environment required by the future community of the master race, the education of people for membership in this community principally but not exclusively by dealing with the "Jewish problem," and the acquisition of both the area and the population necessary for his grand revolutionary experiment. As he said, he set out "to create mankind anew." The job was enormous and the stakes were high:

> If I win, I shall be one of the greatest men in history. If I fail, I shall be condemned, despised, and damned.[1]

He failed because his idealistic revolutionary commitment implied policies that undermined his conduct of a prolonged war, one of the most practical and mundane of human occupations.

Before the Third Reich and its *Führer* disintegrated, however, a number of drastic changes were effected in the style of life and in the expectations of tens of millions of Germans and other Europeans. The positive part of Hitler's program, the creation of a community among those "Germanics" destined to become the master race, has had an apparently lasting influence, but one that ironically has strengthened the tendencies toward bourgeois democracy, the precise form of society he wished to destroy. The ultimate results of the negative part of his pro-

45

gram, the creation of the sentiment of racism that relied primarily upon the treatment of the "Jewish question," are still in doubt. His efforts in the area of culture were quite futile, and his indifference to economics precluded any innovations in this field. Finally, his attempt to restructure the European political system served principally to bring Soviet power well into Western Europe.

Revolutions cannot be made without a certain expenditure of human life. Hitler repeatedly referred to his "bloodless revolution," but by this phrase he meant only the period of his struggle to capture German state power. The "legal" way to power strongly inhibited violence, although the street brawls and other occupations of the SA resulted, toward the end of the Weimar Republic, in several hundred deaths per year. After January 1933, Hitler physically removed the Communists and certain Socialists and liberal Democrats, and the lower orders of the NSDAP enjoyed some months of molesting their real and fancied enemies. This immediate posttakeover period appears to have contained deaths also into the hundreds.

Hitler did not favor the method of "purging" his revolutionary apparatus. Only twice, in the "Röhm purge" of 1934 and in the reaction to the attempt on his life in 1944, were the lives of functionaries taken, perhaps 150 in 1934 and several thousand in 1944. The concentration camps for those accused of political opposition or of being generally antisocial—that is, for counterrevolutionaries—contained about 27,000 people in 1933 and about 25,000 in 1939.[2] Once in power, Hitler had few conscious opponents to destroy; his revolutionary zeal was turned toward those who opposed him merely by their existence.

The great loss of life caused by National Socialism occurred after 1939. World War II in Europe was indeed "Hitler's war," and all its casualties can be attributed to his foreign policy. The military and civilian casualties were about six million for Germany and Austria, twenty million for the Soviet Union, and about ten million for all other European countries, for a total of about thirty-six million. Another wartime measure, the so-called Final Solution to the Jewish problem, took the lives of from five to six million Jews and other people of "inferior races."

For a revolutionary regime, the Third Reich used very little violence against non-Jewish Germans. About 60,000 patients in mental hospitals and an undetermined number of the senile were killed, but the contemplated program to weed out all the physically unfit (discussed below) was never initiated. The creation of "terror," an awareness that one is constantly faced with the possibility of severe and unpredictable physical or mental pain, was not a principal technique of National Socialism. The

SS was feared by most people, the various security agencies were ubiquitous, ordinary people were forced to spy upon one another, the definition of Jewishness often was vague, and those who challenged the regime or expressed their disaffection regularly disappeared. All this was repressive and unpleasant, but it did not require an entirely new attitude toward life. The majority of Germans seem to have experienced the Third Reich as a police state that repressed them but did not seriously interfere with their daily routine.[3]

Hitler was willing to use violence against his enemies, but not against the people he was going to educate: "Too much frightfulness," he said, "produces apathy."[4] The community of action-oriented Aryans could not be apathetic; old ways of acting and thinking were not to be extirpated by the cleansing action of terror. Hitler's principal method of education—and he no doubt would have accepted this designation—was perversion.

The German-speaking people of the Greater Reich (Germany proper, Austria, and the incorporated territories) who were to be made into the Aryan race had to develop not only a sense of difference from other people but also a sense of sameness among themselves. In order to encourage this sense of sameness, the regime made a massive attempt to eliminate the social forces and practices that in the past had kept the Germans apart from one another.

The regime either prohibited or took over all nongovernmental organizations that predated the Third Reich, and it created a number of new organizations intended to encompass as many as possible of the people not otherwise organized and to supervise the activities of all in their so-called leisure time. This policy served to eliminate the possibility of organized opposition, but its main purpose was to bring everyone together, in both work and play and under National Socialist supervision, into (it might be said) one big happy family. The best example of this type of National Socialist organization was the gigantic Labor Front that "coordinated"—that is, incorporated—both the labor union movement and the employers' associations. The Labor Front was to demonstrate that employers and employees shared the same material interests and commanded the same social respect.

The regime's program of social equalization included an effort to eliminate the usual social distinctions between manual and nonmanual workers. In accordance with Hitler's theoretical bias against expertise, this effort took the form of an attack upon intellectuals. "We want," he said, "to abolish forever that attitude of superiority which unfortunately so many of our intellectuals adopt toward the manual workers. . . ."[5] His belief that the masses had slavelike souls did not mean he was an "elitist" in the normal sense, but only that most people, including old-fashioned elitists, were incapable of revolutionary leadership.

From his careful study of the National Socialist program of eliminating social differences among the future master race, David Schoenbaum concludes that the various status and occupational groups were "homogenized." Since the special interests of all groups were both satisfied and frustrated, parochial loyalties and hostilities were at least severely weakened. Working people improved their opportunities and their status and lost much of their former sense of inferiority.[6] Although schools and universities were not really open to the former lower-status groups, there was genuine opportunity for advancement in the critical institutions of the army, the economy, and the civil service. With its use of uniforms, badges, and titles of almost numberless organizations, the Third Reich, "like a super Elks Club, . . . pampered the familiar human weakness for distinction on a scale probably without precedent." "There was no new class, still less a new elite," and although the older status and interest relationships persisted in constant tension with the newer world of radical egalitarianism, the net result was very close to a "psychologically classless society."[7]

Hitler's ultimate plans for the Aryan community probably did not include much in the way of material affluence, since Spartan simplicity is more consistent with dedicated activism. In the meantime, however, to maintain their morale and cohesiveness, these "homogenized" Aryans-to-be could not suffer any severe material deprivations, and the appearance of significant differences in living standards among them had to be avoided. The results of this policy became evident only after the first military reverses on the eastern front. Despite the desperate need to maximize the use of labor and materials in war production, Hitler refused to make significant cuts in civilian consumption. This pampering was not designed to keep the Germans behind the war effort, for like other belligerents they would have sacrificed their material comforts if they had been asked to. It was a matter of emphasizing their equality among themselves and their superiority to lesser mortals.

Preparing the raw material for conversion into the finished master race was not, however, entirely a matter of comfortable togetherness. The Aryans were to be not just a community but a community of activists, and only the healthy can act. According to the regime's psychologists, insanity and feeble-mindedness—those "sicknesses of the soul"—create a "psychic inability to relate,"[8] and thus they were inconsistent with community-building as well as with understanding through action. From 1939 until 1941, the regime pursued a program of euthanasia and put to death perhaps 60,000 patients in German mental hospitals and an undetermined number of the very old. During the war, Hitler discussed the promulgation of a "Reich Health Law," according to which the families of people who were sick, particularly with lung and heart diseases, would "no longer be able to remain among the public" and "no longer be allowed to produce children."[9] This policy never came into effect, but it was the logical continuation of the sterilizations of mental and physical defectives during the early years of the Third Reich.

Among the physically and mentally sound, a high birthrate was encouraged in order to provide replacements for military casualties, to overcome the labor shortage, to increase the total population in response to the long-term threat of the "eastern hordes," to replace the exterminated races, and to get a younger and thus more politically pliable population. In addition, an emphasis on breeding was an excellent way to focus the attention of the nucleus of the master race on its own collective identity.

The other part of Hitler's attempt to create racial consciousness was the construction of an inferior race, and people who could be plausibly described as Jews, in both Germany and the occupied areas, served as his bricks and mortar.

Soon after he became chancellor, the power of government was harnessed to his racial anti-Semitism. In 1933, all Jews employed in governmental institutions were dismissed, and all professions and educational institutions were closed to them. Jews were deprived of German citizenship in 1935, and forbidden to marry Germans. In 1938 all Jews were required to have certain given names drawn principally from the Old Testament, to carry identification papers, and to wear a yellow "Star of David" with the black inscription "Jew." Throughout this period they progressively lost their rights to own property, to serve as managers, and, by being barred from the Labor Front, even to be employees. They were then confined to ghettos and concentration camps, and by 1941 they had been removed from virtually all contact with the inhabitants of the Greater Reich. Nothing more drastically undermined the concept of a German national community than the application of these policies to Jewish veterans of World War I. Very few non-Jewish Germans publicly objected to this course of action, and the Jews themselves put up little resistance. Education in racism had taken another step forward.

The Jews were then removed from Greater Germany and the occupied countries and confined in Eastern Europe in ways that kept them from establishing contacts with non-Jews and from stabilizing their internal relations.[10] Then, in March 1941, when the war with Britain was going rather badly and preparations were being made for the attack on the Soviet Union, Hitler issued an unwritten *Führer* order initiating the "final solution to the Jewish problem," the killing of all Jews throughout the area he controlled. This order was communicated by stages, from his principal lieutenants to the functionaries who were to execute the details, and, although many people were surprised, there was no significant opposition. In fact, enthusiasm, tempered by the realization of the enormity of the operation, seems to have been more typical. The result was the killing of perhaps six million human beings.

The complete segregation of the Jews created certain problems in logistics, but the Final Solution was not designed principally to solve these. On the contrary, the movement of millions of people to the extermination camps interfered seriously with the transportation of troops and military supplies, occupied badly needed labor, and otherwise hampered the war effort.[11] The Final Solution was not to the problem of what to do with the Jews physically, but how to use them to the fullest advantage in demonstrating the existence of inferior races.

The method by which the Jews were killed is one of the most significant aspects of the Final Solution. The procedure was as highly formalized and rationalized as possible, given the size of the task and the wartime environment in which it was undertaken. If anyone killed a Jew without orders from his superiors, the case was treated as murder or manslaughter.[12] Everyone involved in the operation had to understand that the Final Solution was dictated by the most abstract revolutionary logic, and it was to be undertaken only upon the command of the masters of that logic; its fundamental difference from wanton killings of the defenseless and the innocent in the past had to be emphasized. The whole affair was planned to dehumanize the victims, and it strikingly resembled the "delousing" Himmler spoke of.[13] If certain human beings could be seen as insects, racial consciousness would indeed be advanced.

The Final Solution was treated, throughout its implementation, as a top secret, for Hitler realized that, if it were acknowledged, public opinion in both Germany and the occupied and satellite areas would turn against him. He could not afford to jeopardize his program of racial education by getting too far ahead of the masses. The regime, however, made sure that a large number of typical people were directly involved in the killings. By 1944, the special SS detachments assigned to the extermination camps were supplemented by units of ordinary soldiers of the regular armed forces, and the executioners became "a remarkable cross-section of the German population."[14]

Despite this compromised procedure, most ordinary people had heard rumors and stories. Even those interviewed by Mayer and Allen, those who lived in backwater areas and had no family or other connections with Jews, were aware that something unspeakable was occurring;

their response was not to speak, and not even to think, about it. Hitler thus not only involved a cross section of his future Aryans directly in the Final Solution, but he also created a situation in which most of them refused to evaluate their association with what was, according to normal morality, mass murder. This was not a negligible accomplishment.[15]

Although the Final Solution was a successful exercise in perverting the morals of ordinary society, it met resistance from the bourgeois commitment to the principle of the national community. Before the war Hitler had recognized that deporting Jews from Germany would create anti-Semitism in the countries where they were sent, and during the war the governments of his satellite states cooperated in the elimination of these deportees. However, many people in both the eastern satellite states and the occupied countries in the west resisted the application of the Final Solution to their own Jewish nationals.[16] Non-Jewish Germans, on the other hand, were in a more ambiguous position. Those cultural Jews who were their fellow nationals had been physically removed from Germany, and the non-Jews had not objected to this initial violation of the democratic rights of the citizen. Their own government, which had come to power legally, had treated them well enough, and had acted as if it were pursuing the national interest in most matters, was the creator and executor of the Final Solution. With the German Jews out of sight and with the government, which the remaining Germans had accepted as more or less legitimate and whose largess they had willingly received, pursuing its policy in a very quiet way, the inhabitants of the Third Reich chose the easiest response and kept quiet. It does not follow that they were happy in their silence; even Adolf Eichmann could not accept the killing of Jews who were German.[17]

Not all the Jews who remained until 1939 under the regime's control perished in the Final Solution; probably 33,000 in the Greater Reich and the Protectorate survived until 1945. Hitler had his 340 "first-rate Jews," and Himmler allowed Jews to be ransomed, usually for practical purposes such as obtaining needed funds. In its most interesting exception, the Final Solution did not apply to Jews who had criminal records and thus ties with the Germanic community. Hitler, Eichmann, and the National Socialists had nothing against Jews "personally"; the point was only to establish that as a race they had died out. Even after the Jewish race had become extinct, it could be used to remind everyone of the fact of racial inferiority, and officials of the regime competed briskly with one another in collecting items for "museums of Jewish culture."[18]

The Final Solution can be understood only in conjunction with Hitler's "social revolution" within Germany itself. Too often his policy of social equalization has been attributed to a kind of populist nationalism, an interpretation that has supported the view that his Jewish policy was the irrational action of a deranged cultural anti-Semite. As he said, he needed a conception to provide an intellectual basis for a new and antihistoric order, and his ice-cold logic explains the rest. Just as he refused during the war to shift goods from civilian to military consumption, he insisted that, despite the deteriorating military situation, anti-Semitic propaganda still had the highest priority. After he finally had realized that his thousand-year Reich was doomed, he devoted much of his political valedictory to a last effort in educating for racial consciousness.[19]

The Final Solution was designed as a total affront to the bourgeois-democratic rights of man and of the citizen, and official bourgeois-democratic opinion has appropriately elevated it to first place among a deplorably large number of twentieth-century atrocities. To the extent that this revulsion persists, the negative part of Hitler's racial policy was a failure. Racism, however, did not die in 1945, and contemporary racists, who include anti-Semites, can only be heartened by recalling that the absolute distinction of one human being from another was manifested in the Third Reich as a routine social policy.

The racial new order required radical changes in areas of human existence other than that of political community. National Socialism considered social systems, such as the family and the economy, of secondary importance, and hence it left intact the forms it had inherited. The important thing was to change people's attitudes and their manner of viewing reality.

The regime soon took complete control of the schools and all media of communication. Contacts with the world outside the Third Reich were not completely eliminated, but there was strict censorship. As in most revolutionary situations, a strong appeal was made to youthful idealism and advantage taken of youth's lack of specific social commitments. Said Dr. Joseph Goebbels: "Don't let the older generation influence you. We will win. For youth is always right!"

According to Bernhard Rust, the minister of education, "action and action only, not indolent pondering of the past, is the soul of education," and he warned college students not to consider themselves superior to the rank and file of the people. Knowledge was not to be departmentalized, and minds must not be made too critical. The end of education is training for a life of power.[20] National Socialism emphasized the dignity of work and insisted upon proper respect for manual labor.

The principal fare for small children consisted of unquestioning loyalty to the *Führer,* readiness to help him defend himself against his many enemies by means of military service or motherhood, and contempt for the non–National Socialist world. The handbook for the Hitler youth (ages fourteen to eighteen) stated that "all questions of our national life have become so clear, simple, and definite that every comrade can understand them and cooperate in their solution."[21] The handbook discussed the history of European cultures, languages, and tribal groups in an effort to encourage thinking in "racial" terms; it relied heavily on national sentiment but suggested an identification with non-Germans who had similar "cultures" or a common "heredity." Children and youth were also exposed to many stories, plays, and songs designed to create the proper attitudes of loyalty and self-sacrifice.

Higher education was severely curtailed. The terms were shortened from thirty to twenty weeks a year, in order to leave more time for political activities, and classes had flexible schedules so that students could meet their political responsibilities. No student was penalized, or even required to make up the work missed, if he were called from class for a military parade or a political meeting. From 1933 to 1939 the number of university students decreased from 127,920 to 58,325 and the number of students in technical institutes from 20,474 to 9,554. From 1932 to 1938, the number of active professors decreased by 29 percent and university instructors of nonprofessorial rank by 33 percent; the faculties of economics, social science, mathematics, geography, humanities, and law experienced the greatest declines. By 1937, there was a grave shortage of teachers, engineers, and other professional men. The content of courses stressed the practical. Chemistry classes, for example, were concerned with explosives, fire-fighting chemicals, gases and their antidotes, and synthetic foods.[22]

No frontal attack was made on standard religious beliefs and attitudes, nor on the organized churches, despite Hitler's recognition that they were formidable obstacles to his revolution and despite his determination eventually to eliminate both. The regime concentrated instead on trying to prevent the younger generation from contact with religion and to direct youth's natural interest in the mysterious to its own revolutionary purposes. It made a tentative attempt to identify the concept of an ultimate supernatural power with the "forces of nature" and to present the *Führer* as the only person who understood these forces. The principal theme of courses in the philosophy of religion at the University of Berlin was that the "best possible religion" was the people's faith in their leader.[23]

According to Hitler's world view, he alone understood the logic of history and the vital forces of the masses, but the adulation this postulate implies was not fully realized in the Third Reich. Absolute personal loyalty to the *Führer* was required and his infallibility was stressed but, for a movement of total revolution, his presentation as a universal genius with supernatural powers was relatively modest. Although his closest revolutionary associates correctly saw him as, in Goebbels's words, "the automatically creative instrument of a divine fate," apparently the German people's rational and pragmatic common sense was perceived as a temporary impediment to the propagation of this logical position.

A new society implies new ways of approaching reality, both intellectually and artistically. Final understanding could not be had until the racial new order had been established, but in the meantime the old ways of looking at things could be rooted out and the ground for the new perspectives could be prepared.

Science, said Hitler, is a function of the society in which it occurs.

> The simple question that precedes every scientific activity is: who is it who wants to know something, who is it who wants to find how he stands in the world around him? It follows necessarily that there can only be the science of a particular type of humanity and of a particular age. It is reasonable to say that there is a Nordic science, and a National Socialist science, which are bound to be opposed to the Liberal-Jewish science, which, indeed, is no longer fulfilling its function anywhere, but is in the process of stultifying itself.[24]

A number of prominent scientists published works with titles like "National Socialism and Science," "German Physics," and "German Mathematics." It was argued at length that Einsteinian physics aimed at transforming the "world of living essence, born from a mother earth and bound up with blood," into a "spectral abstraction in which all individual differences of peoples and nations, and all inner limits of the races, are lost in unreality. . . ."[25] Most of this material attacked the theories and premises of Liberal-Jewish science, insisted that they be replaced by their National Socialist counterparts, and pointed out the directions that the new science should take, for example, that empirical knowledge should be "integrated into the total biological picture" where the "basic spiritual fact of Volkish belonging is primary."[26] These revisionist scientists, however, developed no concrete axioms or hypotheses of the new way of knowing. In the natural sciences that were relevant to military production, the technicians were by and large left alone, but the attack upon non-Volkish basic theory may well have impeded the war effort.

The Liberal-Jewish biological sciences were virtually destroyed. The National Socialist rector of the University of Berlin, a veterinarian, initiated twenty-five courses in "Race Science," and the director of the University of Kiel Hospital announced that medical science had become alienated from the Volk because of "its dogmatic rejection of all lay medical thought."[27] The social sciences were reduced to meaninglessness, and sociology, the epitome of bourgeois science, was stamped out.

Since history is understood only by making it, Hitler considered written history to be merely propaganda serving the interests of socially dominant groups, and he intended to "re-write history, from the racial point of view," in order to serve his own program of education. "In all this troublesome business we are only interested in one thing—to project into the dim and distant past the picture of our nation as we envisage it for the future."[28] He compared this enterprise with history as written by "liberals," who select events from the past in order to suggest the antiquity of liberal ideas and practices and their inevitable triumph. His own written history asserted that all great men of the past were Aryans and that all culture has been produced by Aryans; even those who best resisted the National Socialist revolution itself were of Germanic origin.

Artistic expression was a field in which Hitler had great interest and firm opinions. He stated his basic position when he opened the House of German Art in Munich on 18 July 1937: "An art which cannot count on the readiest and most intimate agreement of the great mass of the people . . . is intolerable."[29] Goebbels expanded on this theme: freedom of artistic expression does not include the artist's right "to withdraw from his times and lead an eccentric life that exists for itself, which must defend itself against the invasion of the people." The professional critics did not judge "in terms of a healthy instinct linked to the people," but rather in terms of "intellectual abstractness." Hence art criticism had been forbidden, and "now the public itself functions as critic."[30] By allowing artistic expression only for the "mass market," the regime encouraged social egalitarianism and thus facilitated its community-building; popular art was thought to have an homogenizing effect. The popular, moreover, was also the most realistic: painting and sculpture left nothing to the imagination, fiction was literal and unambiguous, music was straightforward and complete, and architecture was solid and massive. National Socialist art was to represent the physical, active side of life—manual work was a favorite theme—and to eliminate the realm of imagination, speculation, and spiritual striving. The physical and the obvious also symbolized the community and the public in contrast to the individual and the private, with architecture being the clearest example. Art for the masses, however, could allow them to imagine themselves "in an enchanted world of the Ideal" and to experience a "world of wonder and gracious appearance."[31]

A society can survive well enough in the short term without art, history, social science, and even theoretical natural science. It cannot exist, however, without an economy, and thus the transition from the bourgeois economy of the Weimar Republic to the Aryan economy of the future racial community was difficult to make and interesting to observe. Consistent with his contempt for technical expertise and with his unlimited faith in the power of human will, Hitler aimed not at organizing the economy but at subjecting it to the revolutionary thrust of National Socialism. The result was what Schoenbaum has called the "anti-economy of the Third Reich."[32]

Prior to 1933 Hitler needed the financial aid of German big business, and the businessmen gave it principally as a means of supporting what seemed to be the currently most powerful "antisocialist" political force. The alliance was only an expedient for both parties: Hitler's *Volksgemeinschaft* propaganda was weakened by his association with the "capitalists," and they in turn began to desert him as his electoral power faded at the end of 1932.[33] Once he obtained control of the government, he allowed most of these men to remain in their previously powerful positions, for, as he said to Rauschning, he intended to use them in his construction of the new order.[34] To the end, big business cooperated with the regime, as did everyone else, "as instruments and objects" of his policies.[35] Formalities of title, position, and ownership meant little to Hitler: "Why need we trouble to socialize banks and factories? We socialize human beings."[36]

All employees, except civil servants and those in the liberal professions, could leave or change jobs only with the regime's permission, and unexcused absence from work could lead to imprisonment. The economic life of the farmer was thoroughly regulated through the Reich Food Estate, and the entailment program was designed to tie the farmer to the land in a most unbourgeois fashion. The small businessman, a favorite of pre-1933 propaganda, also received unfavorable treatment: by 1939 about 10,000 shops and stores in Berlin alone had gone out of business. Investment was controlled, prices were fixed, and corporation taxes were doubled.

Behind this regimentation was the National Socialist concept of community, which did not admit the institution of private property and other economic claims of the individual against the collectivity. In official theory, property was a concession of the group to the individual, and the *Führer* could rescind it at any time in the interests of the group. The great economic empire of Himmler's SS had a strong bias against "capitalism" and the "private economy," and SS leaders apparently envisioned it as the model for the economy of the future Reich.[37]

For the National Socialists, work took priority over consumption, but the material well-being of the German public could not be ignored. The apathy and discontent of depression and unemployment had to be overcome, morale built up to prepare for future innovations in domestic and foreign policy, and the standard of living kept reasonably high and more or less equalized. Immediately after assuming power, Hitler reduced unemployment by relying on public works programs initiated under the Weimar Republic, by keeping workers in these programs at minimum wages, by removing women from the job market, and by driving down the general level of earnings by share-work plans. From 1935 on, the rearmament program resulted in a shortage of labor. Social welfare programs remained at about their 1932 level, although insurance premiums were increased in order to cut purchasing power and to accumulate funds for capital expenditures. In 1940 gross income per taxpayer was down about 3 percent from the 1933 level. No interest, group, or social stratum was economically favored. Despite the great increase in arms manufacture, only I. G. Farben among the large industrial firms realized significant profits. The great *Junker* estates fared better than other agricultural units, but only because of their better initial competitive position.[38] The smaller farmers, despite the theory of "Blood and Soil," at the very least failed to improve their position; 70,000 farmworkers and their families left the land during the Third Reich, and women came to make up almost half of the agricultural work force.

The entire process of economic production in the Third Reich was highly confused and inefficient. This situation resulted in part from the way in which power was arranged according to the leadership principle (to be discussed in Chapter 5), and in part from National Socialism's indifference to mundane matters of economic production, including the production of vital war materials.

Although the regime had virtually full control of the economy, it undertook no real economic planning, except to ensure that heavy industry remained concentrated in Germany proper.[39] Although the Four-Year Plan (initiated in 1936 and continued beyond 1940) was advertised as a means to self-sufficiency in basic war materials, its principal effect was to reduce even further the independence of German industry. The Hermann Göring Works, set up by the Four-Year Plan, was no more than a device to check the steel industry, which could have produced more and better steel if the Göring Works had never been founded.[40] Many businessmen and officials responsible for production had to hire specialists to help them deal with the multitude of regulatory agencies and figure out the flood of special decrees and laws, which they nevertheless very often deliberately had to ignore.

Hitler, as many writers have pointed out, made such a shambles of the German economy because he did not understand economics. The economics he did not understand, however, was bourgeois economics, and the shambles he made were shambles only from the bourgeois point of view. For National Socialism, "economics" was the theory and practice of using as many resources as could be made available to accomplish a number of short-term goals. The net effect resembled plundering: the occupied territories were plundered in the old-fashioned way; the uninhibited expenditure of Germany's own resources was a more subtle form of plundering. This completely unstructured approach to economizing has misled many observers who assume that economic systems must be either "capitalist" or "socialist" and who thus infer from Hitler's indifference to such theorizing that he somehow "retained capitalism." As he pointed out, in the Third Reich there was "neither a socialized economy, nor a free economy, but only a national economy which is subject to obligations."[41]

The distinctive social and psychological characteristics of the racial new order described above required a special geographical setting. The revolution had to expand to the east and to prove itself in a necessarily fatal struggle with Bolshevism and the "hordes of Asia."

Operating within the framework of the standard international political system, by 1939 Hitler had accomplished diplomatic miracles. He not only had wiped out Germany's Versailles-imposed second-class status, but he had collected in one state virtually every person who could be seen as a member or potential member of a German national community. His success depended upon his own skill and nerve, but even more upon the people who had to respond to him. Both the Germans willing to support him and the British and French unwilling to oppose him based their responses on the principle of national self-determination. Precisely for this reason, Hitler could not be content with his peaceful conquests. He could not acknowledge the validity of nationalism without undermining his entire revolution. He could not "build racism in one country" because that country was seen by its own inhabitants and by much of the world as a nation-state. By 1939 he had acquired most of the people he needed for the raw material of his master race, but his revolutionary ideology was geographically imprisoned.

Hitler believed that eventually the entire world, or at least the important parts of it, would be ordered according to the principle of race, but he did not intend to accomplish this by establishing any National Socialist world empire. Once the "thousand-year Reich" existed in the heart of Europe, he expected that other areas of the world would have to follow his example, as previously other areas had to follow the European example of the nation-state. Once his Eastern European policy was successful, he was willing to "let the democracies die of their own accord."[42]

The eastern policy, "the conquest of wide spaces in the East" and "the destruction of Bolshevism," was the essence of Hitler's approach to foreign affairs, the "ambition of his life" and the *raison d'etre* of National Socialism."[43] The human material he needed for the future subraces could be obtained in the proper quantity only in the east, where, moreover, the people were clearly culturally different from the Western Europeans. The east also had the physical space he required for political independence and for the proper interplay between the races, and hence "living space" (*Lebensraum*) was another slogan that evoked nationalist sentiments for racist purposes. His strong eastern orientation also resulted from his conviction that Stalin had been busy setting up another antihistoric order that presented the only real challenge to National Socialism in Europe. His revolution and Stalin's revolution had to clash:

> We cannot in any way evade the final battle between German race ideals and pan-Slav mass ideals. . . . We must win the victory of German race-consciousness over the masses eternally fated to serve and obey.[44]

When Bolshevism proved stronger in the war in the east, Hitler's logic did not desert him. He was prepared to destroy Germany because the Germans had proved themselves unfit to become a master race.

According to Hitler's theory of social progress, struggle is necessary, and warfare naturally is one of the most demanding forms of struggle. He apparently considered a war with Eastern Europe, and particularly with the Soviet Union, to be highly desirable as well as politically unavoidable. In any event, he was going to seize Europe to the Urals, and presumably enough struggle would develop during this process to satisfy his theory of progress.

His policy toward the west was determined by his policy toward the east. When the western powers could no longer tolerate his eastern expansion, he was forced to deal with them militarily. He had no use for the "Latins," because they did not have enough spirit to make good supermen and did not differ enough culturally from Nordics to serve as submen. Despite the ability of the SS to recruit in several "Nordic" countries, the general lack of enthusiasm shown by most of the Dutch, Flemish, and Scandinavian people for his racial grand design was a serious setback.

Hitler fought the British because they were impeding his eastern policy, but he also considered Britain the most successful example of the bourgeois-capitalist order he was determined to supplant. He appreciated Britain's interest in the status quo, but he still could not understand why the British, successful revolutionaries and imperialists in the past, people who acted first and thought about it later, did not perceive the progressive nature of his own revolution and especially why they did not recognize the threat presented by the mobilization of the Asian hordes by Bolshevism. He thus spoke of Churchill and other British leaders only in invective, while maintaining his admiration for the British people.

The Third Reich was reduced to a heap of rubble not because Hitler made a large number of specific mistakes. His foreign policy did not collapse because the "Latin" countries let him down, or because he began the war too soon or too late, or because his attack on the Soviet Union was delayed, or because he ordered a stand at Stalingrad, or indeed because of all of these. His foreign policy was a disaster because he believed he could not separate it from the other principal element of his revolutionary grand plan, the creation of racial consciousness. His anti-Semitism and contempt for liberal bourgeois society antagonized the western powers and created uneasiness within Greater Germany. His indulgent treatment of his future Aryans and his "destruction" of the Jews seriously impeded the mobilization of his resources for war. Finally, and probably most important, his treatment of the people of the conquered eastern areas, including the western part of the Soviet Union itself, as subhumans lost him an incalculable amount of indigenous support in his war against Stalin.

> I have been Europe's last hope. She proved herself incapable of refashioning herself by means of voluntary reform. She showed herself impervious to charm and persuasion. To take her I had to use violence.[45]

His fatal mistake was to use, simultaneously, both physical violence and moral violence.

Notes

1. Albert Speer, *Inside the Third Reich* (New York: Macmillan, 1970), p. 101.
2. Martin Broszart, "The Concentration Camps, 1933–45," in *Anatomy of the SS State* (New York: Walker & Co., 1968), pp. 410, 459.
3. E. g., Elisabeth Noelle and Erich Peter Neumann, eds., *The Germans: Public Opinion Polls, 1947–1966* (Allensbach: Verlag für Demoskopie, 1967), p. 204.
4. Hermann Rauschning, *The Voice of Destruction* (New York: G. P. Putnam's Sons, 1940), p. 282.
5. Norman H. Baynes, ed., *The Speeches of Adolf Hitler* (London: Oxford University Press, 1942), 1:893.
6. Schoenbaum, *Hitler's Social Revolution* (Garden City, N.Y.: Doubleday, 1966), p. 256. See Karl Dietrich Bracher, *The German Dictatorship* (New York: Frederick A. Praeger, 1970), p. 338.
7. Schoenbaum, pp. 285, 65, 296–97.
8. See George L. Mosse, ed., *Nazi Culture* (New York: Grosset & Dunlap, 1966), p. 221.
9. *Nazi Conspiracy and Aggression* (Washington, D.C.: U. S. Government Printing Office, 1946), 7:175–76.
10. Gerald Reitlinger, *The Final Solution* (New York: A. S. Barnes, 1953), p. 48.

11. Raul Hilberg, *The Destruction of the European Jews* (Chicago: Quadrangle Books, 1961), p. 646.

12. Hilberg, p. 648.

13. *Nazi Conspiracy and Aggression*, 4:547. In a conversation reported for 1935, Hitler said about the Jews, "fence them in somewhere where they can perish as they deserve while the German people look on, the way people stare at wild animals." Helmut Krausnick, "The Persecution of the Jews," in *Anatomy of the SS State*, p. 34.

14. *Nazi Conspiracy and Aggression*, 7:211; Hilberg, p. 649.

15. See Hannah Arendt, *Eichmann in Jerusalem* (New York: Viking Press, 1963), p. 111.

16. Reitlinger, pp. 10, 413, 305, 379.

17. Arendt, p. 90.

18. Arendt, pp. 23, 27, 33.

19. François Genoud, ed., *The Testament of Adolf Hitler* (London: Cassell, 1961), pp. 50–57, 89–90, 105.

20. Gregor Ziemer, *Education for Death: The Making of the Nazi* (London: Oxford University Press, 1941), pp. 18, 22.

21. *The Nazi Primer: Official Handbook for Schooling the Hitler Youth* (New York: Harper & Brothers, 1938), p. 3.

22. Ziemer, pp. 171, 17, 160.

23. Ziemer, p. 172.

24. Rauschning, p. 223.

25. William L. Shirer, *The Rise and Fall of the Third Reich* (New York: Simon & Schuster, 1960), p. 250.

26. Mosse, p. 200.

27. Mosse, p. 232.

28. *Hitler's Secret Conversations, 1941–1944* (New York: Farrar, Straus & Young, 1953), p. 72; Rauschning, p. 227.

29. Baynes, 1:591–92.

30. Mosse, pp. 153–54.

31. Mosse, p. 157. The minister of public enlightenment appears to have been thinking along the lines of Disneyland.

32. Schoenbaum, p. 120.

33. Bracher, pp. 186, 248; Ralf Dahrendorf, *Society and Democracy in Germany* (Garden City, N.Y.: Doubleday, 1967), pp. 396–97.

34. Rauschning, p. 161.

35. Bracher, p. 335. William Ebenstein, *The Nazi State* (New York: Farrar & Rinehart, 1943), and Frank Munk, *The Legacy of Nazism* (New York: Macmillan, 1943), already had recognized the "anticapitalist" nature of the Third Reich's economy.

36. Rauschning, p. 193. See Bracher, p. 337.

37. Alan S. Milward, *The German Economy at War* (London: University of London Press, 1965), p. 160.

38. Schoenbaum, pp. 157, 180, 182; Bracher, p. 335.

39. Milward, p. 30.

40. Milward, pp. 3–4; Munk, p. 146; Bracher, p. 333.

41. Baynes, 1:943.

42. Rauschning, p. 74; Genoud, p. 83; *Hitler's Secret Conversations*, p. 397.

43. Genoud, p. 34.

44. Rauschning, p. 133.

45. Genoud, p. 101.

5
The Leadership Principle
in Action

If someone wants to make a revolution, he must acquire a great amount of concentrated social power. This judgment, for National Socialism, was not a matter of common sense but rather a necessary corollary of its world view. In order to understand history, action is required, action depends upon willpower, and the highest concentration and the best utilization of willpower are obtained by a revolutionary movement responsive to the will of a single leader. Revolutionary world views, however, like practical maxims, require implementation in complex and confusing social contexts. Hitler sought arrangements of power that would enable him continuously to educate the people in the spirit of his mission by means of (in his words) the "total domination" of every individual. For a number of reasons, he never achieved this degree of power; but, despite practical difficulties and the later burden of military affairs, he instituted and maintained a remarkable concentration of power in his own hands, enough to enable him to challenge all the basic assumptions of European domestic and interstate society.

As soon as Hitler became chancellor of the Weimar Republic in January 1933, he began to destroy its political institutions. Within a month of his investiture, an "Emergency Ordinance" nominally suspended, and in fact terminated, the rights of individuals, and within two months an "Enabling Act" gave all formal governmental power to the executive branch of government. The trade unions were captured by National Socialists during April and May of 1933. In February Göring had taken over the

Prussian police, in early March the Bavarian *Land* government came under National Socialist control, with Himmler becoming chief of police, and by the end of the month the entire federal system had been eliminated. In March the Communist Party was outlawed, in June the Socialists and the Nationalists were banned, and in July the NSDAP became the only legal party. These actions were made possible by the physical power of the activist sections of the movement, by National Socialist control of the police, and by vast popular indifference to the political organizations and institutions of parliamentary democracy. "Almost unnoticed, the formerly imposing structure of German liberalism crumbled," and within six months the Weimar Republic had disappeared.[1]

There was more to Germany, however, than the Weimar Republic. Among political institutions alone, there remained the police, the judiciary, the military services, the foreign office, and the many ministries dealing with economic and social affairs. These vast networks of human relationships had to be revolutionized rather than eliminated, although a few were retained in their original conditions during the interim period when the German state was to be used to establish the new order throughout Europe.

The regular police were used to help eliminate the Weimar institutions, but police power in itself was counterrevolutionary, a condition that could not be overcome merely by putting it under the control of National Socialists. The solution was to merge ordinary criminal law with "revolutionary law" and thus to eliminate the normal police functions of investigation and fact collecting and the rational organization that these functions required.

The courts and the judicial function were subject to similar treatment. Although there was relatively little turnover in personnel, the judges soon lost their independent tenure, actions of the State Police were withdrawn from their jurisdiction, and their functions were changed from interpreting a legal code to trying to act as the *Führer* would act under similar circumstances. Only in the area of the civil law of (Germanic) consumer's property did normal law and legal procedures remain.

The structure and operations of the great civil bureaucracies were subject to relatively little change during the Third Reich. Jews and political opponents, of course, were removed, and the top positions were given to veteran National Socialists. Although the ordinary civil servant joined the mass party and was very careful of what he did and said, his world remained "fairly normal, almost traditional."[2] The complex normal society needed the expertise of the civil servants, who offered no immediate challenge to the revolutionary regime.

The two most traditional branches of pre–National Socialist government, the military and the foreign service, retained most of their top-level personnel and their independence of operation longer than the agencies concerned with domestic affairs. Hitler's reason for tolerating them was that, despite his contempt for both expertise and the "German tradition," he was not sure that he could succeed in his radical foreign policy without their help. At the beginning of his regime, he talked about revolutionizing the military, and at the end of it he bitterly lamented his failure to do so.[3] When in retrospect he placed a large part of the blame for the collapse of the Third Reich upon the traditionally oriented soldiers and diplomats, he was not merely seeking scapegoats, for their expertise may well not have outweighed their inability to appreciate his grand design.

Although a considerable number of the younger military officers saw the National Socialists as activists who would promote a strong Germany and thus a large army, most of the officers considered Hitler and company as upstarts far outside the imperial tradition and as rowdies without anything resembling the honor of a German officer. No matter how the officers saw Hitler, very few of them felt any obligation whatever to the Weimar system; the great majority was perfectly content to stand by while National Socialism destroyed the Republic. Prior to 1933, the army had insisted upon a status "above politics," which meant that it wanted to preserve its autonomy and to avoid any commitment to the defense of the Weimar Republic. After 1933, Hitler was careful to promise that this "nonpolitical" status of the army would continue. To the army, this arrangement meant that it would remain "a state within a state"; to Hitler, it meant that he would have a free hand for revolution. The officers' "remaining aloof from politics" when Hitler purged Röhm and the SA in 1934 led straight to their complete acquiescence in his purge of Generals Blomberg and von Fritsch and the resulting destruction of their own independent power in 1938.[4]

Hitler's political mastery of the officers was demonstrated again in the matter of the oath of allegiance. On the day of the death of President Hindenburg, 2 August 1934, Hitler unconstitutionally combined the offices of chancellor and president and became himself head of state and commander-in-chief of the armed forces. He then ordered the officer corps to take an oath of "unconditional obedience to Adolf Hitler." The officers, apparently motivated by a need for some person to be loyal to, took the oath and henceforth found it an almost insurmountable barrier to opposition to the Third Reich.[5] They were never able to understand that the twentieth century does not allow nonpolitical armies and has no place for the antique concept of personal loyalty.

When, in July 1944, a number of officers broke out of their political paralysis and made an unsuccessful attempt on Hitler's life, he had little difficulty in destroying all military men he suspected of active or passive complicity. At least by this time—and perhaps as early as the fall of the Weimar Republic—the German enlisted men no longer acknowledged the superiority of the officer caste. In 1944, Hitler, despite his recent disastrous reverses, had, as the only available manifestation of popular government, if not their loyalty at least their tolerance.

Hitler was opposed to anything that resembled a constitution for the Third Reich, because "the moment the new status could be formulated constitutionally, its revolutionary force would be exhausted. . . . It was the fundamental error of the jurists and lawmakers to think they could create life by means of a constitution and a code of laws."[6] Revolutionary creativity required fluidity and flexibility, and whenever National Socialist writers attempted to describe the formal nature of the Third Reich, they were unavoidably either negative or vague. They insisted that concepts such as that of state did not apply to the Reich, which was "the community order of the totality of Volkish life" or "the political-Volkish organization of the people." Politics had absorbed the former functions of law and the movement (or the "party") had replaced the state. Although the Reichstag had been rendered powerless and elections to it noncompetitive, it was dissolved and reelected four times between 1933 and 1938. Apparently Hitler wanted some form of community participation in political life and, in this period of transition to the new order, could not think of anything to replace these now meaningless bourgeois devices.

Ordinary criminal and civil law was, of course, counterrevolutionary. Under National Socialism, law was no longer an objective norm but "a spontaneous emanation of the will of the *Führer*." Hans Frank, as commissioner of justice, told the judges, "Say to yourselves at every decision which you make: How would the *Führer* decide in my place?" Legal offenses were no longer specified: a person could receive severe punishment for having violated "the healthy sentiment of the people," and "preventive custody" was commonplace. There was nothing resembling due process, and no appeal could be made of any action by an agency of the regime, such as the police, that was defined as "political."

Ordinary crimes, such as assault and theft, became indistinguishable from political crimes. Even the revolutionary Third Reich could not dispense with the kind of social stability that depends upon criminal law, but the norms of criminal law interfered with the fluidity demanded by the revolution. To resolve this contradiction, ordinary crimes were reinterpreted as acts inconsistent with the building of *Volk* consciousness, which was also the definition of "political crimes." The novelty of the norm of "building *Volk* consciousness" meant that legal punishment tended to serve more as a deterrent of future acts than as means of indicating that a committed act had been antisocial.

The law was applied in one way to those people who had placed themselves fully within the spirit of the new racial community and in another to those who had not. Since the revolution was designed for all of Europe and since its legitimacy was established with the founding of the National Socialist movement (and not with Hitler's takeover of any preexisting political unit), any action judged especially counterrevolutionary, such as active resistance to the movement, that occurred in pre-1933 Germany or in any part of Europe prior to its political or military acquisition was treated as normal political systems treat treason.

Civil law, on the other hand, retained more of its former nature. The German economy, as shown below, was subject to considerable disruption, but it was never completely revolutionized. The regime maintained the rights of consumer property, when they did not conflict with some immediate political goal, and the courts substantiated these rights.[7] The kind of civil law that affected the average man was severely attacked only by the withdrawal of the property rights of the Jews. National Socialism had in mind, if only vaguely, an entirely new conception of property, but for most inhabitants of the Third Reich the normal civil law remained.

The maintenance of the Third Reich required agencies and men to perform the two different and basically incompatible tasks of furthering the revolution and conducting the normal business of a society in a nonrevolutionary world. These tasks were carried out by an unstructured collection of independent agencies that reported directly to Hitler in his capacity of *Der Führer*, a title indicating his status as the leader of a revolution rather than as head of a state or a government. Some agencies were called "party" agencies and others "governmental," but these labels corresponded to no objective differences. The NSDAP, however, maintained a separate existence as the single "legal party"; although it had as many as 25,000 full-time administrators, its functions were uncertain and it was uncertain of its functions.[8] It had an effect upon public opinion, but Hitler always considered it only one of a number of means, and a not very important one at that, to carry out his reeducation of the German people.[9]

Some of the many agencies under Hitler had unusual concentrations of power. The most powerful was the great empire of the SS, led since 1929 by Heinrich Himmler. It included the schools for training the elite of the future master race, its own medical and legal services, all police organizations, the concentration and extermination camps, the forced labor of captured civilian and military personnel, approximately 150 business firms, 600,000 or so *Waffen-SS* troops engaged in regular military activity, and (eventually) military intelligence. In 1943, the Ministry of the Interior, a "governmental" agency, was added to Himmler's collection.

Martin Bormann, who succeeded Rudolf Hess as head of the Party Chancellory, controlled all NSDAP personnel, handled all contacts between the NSDAP and other agencies of the regime, and, most important, was in charge of the forty-five *Gauleiter* who were supposed to direct the lives of the people in their districts (*Gaue*) according to National Socialist principles. The *Gauleiter* functioned as small viceroys, handling most of the normal business of government that affected the general populace, and thus tending to identify at least as strongly with their clientele as with the regime. Once appointed, always by Hitler himself, the *Gauleiter* had remarkably secure tenure. After 1943, Bormann gained additional power from his continuous physical proximity to Hitler in his capacity of the *Führer's* personal secretary.

Robert Ley ran the German Labor Front, a vast conglomerate based on the dues-paying membership of all those people formerly in trade unions and employer associations. The Front, a "party" organization, administered the "Strength through Joy" agency that supervised all organized leisure activities of the general populace, including the People's Colleges that provided adult education, and it controlled the training academies for future NSDAP leaders. It also operated a number of economic enterprises, including a bank, a publishing business, a life-insurance concern, and the People's Car Works. It had a large income and many functionaries.

Joseph Goebbels, as minister of propaganda and public enlightenment, a "cabinet" office, controlled most of the writers, speakers, teachers, and artists of the Third Reich. This post provided Goebbels with a substantial bureaucracy, he was also *Gauleiter* for Berlin, and he had more or less unlimited personal access to Hitler.

Hermann Göring had charge of the Office of the Four-Year Plan, a "government" agency in charge of a large sector of the economy, including the steel works named after its head. Göring was also minister for air and minister president for Prussia, both "governmental" positions. His great talents as a revolutionary, so useful to Hitler during the time of struggle, were wasted in these positions that dealt principally with mundane matters of economics and government, and he exercised his considerable powers only sporadically.

The Ministry for Armament and War Production gained real power in 1942 when Hitler realized that the war was going to require a higher level of economic coordination than originally envisioned. Its last and most famous head was Albert Speer.

A number of other men and their agencies could not be ignored in the conduct of the affairs of the Third Reich. Walther Darré was minister of nutrition and agriculture ("governmental") and Reich peasant leader ("party"), with a sizable staff and direct contact with the agrarian population. Ribbentrop as head of the Foreign Office, Funk as minister of economics, Seldte as minister of labor, Thierack as minister of justice, Schwerin-Krosigk as minister of finance, Rust as minister of science, education, and popular culture, and Schirach as leader of the Hitler Youth all had some discretion and could not be ignored by the more powerful members of the regime. Finally, the occupied territories were run by governors who were not without independence.

These men and their subordinates performed both the normal business required of any autocratic government and the far from normal business required by the racial revolution. At the extremes were Albert Speer and Heinrich Himmler. Speer's job was to deal with a current practical problem; he was responsible for no changes in the direction of a new social order, although by performing his task he was aiding the revolution. He was an anomaly in the regime and was so recognized by its other principal figures. Himmler's job was to establish racism, to select, train, and educate the nucleus of the master race, and to experiment with new social relations and arrangements, for the *Führer* had given him the task of "carrying forward the concept of the Germanic Reich."[10] In addition to these assignments in constructing revolution, Himmler was charged with the negative chore of policing the population to prevent counterrevolutionary deviations, and he had to rely on his own devices to provide the SS with a firm political and economic foundation during the transitional period.

The rest of the regime's powerful men divided their time and efforts between the ordinary and the revolutionary. For example, that formidable ideologue, Joseph Goebbels, had to spend less and less time on implanting National Socialist culture and more and more on keeping up public morale in a deteriorating military situation.

The National Socialists' leadership principle *(Führerprinzip)* stated that the power of the *Führer* was complete and all-embracing, unbounded by any organization or by public opinion, and "free and independent, all-inclusive, and unlimited."[11] This piece of revolutionary theory was approximated to a remarkable degree in the practice of the Third Reich.

All the regime's powerful men reported directly to Hitler and all were dependent upon him for the retention of their power.[12] His method for establishing this dependence included the time-honored device of using them to counterweight one another, as (for example) he allowed Bormann, Speer, Göring, and Himmler to work at cross-purposes on economic matters. His specialty, however, was the technique of assigning to his various lieutenants specific, yet ill-defined tasks that tended to overlap, and as a consequence only he could decide finally who was supposed to be doing what.[13] Although his principal lieutenants frequently conferred with one another on issues of common concern, they could not reach firm agreements on important matters until they had discovered from the *Führer* their respective responsibilities. Any disagreements among them, naturally, could be resolved only by Hitler.

Formal offices and titles meant little under this arrangement. According to his hatred of "bureaucracy" and his need to maintain a fluid revolutionary situation, Hitler tried to minimize the areas of power that his lieutenants could call their own. He operated by assigning a specific task to an existing or ad hoc group and by then relying upon the personal drive of the group's leader.[14] According to his hatred of expertise, he paid little attention to formal qualifications for positions of power. This policy had the desired practical effect of maintaining fluidity in personnel management, and it also corresponded to his belief that things were accomplished solely through willpower. Although only about one-quarter of the men in positions of great power had had previous administrative experience, most of them performed their assigned tasks with a remarkable degree of competence. Again the extreme cases, Speer and Himmler, are the best examples.

The leadership principle concentrated responsibility and authority to a degree unprecedented in the context of an industrial society. In addition to his monopoly of decision on important issues, Hitler settled matters, even during the most critical periods of the war, that would have been much too trivial for a president or a prime minister.[15] His lieutenants, applying the leadership principle to their own subordinates, used all the same techniques.

Directly beneath Hitler and throughout the regime, the leadership principle led to an unchecked struggle for power. Encroachments on and duplications of the functions of others, temporary alliances against a common rival, the establishment of private financial and administrative empires—all these practices occurred with Hitler's tacit approval and despite their considerable interference with the solutions to many pressing practical problems. (Hitler's famous "indecisiveness" had its roots in his refusal to commit himself in these conflicts until it was absolutely unavoidable.) The leadership principle in action necessarily resulted in an enormous amount of confusion and inefficiency in the handling of

some of the most routine functions of normal government. Revolutionary change depended upon a minimum of operational routine, and, if this
meant that the day-to-day business of maintaining a complex society was
impeded, so much the worse for that business. Flexibility and confusion
were probably most advanced in the SS, the vanguard of the purely
revolutionary thrust, a "random and self-contradictory world," "devoid
of all logic," where Himmler faithfully followed the means as well as the
ends of his master.[16]

In 1942 Hitler finally had to acknowledge that the unrevolutionary
business of production for war needed serious attention, and so he gave a
considerable amount of power to the Ministry for Armaments and War
Production. By this act, he created a classic case of the unavoidable
conflict between the revolutionary's effort to effect fundamental social
change, with its corollary of undiluted power in the hands of the leader,
and the need to deal with urgent practical matters in a context defined by
normal, nonrevolutionary premises.

Although his grand design required extensive military action, Hitler
recognized the contradiction between his revolutionary goals and the
efficient direction of the conventional areas of social life implied by this
action.[17] With perfect logic, therefore, he did what he could, as Milward
has put it, to avoid "a properly planned war economy." Until 1942, he
was able to rely on the method of *Blitzkrieg,* which, in addition to applying massive military force for the rapid accomplishment of a specific
military objective, involved the provision of military goods on the same
basis. The method, in other words, avoided long-term economic planning by providing only enough war material to accomplish the short-term
military objective, and priorities were "decided by the simple device of
issuing a *Führer*-Command." Since *Blitzkrieg* worked by shifting reserves
of material, it was effective only when many unexploited reserves—
namely, those accumulated in prewar Germany—were available. Its advantage was that it did not upset the pattern of competition among the
regime's many formal agencies and other power groups: "The running of
the German war economy therefore was originally left in the hands of a
number of competing administrators and administrative organizations.
To have reorganized the economy for a full-scale war would have meant
abandoning these administrative practices. . . ."

When Hitler realized that the war's prolongation had destroyed the
feasibility of the economic policy of *Blitzkrieg,* he gave Albert Speer, as
minister for armaments and war production, the power to bring some
centralized control and planning into war production. Speer was soon
able to achieve some rather spectacular rises in output by initiating a few

fairly simple rationalizations of the productive process, but before long his attempt to introduce planning met stubborn and successful resistance from a number of powerful people. Although he maintained tolerable personal relations with Göring, the Office of the Four-Year Plan continued to go its independent way. The *Gauleiter,* supported by Bormann, repeatedly refused to allow workers to be moved from their districts to where they were needed in war industries and to allow plants in their districts to be converted from civilian to military production.[18]

The minister also experienced opposition from the SS. By 1944, a severe shortage of labor for armaments production had developed, but (according to Speer) the SS would not release any of its large labor forces that were inefficiently engaged in various inessential tasks. In the same year, he had trouble with aircraft production because the SS controlled the manufacture of certain key parts and refused to coordinate its actions with the rest of the industry.[19] As Speer gradually gained some control over other sectors of the economy, the SS became even more independent.[20]

The leadership principle created other difficulties. In August 1944, Speer calculated that he could obtain from six to eight hundred thousand workers for war industries if the system of checking and counterchecking—he has called it "mistrust"—were eliminated from the regime's administrative apparatus. Once, during a Berlin air raid, it was necessary to use Hitler's private telephone to summon fire engines for a local fire; when an excessive number arrived at the place, it proved impossible to send them to other areas where they were badly needed because their original order had come from the *Führer* himself. Finally, as Speer has put it, Hitler "arrived at the core of matters too easily and therefore could not understand them with real thoroughness."[21]

In short, Speer succeeded in rationalizing parts of the process of war production when he received Hitler's support, and he failed to rationalize other parts when Hitler supported those people whose principal concern was the racial policy.[22] Only a master juggler could have kept things going for even so short a time.

The National Socialist regime was a hodge-podge of individuals and organizations promoting the revolution or maintaining the essentials of normal life or doing both at once. It included a rudimentary political system, because the revolution had not progressed to the stage where reality and "facts" could be entirely ignored and consequently governmental power had to be used to promote some regularity of interpersonal relations. Although the Third Reich thus was a kind of state, it was also, and more significantly, an experiment in creating a brand-new, antihistorical social order. The experiment depended entirely upon the mode of operations described above, and this mode in turn depended upon the power of the single leader.

When the leadership principle was in operation, it went a long way toward guaranteeing that everyone would be subject to the daily shifting confidence of the *Führer*, but Hitler's power was not solely a matter of mechanical arrangements. It also depended upon the voluntary support of the different types of people who, consciously or unconsciously, cooperated with him in furthering the revolutionary goals of National Socialism.

One reason for Hitler's domination of all who served him was the force of his personality. His belief in his mission and his confidence in his ability to carry it out gave him, even when he was failing physically and mentally, an aura of total assuredness that overawed virtually everyone, from the wildest revolutionary to the most practical man of affairs, who came in contact with him. When he assigned a task or agreed to support a project, his lieutenants could not help believing that they had been given real power to carry out a crucial assignment. Such personal contacts, however, were necessarily relatively infrequent.

A more mundane reason for Hitler's power was that many saw him as the principal or even sole representative of the German people. Since all the men and institutions of bourgeois democracy had been destroyed, those who identified with the German national community, both among the regime's functionaries and among the general population, could find no one else who symbolized it.

Hitler's own claim to power was based on his capacity as a revolutionary. Although his claim undoubtedly was effective among the Third Reich's functionaries, it cannot be assumed that all of them fully understood and enthusiastically accepted his vision of the new order. Not everyone demonstrated the "faithfulness" of Himmler, who always unquestioningly obeyed Hitler, "the only man who could say no to the SS," even when Hitler was supporting one of his rivals, and who, although dumbfounded and appalled by the order to commence the Final Solution, rigorously carried it out with the clearest realization of the limitations of his own bourgeois mentality compared to the ice-cold revolutionary logic of the *Führer*.

The case of Goebbels illustrates the difficulty of the revolutionary leader's demand for total acceptance and compliance. Goebbels had come under Hitler's spell in the early 1920s, and he continued thereafter to be "recharged" (as he said) upon every personal contact with the *Führer*. He advocated the extermination of the Jews and was privy to the Final Solution in its early stages. During the war, however, as his responsibilities for domestic order and morale increased, he became more and more practically oriented. He came to believe in a rational organization of the eastern occupied territories, a less brutal treatment of the Soviet peoples, and a more flexible foreign policy. He repeatedly complained about the inefficiency of the war effort and about Hitler's tolerance for incompetents in positions of power and his inability to "make up his mind," but his only recourse was to hope that the *Führer* would change his ways.[23]

The important personages of the Third Reich, beyond any doubt, followed Hitler as a revolutionary leader and a visionary, although many of them had serious reservations about some of his policies and some of them denounced National Socialism after the fall of the Third Reich. The rank and file of the SS, the vanguard of the master race carefully selected and conditioned to Hitler and Himmler's view of the new order, undoubtedly contained some cynics. Nonetheless, most of this new breed of viceroys probably resembled Eichmann in seeing themselves as idealists who sacrificed everything and everybody for their idea,[24] a conclusion supported by their postwar inability to see that they "had done anything wrong." It will be recalled, once again, that even Eichmann balked at the killing of German Jews.

The fanatical commitment to change of the National Socialist movement meant that it had to depend upon a community of true believers, but its scope and diversity meant that it was also subject to ideological deviation, misunderstanding, and ignorance. The leadership principle guaranteed that these ideological failings would not impede the furthering of the *Führer's* grand design.

Although the Third Reich was one of history's purest autocracies, there were obviously limits to Hitler's power, but limits resulting not so much from imperfections in the machinery of power as from the context within which it had to operate. The environment of the leadership principle was not the future but the present, and inseparable from the present were not only the need to maintain basic normal social systems but also the great force of the opinions and attitudes of a people seeking a political community and a popular government.

In order to have the economy, polity, and army necessary for existence and expansion in the international political system, the regime had to make the obvious compromises by relying on bourgeois methods and expert personnel; but, much more importantly, it had to compromise by accepting the German people's acceptance of it. This acceptance was in part a matter of not violating too seriously their expectations, as when the Final Solution was impeded and the euthanasia program halted by the force of public opinion. Popular acceptance, however, had another, more fundamental aspect. Most Germans had accepted a number of Hitler's policies as beneficial to themselves and to the German national community and as coming from a man who represented that community. His early, costless victories in foreign policy and his continuing solicitude for the material well-being and social standing of the average German gave his regime a popular legitimacy that was a direct impediment to his main goal of creating an entirely new way of looking at political life. His acceptance by normal society was one of the greatest limitations to his power.

In a more basic sense, Hitler was limiting his power to effect revolution by inadvertently strengthening the bourgeois society he was trying to destroy. His program of social homogenization was reinforced by the movement of population from rural areas and the shift of labor into industrial and service occupations resulting from the finally unavoidable mobilization for war production, and he became involved in the construction of a democratic national community. His unwanted success in this counterrevolutionary direction may be measured by the most un-Weimar-like stability of the Federal Republic.

The brief life of the Third Reich was a final limitation to Hitler's power, for he did not have the time to educate even one generation in the spirit of his mission. Yet, as he so clearly realized, "everyone knows" that mankind is divided into races. Future revolutionaries may well derive encouragement from his effort to build upon this "knowledge."

And even if our endeavors should end in failure, it will only be a temporary failure. For I have opened the eyes of the whole world to the Jewish peril.[25]

Notes

1. Karl Dietrich Bracher, *The German Dictatorship* (New York: Frederick A. Praeger, 1970), pp. 203, 215–16, 220–22; Dietrich Orlow, *The History of the Nazi Party, 1933–1945* (Pittsburgh: University of Pittsburgh Press, 1973), pp. 23–24.
2. Edward N. Peterson, *The Limits of Hitler's Power* (Princeton, N.J.: Princeton University Press, 1969), p. 430.
3. Hermann Rauschning, *The Voice of Destruction* (New York: G. P. Putnam's Sons, 1940), p. 157; François Genoud, ed., *The Testament of Adolf Hitler* (London: Cassell, 1960), pp. 59–61.
4. Joachim C. Fest, *The Face of the Third Reich* (New York: Random House, 1970), "General von X."

5. Fest, pp. 236, 243.
6. Rauschning, p. 201.
7. Ernst Fraenkel, *The Dual State* (New York: Oxford University Press, 1941), pp. 73–80.
8. Orlow, pp. 136, 137, 169, 222, 261; David Schoenbaum, *Hitler's Social Revolution* (Garden City, N.Y.: Doubleday, 1966), pp. 233, 234, 237.
9. Joseph Nyomarkay, *Charisma and Factionalism in the Nazi Party* (Minneapolis: University of Minnesota Press, 1967), p. 27.
10. Orlow, p. 401.
11. *Nazi Conspiracy and Aggression* (Washington, D.C.: U.S. Government Printing Office, 1946), 1:191.
12. Bracher, pp. 212, 236; Nyomarkay, p. 32.
13. Orlow, pp. 139, 283; see Albert Speer, *Inside the Third Reich* (New York: Macmillan, 1970), p. 210.
14. Alan S. Milward, *The German Economy at War* (London: University of London Press, 1965), p. 9; Colin Cross, *Adolf Hitler* (London: Hodder & Stoughton, 1973), p. 109; Orlow, p. 287.
15. For example, see Louis P. Lochner, ed., *The Goebbels Diaries, 1942–1943* (Garden City, N.Y.: Doubleday, 1948), pp. 214, 217, 229, 235, 236, 314, 527.
16. Heinz Höhne, *The Order of the Death's Head: The Story of Hitler's S.S.* (New York: Coward-McCann, 1969), pp. 12, 13; Roger Manvell and Heinrich Frankel, *Himmler* (New York: G. P. Putnam's Sons, 1965), p. 156; Gerald Reitlinger, *The SS* (London: Heinemann, 1956), p. 219; Nyomarkay, p. 31.
17. This paragraph relies on Milward, pp. 2, 9–10, 25, 52.
18. Milward, pp. 80, 154; Orlow, pp. 377, 378, 379, 472; Speer, pp. 215, 218, 274.
19. Milward, pp. 145, 157; *Nazi Conspiracy and Aggression,* 1:916–17.
20. Milward, p. 159.
21. Speer, pp. 537, 289, 232.
22. Milward, p. 117; Orlow, pp. 434, 471.
23. Lochner, passim.
24. Hannah Arendt, *Eichmann in Jerusalem* (New York: Viking Press, 1963), p. 37.
25. Genoud, p. 52.

III
Stalin's Union of Soviet Socialist Republics

*Can such a radical transformation
of the old bourgeois system of society
be achieved without a violent revolution,
without the dictatorship of the proletariat?*
JOSEPH STALIN

6
Stalinism

During the twenty-five years he dominated the Soviet Union, Joseph Stalin brought about social changes of unprecedented scope and comprehensiveness, and, despite a surprisingly persistent belief to the contrary, his most important revolutionary policies were based upon a system of ideas he had derived from the theories of Marx and Lenin. He believed that he was the logical successor to Lenin, as Lenin had considered himself the logical successor to Marx; and, as Lenin had "proved" his claim by capturing and holding state power in Russia, Stalin "proved" his by succeeding Lenin and carrying out the First Five-Year Plan. An understanding of Stalin's policies is impossible without reference to his ideas, but since he adopted some of them more or less intact from Lenin or from Marx, his presentation of them is incomplete. This incompleteness makes it necessary to refer on occasion to the writings of his predecessors, with the result that his world view is more difficult to elucidate than those of the other great twentieth-century revolutionary leaders here under consideration.

Stalin continued the simplification of Marxism begun by Lenin until he arrived at a few fundamental propositions concerning the basis of human knowledge, the nature of man, the essence of history, the dynamics of social change, and the conditions necessary for an ideal society. In this process he eliminated all vestiges of social science from Marxism-Leninism; all his propositions were in the form of postulates that provided orientations to experience and prescriptive grounds for action. Stalinism is the refinement of a number of immutable postulates and the deduction of their implications, which may or may not correspond to what social science and common sense perceive as reality.

Stalin, unsurprisingly, was principally a man of action who believed that the basis of action was willpower rather than theoretical knowledge. In 1907 he emphasized the importance of human will and striving, and in 1952, quoting Engels, he insisted on the "subjection of social forces to our will." The spirit of Leninism, he said, is "The consciousness that the victory of socialist construction in our country is possible and necessary," and he fully appreciated Lenin's practical emphasis on stubbornness, enthusiasm, will, and tenacity. His admiration for American efficiency, "that indomitable force which neither knows nor recognizes obstacles," nicely expresses his fundamental commitment to the power of the human will.[1]

Stalin's belief in willpower as the principal force of social action was not solely the natural posture of a self-styled man of steel, for it was based upon, and continued and refined, a main strand of Leninism. Lenin's well-known "voluntarism," which many have seen as inconsistent with the "materialism" and "determinism" associated with the Bolsheviks' Marxist heritage, was a statement, fully relevant to the Russian environment, that fundamental social change can occur only when some people have succeeded in freeing themselves of the bonds of the existing society. This proposition that the human will can dominate man's social, as well as material, environment is supported by the concept of "materialism," which rejects the thesis of the "bifurcation" of reality and thus admits the possibility that beliefs, attitudes, and other ideational phenomena are amenable to human control in the same way that material objects are generally assumed to be. "Materialism," said Lenin, implies that "things in themselves" can be known "directly, immediately, face to face," and thus the way is open for the revolutionary's mastery of the world.[2] Similarly, the famous "determinist" element in Leninism gives positive encouragement to revolutionary initiative, for it guarantees the success of action taken in conformity with the march of history; it has nothing to do with a fatalistic view of the futility of action. Revolutionary change in human affairs is inevitable, and once a change has occurred it can be seen that no other development would have been possible. Such change is perfectly compatible with, indeed depends upon, conscious revolutionary activity, even though the revolutionaries themselves cannot fully predict the direction of history's march.

Voluntarism, materialism, and determinism are logically associated with the theory of the "unity of theory and practice," the belief that understanding comes only through action.[3] In his first thorough account of Leninism, Stalin defined theory as "the experience of the working class movement in all countries taken in its general aspect" and said that the only way to create "a truly proletarian party armed with revolutionary theory" is to "restore the disturbed unity between theory and practice" by testing socialist theories "in the crucible of the revolutionary struggle of the masses, in the crucible of living practice." Stalin gives every indication that he fully appreciated Lenin's claim to superior revolutionary theory based upon the fact that he alone "had made a revolution," although his appreciation appears more instinctive than cerebral.[4]

The unity of theory and practice implies that the only meaningful human life is a life of action, that reflection and speculation can serve only to obscure reality, and that reality is the interaction of the human will with the material and social environment and thus is identical with change. Since change is the goal, power is the indispensable means. Stalin inherited a ready-made justification for his sound commonsense conviction that success is the only criterion of truth.

Like most convinced activists, and especially political activists in imperial Russia, Stalin saw human life and human history as struggle, and again he could draw on Marx and Lenin to support his view. Most varieties of Marxism rely heavily upon so-called dialectics, the principle that change and thus progress result from the interaction of opposing forces. Underlying this concept of dialectics is Marx's definition of man as that being who interacts with his environment in order to master it and eventually to render meaningless the distinction between the actor and the thing acted upon. Although this view of man as a "producing animal" reappears in Stalin's intense concern with the economic aspects of human life, his own concept of struggle probably received its principal reinforcement from the idea that the dynamic element in human history is provided by the struggles of men against men or, as the Bolsheviks usually phrased it, the "class struggle." The concept of struggle, of course, is closely related to the idea of power and thus, to Stalin, to the idea of will. History is struggle among people, one cannot struggle successfully unless he has power, and the power of the will can overcome the powers of expertise, wealth, and position.

To Stalin, moreover, struggle was desirable because human progress depended upon it. During its history, mankind more than once had moved from one type of society to another completely different type, this movement had been progressive in nature, and therefore progress depended on revolution.[5] The next stage of social development, which his own revolution was to create, was to be a type of human association without historical precedent, and he was optimistic enough to believe that he had gone at least part of the way to its realization. In 1936 he announced that since "socialism" had been achieved, the Soviet working class, peasantry, and intelligentsia "have no counterparts in the history of mankind." In his last work he reaffirmed his conviction that, for the first time in history, the exploitation of man by man had been eliminated.[6] Although under socialism dynamic changes still occur, there is a specific and concrete goal—namely, the communist society—which at least can be closely approximated by the proper handling of these dynamic forces. Because there are no precedents for communism, its details cannot be anticipated, but its basic principles and working logic can be stipulated.

Since in human history the old has repeatedly been replaced by the superior new, the new is "inevitable," its superiority is a logical not a factual matter, and the present is doomed.[7] "Historical determinism" means that the proper understanding of the past allows one to deduce, on the grounds of pure logic, that a new and desirable social order will come to pass and that anything done to effect this transition is both justified and guaranteed of success.

By means of a curious disregard of the facts, both conservative realists and revolutionary idealists have made it currently fashionable to consider Stalin a power-mad paranoid with the tyrant's lack of any goal other than self-gratification. The evidence, however, shows that (no matter how unpleasant personally) he was a dedicated revolutionary who unambiguously expressed a perfectly clear conception of the historically unprecedented society his labors were to bring into existence. This new society was to be communism, the ideal order of human life envisioned by both Marx and Lenin and describable by the slogan, "from each according to his ability, to each according to his needs." The exploitation of man by man will become logically impossible in a society in which "work" has become "life's prime want" and "social property" is seen as "the sacred and inviolable basis of the existence of society." In communist society, "production will be regulated by the requirement of society, and computation of the requirements of society will acquire paramount importance for the planning bodies." The amount of labor will be measured not through value (as in commodity production) but directly by the amount of time expended on the production of goods, and labor will be distributed not according to the law of value but "by the growth of society's demands for goods."[8]

Despite the tendency of outside observers not to take seriously these clear expressions of Stalin's purpose, all his most important innovative policies can be understood only by reference to his commitment to a new society of the future. One can see how his practices of "purging" and "terror" have given comfort to those who have characterized him as pursuing power "for its own sake," but such an interpretation of this part of his behavior cannot possibly apply also to his great innovations in the economic and cultural fields. There is, moreover, an element of hypocrisy in this dismissal of Stalin as a tyrant, for many who practice it, including a number of post-Stalinist Soviet intellectuals, profess their faith in Lenin's idealism despite Lenin's straightforward acknowledgment of the cost of his own omelet.

Underlying Stalin's concept of communist society was his belief that man is a producing animal who realizes his true humanness only under the proper conditions of economic production. What is "real" in human life is the relation of man to his fellow men in the productive process. As this process has evolved into higher forms throughout human history, man's ability to produce has increased and his rational nature has been enhanced. The specific productive process structured according to the utilization of power and machinery and the division of labor in the factory of classical capitalism is the ideal form for the fullest development of man's rationality, but its potential has been frustrated by the social arrangements of capitalism. These arrangements—the manager's monopoly of understanding of the goals of production, the accumulation of capital (or "dead labor" parasitic upon "living labor"), and the phenomenon of commodities that are based on value rather than on need—must be eliminated in order for man's true nature to be realized. Their replacement by new social arrangements, combined with the retention of the factory method of production, will create a new society with an entirely new culture and usher in a new era of human history.

Stalin's ultimate goal was to create a new and higher kind of man, a process that required the "remolding of men's psychologies"; a "cultural re-education of society" was required before communism could become a reality.[9] To accomplish this goal was the task of revolutionary leadership, for such basic changes do not occur autonomously: as Lenin said about Bolshevism's favorite candidates for remolding, left to themselves industrial workers can develop only trade-union consciousness.

According to Stalin, the new "psychology" depended principally upon the creation of the proper "forces of production" and the proper "relations of production." The productive forces of society are the "relation of society to the forces of nature, in contest with which it secures the material values it needs," and the relations of production are "the relations of men to one another in the process of production."[10] The forces of production required for the ideal society are those of the large-scale industry of classical capitalism; it is thus necessary, as Lenin had said, to "electrify the Soviet Union." "Only when the country has been electrified, only when our industry, our agriculture, our transport system, have been placed upon the technical basis of modern large-scale industry, shall we achieve final victory."[11] The relations of production that are to be combined with these forces of production to achieve communism are those of "social property," which meant the elimination of all the capitalist impediments to the true society of work in the factory. For both Stalin and Lenin, the agrarian sector of the economy they had inherited from the czars, with its unmechanized, small-scale forces of production and its reliance upon commodities, was absolutely inconsistent with communism, and they thus considered it the epitome of "capitalism."

Stalin never departed from his belief that "modern industry"— which he understood as large-scale, mechanized, and "heavy," that is, the kind of productive process Marx had seen as essential to nineteenth-century capitalism—was a necessary condition for communism. Following Lenin again, he stressed the need, "at the price of extremely great economy in the economic life of our state"—that is, by keeping the standard of living very low—to accumulate savings to pay for "electrification"; he emphasized that the "whole psychology and habits" of the small farmer could be remolded only by the "application of machines to agriculture on a mass scale, electrification on a mass scale"; he insisted that "to beat the internal enemy" the whole economic life of the country must be put on the "new technical basis of modern large-scale production"; and he said that the issue in the countryside was either electrification or a return to capitalism.[12]

The relations of production necessary for communist society consisted in a "concentration of production," such as that of advanced capitalist industry, under "public" ownership. Under the Russian Empire, capitalism had "so concentrated the means of production in industry" that the Soviet government was able to "nationalize" or "expropriate" them and thus make them the "property of society."[13] By this act, the industrial sector of the Soviet economy was freed of the phenomenon of the commodity, a product that may be sold to any purchaser if he commands its value and that once sold becomes the exclusive property of the purchaser, the original owner having no further control of it.[14] The specific type of relations of production that Stalin calls "social property," therefore, makes it possible for need to replace value as the principle of economic distribution. Since the forces and relations of production required by communism do not yet characterize the entire Soviet economy, the USSR is in an interim period of "socialism," during which the "basic economic law" is

> the securing of the maximum satisfaction of the constantly rising material and cultural requirements of the whole of society through the continuous expansion and perfection of socialist production on the basis of higher techniques.[15]

To raise mankind to a new stage of social development, both the forces and the relations of production must be appropriately changed, and a change in either contributes to change in the other. In 1952 Stalin stated that the innovations made by the Soviet regime in the relations of production—the early "expropriation" of industry and the later collectivization of agriculture—had made possible "tremendous strides" in the development of both the industrial and the agricultural forces of production.[16] Nonetheless, the forces of production, the "most mobile and revolutionary forces," "undeniably move in advance of the relations of production even under socialism."[17] In a socialist society, however, steps can be taken "to bring the lagging relations of production into conformity with the character of the productive forces" because socialist society "does not include obsolescent classes that might organize resistance."[18] These steps, according to Stalin's last pronouncement, should be the elevation of collective farm property "to the level of public property" and the replacement of commodity circulation "by a system of products-exchange, under which the central government, or some other social-economic centre, might control the whole product of social production in the interests of society." In addition, however, the forces of production should be improved, with special emphasis upon the "expansion of the production of the means of production."[19]

Although Stalin seems to have believed that the forces of production have some autonomous influence on society, in the above discussion he is saying principally that both the forces and the relations of production required for communism must be created by the leaders of the revolutionary regime. He also recommends the general "cultural advancement of society," that is, the development of everyone's physical and mental abilities so that all people can participate actively in the revolution and, in order to eliminate the superior-subordinate relation of capitalism, can perform a number of roles in the complex division of labor.[20] In all of this, Stalin is unconcerned with the practical relationships between the forces of production and the relations of production and with the problem of how the regime is to accomplish what he is recommending. His "economic theory" is only a statement that once the proper forces and relations of production are realized, a communist society will result; he makes no effort to establish any empirical connection between the utopian end and the stipulated means to this end. His reasoning is principally deductive and, since the precise nature of communism cannot be anticipated, much of it relies upon key concepts that are defined only negatively. A "planned economy," for example, is the absence of the "anarchy" of the capitalist price system, and "profitableness" is the absence of capitalist "crises of overproduction."

Stalin's indifference to the evidence and reasoning of the bourgeois science of economics was probably a necessary condition for the unmatched fanaticism of his belief in the absolute necessity of a given mode of economizing for the realization of mankind's true potential. At a time when the capitalist world was becoming concerned with the problems of automation and mass leisure, he retained the essence of the classical Marxism that saw human life as the never-ending struggle to wrest a living from a recalcitrant natural and social environment.

According to Stalin, the "fundamental problem of Leninism" was not the peasantry—that is, how to bring about the Bolshevik coup of 1917—but the dictatorship of the proletariat—that is, what to do after the coup had been accomplished.[21] The seizure of power in 1917 was part of the first or "political" stage of the revolution; it was concerned with the initial "establishment of the Soviet government" and was directed until his death by Lenin. The second, and really more important, stage was the "economic" stage, which Stalin considered solely his own responsibility.

The first stage of the revolution, said Stalin, was a unique event. Unlike the bourgeois revolutions that had preceded it, it was not a political response to a fundamental change in economic conditions, for prior to its occurrence there existed no "ready-made rudiments of a socialist economy." Upon gaining political control, the Bolsheviks "had to create new, socialist forms of economy, 'starting from scratch,' so to speak."[22] Hence the 1917 coup and the resulting Soviet government were not based on a "social class" in the sense of a group of people sharing a desire for a new kind of society; there was no group in the Russian Empire comparable to the bourgeoisie in pre-Revolutionary France. Like Lenin and all other careful observers of the Bolsheviks' capture and retention of power, Stalin could find no demand for socialism coming from a "class" of industrial workers alienated by capitalism, or, for that matter, from anyone else.

In insisting, however, that Lenin's coup was a capture of power by the "proletariat" and that the subsequent government was a "dictatorship of the proletariat," Stalin was not engaging in rationalization or in double-talk. His "proletarian" was not an assembly-line worker but a man who understood the dialectical nature of human history and who realized that the end of man's exploitation of man was not only possible and desirable but inevitable. The driving force behind the latest and therefore the most progressive social revolution was not an objectively identifiable group of people who had developed an ideology from a common economic experience but a self-selected band of professional revolutionaries. Although the forces and relations of production are of supreme importance in determining the nature of any type of society, they have very little to do with the change from one type to another.

During the period of the dictatorship of the proletariat, said Stalin, the capitalists and landlords are to be eliminated, the peasantry educated, and socialism constructed. Following Lenin again, he insisted that the "class struggle" does not disappear after the establishment of the dictatorship of the proletariat, but "merely changes its form, and becomes in many respects still more bitter."[23] This struggle, however, is "nonantagonistic," for it does not imply the destruction of the proletarian dictatorship, although the regime must control it carefully in order to prevent its becoming antagonistic. The power generated by this struggle can be used by the dictatorship to bring about the projected new society.

The concept of proletarian in this theory is the same as that in the theory of the October Revolution; that is, the second stage of the revolution, like the first, is the autonomous act of a small association of those who have understood history. The landlords, peasantry, and capitalists, on the other hand, are large social groups with shared orientations deriving from their respective functions in the pre-Soviet mode of economic production. These orientations cause them to be unalterably opposed to the goals of the revolution, but this "contradiction" is "nonantagonistic" because the revolutionary regime thoroughly understands its nature and commands irresistible political power. For Stalin, these people who oppose socialism are incapable of political initiative; they can only resist the initiative taken by the proletarian dictatorship.

While smashing the resistance of the residual counterrevolutionary classes, the regime must also "elevate the masses of the working class to the level of the class interests of the proletariat." The "working class" here is defined in terms of its position in the mode of economic production; it contains all those people who work under the conditions of "socialist property" and "electrification," that is, workers in government-owned heavy industry. This group, however, like the post-1917 landlords, peasantry, and capitalists and like the pre-1917 industrial workers, is incapable of generating political power. Even after the successful completion of the first stage of the revolution, the working class remains "inert" and "politically indifferent." It cannot attain the "level of the class interests of the proletariat," that is, come to understand the goals of the revolutionary regime, until the entire economy is structured according to the proper forces and relations of production. In the meantime, the working class is only favorably inclined to the task of revolution; it can give only "sympathy and support" to the dictatorship of the proletariat.[24]

Although the essence of Stalinism is that changes effected by the revolutionary leadership in the forces and relations of production will "remold men's psychologies," during the drive toward socialism, the "first or lower phase of communism," certain elements among the landlords, peasants, and bourgeoisie are so attached to their counterrevolutionary interests that they must remain outside the new society.[25] The most interesting expression of this point occurs when Stalin describes as ridiculous the question whether the kulak can be admitted to the collective farms: "Of course not, as he is a sworn enemy of the collectivization movement. This would appear to be plain."[26]

When by 1936 the proletarian regime, with the sympathy and support of the working class, had removed these objective enemies from society, "socialism" was established in the Soviet Union. Under socialism, the transformation of the economy, although only partial because agriculture has been "collectivized" rather than "nationalized" and "electrified," nonetheless has guaranteed that such hostile "classes" will never reoccur. To carry on the revolution, now from socialism to communism, remains the sole responsibility of the regime, but under socialism it has the sympathy and support of every social group within the Soviet Union.

Although all phases of the revolution are under the exclusive control of the true proletarian movement, the "masses" cannot be ignored.

> But the Party cannot be only a *vanguard* detachment. It must at the same time be a detachment of the [working] *class,* part of the class, closely bound up with it by all the fibres of its being.[27]

The revolutionary leadership is dependent upon its acceptance by the masses; the Party must take care not to become isolated from the needs and requirements of the masses; there must be continuous conferences, consultations, and meetings to "test the mood of the masses" and to aid in exposing the mistakes of the leadership; the revolutionary must not rush ahead of the masses, for to do so is "to lose contact" with them; revolutionary ideas must "force their way through" and become the possession of the masses; and the leaders must allow "the development of the creative initiative and independent activity of the masses."[28] In response to these requirements, the Soviet regime has given itself "the most pronounced mass character" possible under transitional circumstances.[29]

Since leadership of the revolution had been divided between Lenin and Stalin, Stalin never had been politically dependent upon any group outside the revolutionary movement itself, and once his power was assured his treatment of the Soviet people was insensitive when it was not cruel. In theory, moreover, he held that the "masses" could provide at best only sympathetic support for the revolution. These considerations have suggested hypocrisy, but Stalin's agreement with Lenin on the need for the regime to have its roots in the masses was an integral part of his ideology. As with most such ideological principles, however, it cannot be interpreted according to the assumptions and practices of nonrevolutionary politics.

The revolutionary movement must be bound to the masses of the working class by all the fibers of its being because only in this way can it avoid becoming detached from reality and losing itself in a fog of expertise and "bureaucracy." The regime's functionaries must always remember that they do not "possess all the knowledge necessary for giving correct leadership" and that they must go to the masses for assistance.[30] For Stalin, keeping attuned to the experiences of the masses was intended not to discover what most people want or to identify their interests, but to ensure that the revolutionary movement remains faithful to the principle of the unity of theory and practice.

The "masses," furthermore, have a certain purity and naiveté that enables them to grasp the essence of important situations. As Stalin said, "Simple people sometimes prove to be far nearer to the truth than some highly placed institutions."[31] Their ability to get to the heart of the matter resulted in part from their innocence of bourgeois expertise, one of Stalin's principal irritants. In 1928 he complained that bourgeois experts by their various theories "are always ready to proclaim the doom of the Soviet government" and the next year he fulminated against the retention of bourgeois and petty-bourgeois theories:

> Is it so difficult to grasp that without an irreconcilable struggle against bourgeois theories on the basis of Marxist-Leninist theory, the complete victory over the class enemy cannot be won?

All bourgeois theories that question the Soviet achievements should be "exterminated root and branch." Twenty-three years later he was still seeking new economic concepts and scolding his economists for their failure to devise them. He once had hoped that the working class would "create its own technical and industrial intelligentsia," but his hope was never fulfilled.[32]

Stalin's emphasis on the mass character of his regime also served to guard against the danger of its becoming bureaucratically ossified. Although he quoted Lenin to the effect that the revolution required "an iron party steeled in the struggle," a party "enjoying the confidence of all that is honest in the given class" and "capable of keeping track of and influencing the mood of the masses," as early as 1926 he made it most clear that the "dictatorship of the proletariat" did not mean the dictatorship of the Party. Identifying the Party with the regime could lead only to complacency and a divorce of leadership from the masses.[33] Stalin's warning was not completely heeded, for (as he later announced) bureaucratic tendencies grew, especially in Party offices and among the staffs of the soviet, economic, cooperative, and trade union organizations, until the revolution itself was threatened. The only appropriate response was "to smash bureaucracy in our institutions and organizations."[34]

In order to maintain the revolution, the regime had to maximize its flexibility, its appreciation of the need for change, and its sensitivity to the masses' capacity for change. It therefore had to avoid at all costs the routinization of its power, especially in the form of a highly disciplined party, and it had to involve as many people as possible in its innovative efforts. The only sure way to smash bureaucracy conclusively was to vest complete power in a single leader, whose revolutionary theory, although often expressed through the Party and other agencies of the regime (thus justifying their existence), then would form a unity with the actions of the masses of the working class. By this train of reasoning, one of history's least popular revolutionary leaders inseparably linked himself with ordinary and average men and women.

The transformation of Soviet society during the second stage of the revolution naturally enough required the elimination of the institutions, values, theories, and attitudes of the old, so-called bourgeois or capitalist society; it was necessary to pursue an *"offensive* against the capitalist elements along *the whole front."*[35] Stalin's offensives against the bourgeois concept of the national community and the bourgeois interpretation of history often have been misunderstood and hence are in need of some special clarification.

Throughout his fairly extensive writing on "the national question" from 1913 until 1936, Stalin correctly treated the consciousness of national community as a bourgeois phenomenon. The October Revolution, he said, had proved that national self-determination, a bourgeois device, was not the only way to liberate oppressed peoples. The idea that the USSR should become "a single, common Great Russian nation with a single, common Great Russian language" is "national chauvinist and anti-Leninist." Indeed, "deviation toward nationalism" must be carefully guarded against, for "the survivals of capitalism in people's minds are much more tenacious in the sphere of the national problem than in any other sphere."[36] The bourgeois principle that all members of society can join together in a single community obviously contradicts the Leninist principle that by creating "classes" capitalism raises insuperable barriers to true community. Said Lenin, in discussing the bourgeois-democratic revolution:

> if it is "national" it means that there *must* be "unity of will" precisely in so far as this revolution satisfies the national needs and requirements. Beyond the boundaries of democracy there can be no unity of will between the proletariat and the peasant bourgeoisie. Class struggle between them is inevitable. . . .[37]

The great majority of non-Soviet commentators has seen Stalin's later theory of history, with its emphasis upon the perennially leading role of the Russian or Soviet people in world affairs, as a rather obvious "national chauvinist and anti-Leninist" repudiation of his earlier views. Stalin's so-called Russia-firstness, however, was perfectly consistent with the basic principles of his world view discussed above. His principal concern was to project the future into the past, and the things that he and his official historians said constituted an original and imaginative attempt to "struggle against bourgeois theories on the basis of Marxist-Leninist theory."

The essence of this new history was the thesis that virtually every important innovation in human civilization during the past few thousand years was accomplished by people who lived within the area occupied since 1920 by the Soviet Union. In recent centuries, the Great Russians have monopolized such innovations, including (of course) the invention of capitalism, but further into the past other people of the area in question served as the vanguard of progress.[38] This account of history, by repudiating "bourgeois objectivism," made the past consistent with the future by stating that past progress was the product of the biological and geographical predecessors of the members of the current socialist society, the people who, by definition, are producing and will produce present and future progress. The "Soviet-firstness" theory served to provide a logical historical context for Lenin's and Stalin's revolutions and thus to reinforce their thesis that their triumph was inevitable.

Stalin's view of world politics was constructed from the several ideas and theories just discussed. International power was divided between the socialist bloc led by the Soviet Union, history's first socialist state, and the capitalist bloc of the bourgeois democracies and their satellite "colonial" areas. Since socialism and capitalism represented two different stages of man's historical development, conflict between them was unavoidable. Since capitalism was at the lower stage and thus by definition obsolescent, it would do everything in its power to impede its own decline, although it could only postpone its inevitable collapse. Any increase in the power of the socialist bloc resulted in the even more desperate resistance of the capitalist bloc. The bourgeois democracies, for example, had set Hitler against the Soviet Union, but this scheme to save capitalism had been frustrated by the virtually unaided heroics of the socialist fatherland.[39] Every effort to improve the domestic situation in the Soviet Union necessarily increased the hostility of the nonrevolutionary world.

Although socialism initially was established "in one country," as the latest and most progressive form of society it had universal applicability. Because it depended upon the existence of large-scale industry owned by society, to encourage "electrification" and "nationalization" anywhere in the world was progressive and to impede them was counterrevolutionary. Similarly, movements of national integration in the "underdeveloped areas" that attempted to build political communities composed of all social strata were inherently opposed to the new order and were the allies of imperialism even if they denounced it.

Eventually socialism would triumph throughout the world as the forces of production increasingly came into contradiction with the outmoded capitalist relations of production. This contradiction, however, had no force until it was exploited by a vanguard of conscious revolutionaries, and hence the construction of such a vanguard was an indispensable condition for world revolution. True revolutionary consciousness naturally was possessed only by those who had directed the process of revolution; it followed that the Leninist-Stalinist Soviet leadership had the only genuine claim to direct the world revolution and that, indeed, it was obliged to control the international proletarian vanguard. The world, according to Stalin, was a vast battleground between the agents of capitalism and what capitalism has called the worldwide "conspiratorial" organization of Communism. Stalin's position that "what is good for the Soviet Union is good for world revolution" was not a kind of protectionist rationalization but a genuine identification of Stalinist leadership with world revolutionary leadership. Anyone who was not completely responsive to Stalin's understanding of what had to be done was not a genuine revolutionary and consequently was in league with the reactionaries.

Notes

1. *Anarchism or Socialism?* (1906–07) (New York: International Publishers, 1953); *Economic Problems of Socialism in the U. S. S. R.* (Moscow: Foreign Languages Publishing House, 1952), p. 95; "Article" (1925), in Joseph Stalin, *Leninism* (New York: International Publishers, n.d.), 1:251; and "A Year of Great Change" (1929), in *Leninism*, 2:167, 168; Stalin, *Foundations of Leninism* (1924) New York: International Publishers, 1939), p. 126.
2. Stalin, *Dialectical and Historical Materialism* (1938) (New York: International Publishers, 1940), pp. 15–16, 17; V. I. Lenin, *Materialism and Empirio-Criticism* (New York: International Publishers, 1927), p. 322.
3. See Karl Marx, *The German Ideology* (New York: International Publishers, 1947), p. 197; and Alfred G. Meyer, *Leninism* (New York: Frederick A. Praeger, 1962), p. 88.
4. *Foundations of Leninism*, pp. 22, 28; "Article" (1925), in *Leninism*, 1:256;

Dialectical and Historical Materialism, p. 20.

5. *Dialectical and Historical Materialism,* pp. 12, 21, 34.

6. Stalin, *On the New Soviet Constitution* (1936) (New York: International Publishers, n.d.), pp. 7, 8, 11; *Economic Problems of Socialism,* p. 9.

7. "The Right Deviation in the C. P. S. U." (1929), in *Leninism,* 2:115.

8. *Economic Problems of Socialism,* pp. 26–27, 74. See his "Interview with the First American Labour Delegation in Russia" (1927), in *Leninism,* 1:387.

9. "Questions of Agrarian Policy in the Soviet Union" (1929), in *Leninism,* 2:198; "Foundations of Leninism" (1926), in *Leninism,* 1:51.

10. *Economic Problems of Socialism,* p. 70.

11. "Report to the Fourteenth Conference of the Russian Communist Party" (1925), in *Leninism,* 1:167.

12. "Speech" (1925), in *Leninism,* 1:229; "Results of the July Plenum of the Central Committee" (1928), in *Leninism,* 2:51, and repeated in "Questions of Agrarian Policy" (1929), p. 198; "The Right Danger in the C. P. S. U." (1928), in *Leninism,* 2:61; "Industrialization of the Country and the Right Deviation in the C. P. S. U." (1928), in *Leninism,* 2:78.

13. *Economic Problems of Socialism,* pp. 14, 15.

14. *Economic Problems of Socialism,* p. 58.

15. *Economic Problems of Socialism,* p. 45.

16. *Economic Problems of Socialism,* pp. 68–69.

17. *Economic Problems of Socialism,* pp. 57, 75, 76.

18. *Economic Problems of Socialism,* p. 57.

19. *Economic Problems of Socialism,* p. 74.

20. *Economic Problems of Socialism,* p. 76.

21. *Foundations of Leninism,* p. 61.

22. *Economic Problems of Socialism,* p. 9. This position follows Lenin and was expressed by Stalin as early as 1926; see *Leninism,* 1:266–67.

23. "Speech" (1925), in *Leninism,* 1:220; "The Right Deviation in the C. P. S. U.," p. 124.

24. *Foundations of Leninism,* pp. 109, 110; *Problems of Leninism* (1926), in *Leninism,* 1:269.

25. "The Right Deviation in the C. P. S. U.," p. 159.

26. "Questions of Agrarian Policy," p. 201.

27. *Foundations of Leninism,* p. 110.

28. "The October Revolution and the Tactics of the Russian Communists" (1924), in *Leninism,* 1:129, 131; "Questions and Answers" (1925), in *Leninism,* 1:236; "Interview with the First American Labour Delegation," p. 370; "Dizzy with Success" (1930), in *Leninism,* 2:220; *Dialectical and Historical Materialism,* p. 23; and "Report of the Central Committee to the Sixteenth Congress of the C. P. S. U." (1930), in *Leninism,* 2:313.

29. *Foundations of Leninism,* p. 59.

30. Stalin, *Mastering Bolshevism* (1937) (New York: New Century Publishers, 1945), p. 41.

31. *Mastering Bolshevism,* p. 43.

32. "Industrialization of the Country," p. 91; "Questions of Agrarian Policy," pp. 181, 195; *Economic Problems of Socialism,* pp. 22, 60; "New Conditions, New Tasks" (1931), in *Leninism,* 2:381.

33. "Problems of Leninism," in *Leninism,* 1:284, 295–96.

34. "Industrialization of the Country," p. 88. "Report of the Central Committee to the Sixteenth Congress," p. 313.

35. "Report of the Central Committee to the Sixteenth Congress," p. 295.

36. "Article" (1927), in *Marxism and the National Question* (New York: International Publishers, 1942), p. 202; "Reply to the discussion of a report to the Sixteenth Congress of the C. P. S. U." (1930), in *Marxism and the National Question,* p. 211; and "A Report to the Seventeenth Congress of the C. P. S. U." (1934), in *Marxism and the National Question,* p. 215.

37. *Two Tactics of Social-Democracy in the Democratic Revolution* (1905) (New York: International Publishers, 1935), p. 71.

38. For the specific elements of the new history, see Klaus Mehnert, *Stalin versus Marx* (London: Allen & Unwin, 1952), ch. 3.

39. Andrei Zhdanov, *The International Situation* (Moscow: Foreign Languages Publishing House, 1947), p. 8.

7

The Bolshevik Revolution, 1917–28

Both Lenin and Stalin divided their proletarian revolution into two stages. The first or "political" stage consisted in the "establishment of Soviet power," and it included both Lenin's coup of 1917 and his more significant accomplishment of maintaining his power during the subsequent Civil War. From the conclusion of the Civil War until the onset of his fatal illness, Lenin had only one year of full energy for shaping and refining the power he had seized and defended, and much of this year was consumed in foreign adventures. Although at his death he had determined the broad outlines of Soviet power, it remained for his successor to establish this power. The first stage of the revolution thus lasted until the succession to Lenin had been determined in a way that made possible the initiation of the second or "economic" stage. Hence Stalin not only directed the second stage of the revolution, but he also continued and consummated Lenin's leadership of the first stage.

The first stage of the revolution had its beginning in the seizure of state power in the Russian Empire by a small group of revolutionaries dominated by a fanatic determined to acquire undiluted power for the purpose of bringing into being a new kind of society. It is clear that, by 1917, political power in the empire was highly fragmented and that Lenin had an unmatched ability to take advantage of this situation; it is much less apparent why the precise configuration of forces that underlay the disintegration of the empire produced a Leninist regime dedicated to the construction of a social order radically different from both the traditional czarist autocracy and the incipient bourgeois society that was undermining it. The difficulty in understanding Lenin's success is increased by the fact that he conducted his coup, the Civil War, and the first years of his peacetime regime without the positive support of any significant social strata. The Bolshevik seizure and maintenance of power obviously did not in any sense "have their roots in" the Russian environment or tradition.

The Bolsheviks would not have triumphed if czarism had not collapsed, and the conditions associated with this collapse thus form the background for their triumph. These conditions included the presence of great numbers of peasants, unruly, disaffected, but accustomed to autocracy, and of a group of industrial workers, unable to organize to pursue their own practical interests; the absence of a constitutional tradition and of experienced bourgeois politicians; and the incredible ineffectiveness of the principle of hereditary autocracy. The political vacuum resulting from these conditions was receptive to a *putsch,* but the principal theoretical question is whether these conditions gave rise not merely to a *putsch* conducted by the most skillful politician on the spot but also to the victory of a movement determined to bring about an unprecedented social order. The question, in short, is whether there was any connection between the reasons why Lenin came to power and the purpose for which he sought power.

Lenin himself considered the triumph of the proletarian revolution inevitable. The political society of the Russian Empire was doomed. Its disintegration made possible the construction of a brand-new society, if only someone with an understanding of "historical necessity" had the will to capture and retain the unconditional power necessary to complete the destruction of the old and effect the creation of the new. The precise time at which conditions would favor the true revolutionary could not be inferred from Marxist theory but had to be determined according to the revolutionary's own understanding of prevailing circumstances. Lenin, in contrast to almost all other Marxists of his time, claimed that the revolutionary period was close at hand in the empire and that by 1917 it had arrived. While other Marxists were trying to decide whether the empire was "capitalist" enough to support a "proletarian" revolution, Lenin dismissed the theory that the industrial worker, because he could understand that the capitalist system made man into a commodity, would gain revolutionary consciousness. Instead, he took the position that left to themselves the workers could develop only "trade-union consciousness," that is, they could never go beyond demanding improvement within the existing capitalist economic system.[1] By recognizing that the workers were an integral part of bourgeois society and thus incapable of imagining its elimination, Lenin laid to rest the theory that the proletarian revolution was to gain its power from something called a social class.

The driving force of the revolution was to be a community of "intellectuals" who could transcend their environment and develop true revolutionary consciousness (*soznatel'nost'*) because they were not bound by their social roles to the existing mode of production. Although the ability of the revolutionary intellectuals to escape the bonds of their own society and its principles of knowledge allowed them to attain a perfect understanding of human history, they had to wait for the time to be ripe for the proletarian revolution. Lenin believed that he had some good reasons for predicting that social conditions in Russia would soon exhibit this kind of ripeness.

In the first place, the industrial workers of the empire, said Lenin, although they cannot understand the goals of Bolshevism, are receptive to Bolshevik slogans and leadership. Since he was fully aware that the industrial workers of highly developed capitalist economies, such as the British and the American, had been relatively unreceptive to the spark of Marxist theory, he must have believed that the Russian workers had some characteristics that distinguished them from their counterparts elsewhere. The further development of the Russian economy, he maintained, would result only in strengthening the industrial workers' tendency to trade-union consciousness and hence lessen the chances for a successful proletarian revolution.

In the second place, Lenin was not deterred by the fact that peasants made up the great majority of the empire's population. Although he never doubted that the peasants were basically "petty-bourgeois" and would fiercely resist the victorious proletariat, he believed that during the first or political stage of the revolution the proletarian vanguard could rely on the cooperation of the peasantry. The Russian peasantry, he said, was "interested not so much in the absolute preservation of private property as in the confiscation of the landlord's land, one of the principal forms of private property." Hence, even though remaining petty-bourgeois in their desire for the Black Repartition, the peasants can come to support, "wholeheartedly" and "radically," the first stage of the revolution. The peasants, unlike the big bourgeoisie, see nothing to fear in a movement designed to establish complete political equality.[2]

In short, Lenin's theory was that a small group of asocial revolutionaries could get control of the apparatus of the Russian state by gaining the support of the industrial workers for an antibourgeois program and by gaining the tolerance of the peasantry for a radical petty-bourgeois program. The coup was not solely a matter of outmaneuvering other aspirants to seize a government that really belonged to no one. It was also a response to objective conditions that made its success virtually inevitable.

The most significant feature of the Russian Empire prior to 1914 was the failure of its political system to keep pace with its changing economy and with the changing beliefs and expectations of significant segments of its population. The traditional autocracy, conceiving itself as over and above those it ruled and as justified because it cared for them better than they possibly could have cared for themselves, clashed with the growing industrialization of the economy, the increasing social awareness of those with modern education, and the beginnings of national consciousness among the empire's many cultural groups. The czarist regime could not eliminate the sources of these incompatibilities without undermining its position of strength in the world political system; it responded only by suppressing discontent and succeeded only in accentuating it. The more or less westernized intellectuals responded to their enforced isolation from political activity by indulging in utopian schemes and self-pity. The larger bourgeoisie had lost confidence in czarist autocracy, but they offered no substitutes because they believed that an attack on the czar would lead to a breakdown of political society itself.[3] The modern sectors, in short, had little loyalty to the czar, little experience in political affairs, and few ideas regarding a reasonable replacement for czardom.

On the other hand, despite this modernization, the great majority of the population was peasants. Although the peasantry was the natural ally of the autocracy, it had become disaffected toward the Romanov dynasty because the land reforms of the nineteenth century had failed to give the rights of landowners to the bulk of the peasant households. The reforms instead had created communes that periodically redivided the land under their control among their member families, an arrangement that hardly satisfied the peasant's desire for his own land. To make the situation worse, about half of all land was retained by the estate-owners. From the abolition of serfdom in 1861 to the beginning of World War I, the rural population of the Russian Empire doubled in size, and its frustrations bred among it a "spirit of sullen contempt for the dynasty" and an "indifference to its fate."[4]

Although large-scale industry had grown rapidly in the empire, the industrial worker remained oriented toward the village and the peasantry. He himself had only recently left the village, and he retained close links with his family, frequently including his wife and children, who remained there. These links were reinforced by the czarist regime's failure to provide him with legal protection in his new economic role.[5] He was dissatisfied with the industrial part of the economy, and he retained the peasant discontent he had brought from the village. He was integrated neither socially nor ideologically into his new way of life.

The situation in the empire was inherently unstable, and, sooner or later, the hereditary autocracy would have been replaced by another kind of political system. Although the new system undoubtedly would not have been liberal democracy, there was no precedent for the rigorously antibourgeois regime of the Bolsheviks. The inability of the empire to avoid involvement in World War I and its inability to fight a modern war against a much more modern enemy did not create the conditions that undermined czardom, but they brought these conditions to a rapid and thorough culmination. The emergency of 1917 created the political confusion that allowed Lenin to seize power from his less adept competitors, but it also sharpened and concentrated social discontents to a degree essential to the success of the movement determined to construct a completely unprecedented social order.

The unusual efforts, both civilian and military, required by the war accentuated the inefficiencies of czarist rule and the incompetence of the current czar. Discontent in urban areas was increased by severe shortages of food and other consumer goods and by inflation. In March 1917, these grievances were manifested in the great strike and demonstration in Petrograd, the czar's capital city. Although the morale of the empire's front-line troops seems to have held up well enough, that of the garrison troops, who were not at all anxious to be sent into action, was considerably lower. When the Petrograd garrison was ordered to disperse the demonstrators, it refused; the soldiers had taken the side of the former peasants now working in industry. This localized but massive defection convinced even Nicholas II that his abdication was unavoidable. The erosion of the belief in traditional autocracy even among the aristocracy itself was strikingly illustrated by the refusal of the Grand Duke Michael, the brother of Nicholas, to accept the crown, unless it was offered to him by a constituent assembly. This decision marked the end of the dynasty.

Without a czar, the old political system could not continue, and a new form of government had to be created. Probably the most likely response to the collapse of a hereditary monarchy in a relatively backward society would have been a military dictatorship, at least as an interim measure. In 1917, however, the disciplined troops were far from Petrograd engaged with the Central Powers. By the time they were available to act as a political force, the issues were muddled and the general population was in a condition approaching anarchy. In the absence of anyone else willing and able to form a government, on 16 March

1917 a provisional government was selected by the Duma (a body indirectly elected under the empire) in consultation with the leaders of the Soviets, the councils of workers and soldiers created during the uprising. This government proceeded to adopt advanced policies of civil liberties and rights and universal suffrage that were fantastically inappropriate to an underdeveloped society in a time of political chaos. Liberal democracy had no chance whatever to succeed the czars, but the liberal democrats apparently were incapable of realizing it.

The mass rising in Petrograd that was the immediate cause of czardom's sudden disintegration resulted from a failure of confidence brought on by material deprivation. The only reason the workers went to the streets was to demand an immediate and substantial improvement in their personal living and working conditions; they had no political orientation other than the belief that the present regime was incapable of satisfying their demands.[6] The forces behind the March uprising, and indeed behind all Petrograd politics until Lenin took over, have been best described by Vladimir Stankevich:

> Not a political thought, not a revolutionary slogan, not a conspiracy, and not a mutiny. But an elemental movement that suddenly reduced the whole old regime to ashes with nothing left over. . . . And not being able to formulate objections nor knowing how to resist, the mass began to repeat slogans alien to it and words not its own, and to permit itself to be inscribed into parties and organizations. Naturally, the least organized and the least demanding of organizations proved the most acceptable to the spirit of this mass. The Soviet, that meeting of half illiterate soldiers, appeared as their leader because it demanded nothing of them, serving only as a facade to cover up a complete lack of definite principles.[7]

This "elemental movement" was a special form of the *stikhiia,* the anarchic urge that always lay just below the surface of the Russian peasant society, and the Soviets were the most disciplined organizations it could produce. Although Lenin was bitterly opposed to "spontaneity" and the *stikhiia*, their transfer from a rural to an urban environment provided him and his band of rootless intellectuals with the power to effect their coup. The aimless force of the workers and soldiers was harnessed by the powerless but purposeful Bolsheviks.

In order to get and keep this elemental movement behind his revolutionary vanguard, Lenin had to outmaneuver other political groups that sought the same goal or that were trying to neutralize the workers and soldiers, and he also had to discredit and eventually destroy these rivals. At the same time, all his skill was required to control his own followers. If his plans for instituting a new kind of society were to be realized, the

Bolsheviks had to seize state power immediately, without any allies and without any commitments, but few of the Bolsheviks understood this. At his death, Lenin had succeeded in creating a monopoly of power for his vanguard, but the proper structuring of the vanguard itself remained to be completed.

During 1917 Lenin not only kept abreast of the shifting moods of the Petrograd workers and soldiers; he also undermined the various socialist and agrarian parties, also seeking popular support, and began the elimination of all institutional alternatives to the Bolshevik dictatorship. Before his coup, he benefited greatly from his ability always to be more radical than his rivals, for his was an all-or-nothing strategy. He out-flanked the Mensheviks by his refusal to cooperate with the bourgeoisie. By condemning the war, he played to the maximal desires of the garrison troops (and later in 1917 to the front-line troops as well). Throughout this period, the German government, seeing support of the Bolsheviks as a good method of reducing Russia's fighting capacity, gave him large sums of money, which he used for propaganda and organization. Once again, he benefited from the occurrence of World War I.

The destruction of institutional alternatives to a Bolshevik dictator-ship was a more difficult task. Czardom was dead and the forces capable of setting up another form of autocracy were in acute disarray, not to threaten until after the Bolshevik coup. Two institutions with claims to political legitimacy not based upon the Petrograd mobs, the Provisional Government and the Constituent Assembly, were already in existence. The Provisional Government was inexperienced, without a broad popu-lar base, and faced with enormous problems. Its duration was obviously limited, but Lenin understood that it had to be completely discredited: "The government is wavering. We must finish it off no matter what."

In destroying the Provisional Government, Lenin had much help from his enemies, including the government itself, and the good luck that they effectively neutralized one another. The non-Bolshevik groups that dominated the Soviets, although mistrusting the Bolsheviks, always de-fended them against the Provisional Government in the name of revolu-tionary solidarity. The war prevented the Provisional Government from competing with Lenin's demagoguery, for it could not make peace with-out dismembering the polity and thus losing the little popular support that it had, and it could not introduce radical economic reforms, such as worker control of industry and land redistribution, without completely disrupting production.[8]

The Provisional Government, however, probably could have pre-vented the Bolsheviks from staging a coup, but its timing was uniformly poor. At first it did not take them seriously. Then, in July 1917, the Bolshevik leaders were charged with being German agents and forced to go into hiding, but within a few weeks they were forgiven in order to get their support against the ill-timed attempt by General Kornilov to overthrow the Provisional Government. The Bolsheviks were again left alone until early November, when the government made a new move to arrest their leaders. At this time, however, the Bolsheviks were able to present the threat to themselves as a counterrevolutionary action against all those involved in the Petrograd Soviet, and under the aegis of the Soviet and by means of undisciplined skirmishing they took physical control of the seat of power and arrested the ministers of the Provisional Government. Luck again was with Lenin because, prior to the government's last move against him, he had failed to prevent the Soviet from moving toward the support of a new regime based on a coalition of all the parties represented in the Soviet.[9] By taking the initiative against the "counter-revolution" of the Provisional Government, Lenin accomplished one of his preliminary but absolutely essential goals: to present the Bolsheviks as the sole rulers of revolutionary Russia, the sole spokesmen for the "masses" represented by the Petrograd Soviet.

Before its demise, the Provisional Government had called for the election of a constituent assembly to determine the legitimate successor to czardom, but the election had not taken place by the time of the Bolshevik coup. Rather than meeting this threat head-on, Lenin made no effort to interfere with the popular selection of the assembly. He also allowed the assembly, in which the Bolshevik representation was only 25 percent, to convene in Petrograd, where on the first day of its meeting it voted against the Bolshevik position. His tactic was progressively to restrict its scope of action and then to dissolve it on the grounds that it represented the old bourgeois rather than the new revolutionary order.[10] Martyrdom was avoided, and no group of any significance attempted to defend "the old bourgeois order."

Once Lenin was established in Petrograd and the Bolsheviks had got control of Moscow and other cities, he could utilize the power of the government he had seized to destroy the effectiveness of all rival political organizations and to subdue the trade unions and Soviets. He bought peace and time by giving the Germans an enormous part of the former empire at Brest-Litovsk. He could not refuse to pay this price because the continuation of the war would have necessitated full popular mobilization, and this could have been effected only by an appeal to the bourgeois-democratic principle of national unity.[11] His luck held again, however, as Germany lost the war in the west. In the urban areas the rigors of Bolshevik rule were soon made clear, but by this time no one could resist. After approving the Black Repartition, the new regime was unable immediately to assert its power outside the cities and in the peripheral regions of the empire where "every village and every town ran its own affairs" in "a time of intoxicating freedom and equality."[12] Before too long, however, Bolsheviks were sent out to replace the "kulaks" and "petty bourgeoisie" of the locally elected Soviets, and "anarchy" in the army, in the factories, among the several cultural groups, and in the villages was vigorously attacked. The promises of the summer of 1917 were steadily abandoned by the new regime, and it came to threaten more and more of the hopes attendant on the fall of czardom. In the spring of 1918, armed resistance to the Bolsheviks sprang up and the Civil War began.

During the Civil War Lenin successfully extended his power from a few cities to most of the former empire, and this period therefore was a direct continuation of the October Revolution and an integral part of the first or political stage of the revolution. It was now the peasants who had to be brought under control, and, despite the urgency of military matters, Lenin never forgot this basic necessity.

In facing his militarily organized opponents, Lenin benefited once again from their inability to unite against him, a result partly of their own ineptitude but primarily of their divergent political ideas and different bases of social support. Among the White forces, the military commanders, who were former officers of the imperial army, worked at cross-purposes to the civilian authorities. Those who thought along traditional lines could not understand the bourgeois democrats, and the bourgeois democrats could not work with the socialists, who could not cooperate among themselves. Each of the many non-Russian cultural groups aspired to national independence and mistrusted the frankly acknowledged Great Russian orientation of the leading military commanders. By the end of 1920, these diverse forces had succumbed to the Bolsheviks, united under the will of Lenin and dependent principally upon the strength of their organization.

In the equally important political part of the Civil War, Lenin gained control of the countryside while maintaining control of the cities. The peasants soon had realized that the Bolsheviks were to be masters no less severe than the old regime, but they remembered that the Bolsheviks had approved the Black Repartition. As long as there was any chance of the landlords' returning, the peasants aided the Bolshevik cause by resisting the Whites, and often enough, when the Whites had succeeded in returning, they behaved in such a way that the peasants actively supported the Bolsheviks.[13] Lenin, needless to say, did not leave to the Whites the business of increasing his rural strength. He instituted in the villages a "civil war within the civil war" by setting poor peasants against those who were less poor, thereby undermining the most popular agrarian organization, the Social Revolutionary Party, and also assuring an adequate supply of grain for the cities. Behind the poor peasant he placed the *Cheka,* an organization "committed to unvarnished punitive actions."[14] To complete his pattern of control, in the cities as well as in the countryside, all manpower was conscripted, the government took over all industry and trade, and rationing was introduced. "War Communism" was one of the most important components of the political stage of the revolution.

Lenin's seizure of governmental power in 1917 and successful defense of it during the Civil War are among the most important yet least understood social events of the twentieth century. The opinion that his revolution was a response to the rejection by the industrial workers of the capitalist system is probably still the most popular explanation, although it has virtually no correspondence with the facts. Lenin himself had said that revolutionary "proletarian consciousness" could not exist within any group defined according to its role in a functioning social system. His theory was confirmed when the grievances of the Petrograd workers led them to demand only improved conditions within the existing industrial order.

Lenin's good fortune and personal ability were necessary to his success, although they cannot completely account for it. He was very lucky in having World War I bring about the sudden collapse of the monarchy at a time when no reasonable replacement was available. His luck held when the Provisional Government proved inept, the traditionalists incompetent, and the Germans weaker than the Western Allies. His tactics and his actions were not flawless, but they were superior to those of any of his opponents. His will, on the other hand, seems to have been unshakable, and his logic impeccable. No one else could have replaced czardom with a regime dedicated to constructing an entirely new form of society.

In the Russia of 1917, political power was fragmented and no one knew what political principles to believe in. This social confusion was ideally suited to a coup, but those who executed the coup were not simple power-seekers. The critical question is whether the victory of Bolshevism was in some way a response to the specific kind of social breakdown experienced by the Russian Empire. The answer seems to be that, although the breakdown released no social forces favorable to the communist society, it occurred at a specific point during the empire's transition from a traditional society to a modern society and thus allowed the Bolsheviks to move the Russians in a third and unprecedented direction. An examination of the two groups critical to Lenin's success, the urban workers and the peasantry, will show the nature of this specific point of the empire's social transition.

Lenin's conviction that the workers in Russian industry would support an antibourgeois program, despite his theory that the industrial workers cannot transcend the bourgeois belief system, makes sense only under the condition that these workers were not genuine industrial workers because they had not yet been integrated into the bourgeois system of production and thus into bourgeois society. They were, that is, still half peasants, and hence they had no stable position in society that could provide them with more than a superficial sense of their own interests. Consequently, the Petrograd workers, although originally seeking only improvements in their working and living conditions, could be induced to repeat Bolshevik words and slogans and to support Bolshevik organizations. They could be used by Lenin precisely because they lacked ideological cohesiveness, and when Lenin eliminated all potential rivals for political power, the workers could do nothing to prevent his continued use of them.

The same observations apply to the peasants of the empire. Because they had not yet got their own land and thus were obliged to seek it by expropriating the land of others, they had no clearly defined social role and no firm sense of self-interest. They were too preoccupied with trying to find a role and a self-interest to object to the Bolsheviks' sweeping attack upon "private property," and after the coup their indecisiveness allowed Lenin to set them against one another. They were not finally defeated until more than a decade later, but they had helped create the power that then defeated them.

In his own theory of the first stage of the proletarian revolution, Lenin had correctly realized that a society was ripe for the kind of revolution he had in mind when its social systems were new and its social roles ambiguous. He focused his attention on the workers and peasants, but the bourgeoisie itself was equally equivocal. There was no way that he or anyone else could have anticipated that the sudden collapse of czardom would give him the opportunity to take advantage of this social situation, but he alone recognized the opportunity when it came.

From the collapse of the monarchy until the end of the Civil War, Lenin was engaged in two struggles, one with his enemies and one with his followers, and the cessation of the former did not mean the end of the latter. Before the coup, he had to mold the Bolsheviks into a force capable of seizing power by itself and in its own name; after the coup, he had to create a force capable of defending the regime; and, after the Civil War, he needed an agency capable of completely transforming society.

His fatal illness prevented him from accomplishing the last task, and he thus was unable to consummate the first or political stage of the revolution.

From March to November 1917, one of his most serious problems was his colleagues' faint-heartedness, their fears that they were not strong enough to capture and then to retain power. He persuaded, argued, vilified, and threatened them; he "was always ahead of his party, pushing it always into bolder, more violent, more irreversible action than it cared to contemplate." He met repeated resistance, even from his most senior lieutenants. He could argue that the confusion of the times made his projected coup feasible, and when argument did not suffice he could rely on his formidable will and terrible temper. He finally bullied his organization into its successful attempt to take power, but even then his problems were not over. Soon after the coup, the Bolshevik Central Committee voted to continue negotiations with the other revolutionary parties. Lenin was furious. "He was ready to stage the October Revolution all over again, and against his own men, if his aim of ruling alone was thwarted."[15]

During the Civil War, Lenin could do little with the Bolsheviks but bombard them with instructions on how military and especially political affairs should be conducted in the many areas affected by warfare. With the completion of the Civil War, he could seriously consider the problem of constructing a genuine Soviet government.

War Communism was basically a device for political control, but it also instituted many practices and policies central to Bolshevik theory. Nevertheless, in 1921 Lenin announced a temporary "retreat" from the principles of War Communism and the initiation of the New Economic Policy, which relaxed the controls on the peasants and allowed the development of a new group of small businessmen. Within a year of the announcement of the NEP, however, Lenin declared that the "retreat" had ended, but his illness prevented him from initiating a new advance.[16]

The NEP is often interpreted as a course more or less forced upon Lenin by the disastrous economic results of War Communism, the rampant inflation, the decline of industrial production to less than one-sixth of the 1913 level, the cessation of foreign trade, and the refusal of the peasantry to produce and deliver food except under force. Although Lenin may well have considered a recovery in economic production to be of some value, his basic theoretical and practical indifference to material well-being, the absence of any internal force that could exploit popular discontent, and the disappearance of any military threat from without strongly indicate that he retreated on the economic front because he wished to attack somewhere else.

During the year 1921–22, when he unreservedly pursued the NEP, Lenin completed the destruction of all potential opposition groups and carried out a thorough reorganization of his own group, now called the Communist Party. In pursuing the policy of "consolidation of the power of the Communist Party," he prohibited all factions, adopted a method for expelling dissenters, and enormously increased the power of the Party's central apparatus. Most of his lieutenants apparently did not understand where he was taking them in 1921; they had not realized that "democracy" within the Party was incompatible with the Party's monopoly of power and that the revolutionary leader required a disciplined instrument completely responsive to his will. Whether or not Stalin fully comprehended Lenin's logic, his self-discipline and organizational abilities prompted Lenin to entrust him with a critical part in this phase of the creation of "Soviet power."

By constructing a governing instrument that would respond to his every wish, Lenin hoped to prevent his revolutionary movement from becoming "bureaucratic," an eventuality that, once he had destroyed all potential internal and external opposition, he feared most of all. His careful plans, however, were frustrated by his physical breakdown; on 26 May 1922 he had his first stroke, from which he never fully recovered. He had just concentrated full control over the Party in its Politburo, an instrument he had intended to dominate by the force of his personality. When his illness prevented him from exercising this force, the Politburo became in his eyes a perfect specimen of the "bureaucracy" against which he had always fought. He thus disobeyed his doctor's orders to avoid work—and circumvented the Politburo's efforts to enforce these orders—in an attempt to reduce the Politburo's independence by returning power to the larger body of the Party's Central Committee.[17] The members of the Politburo—Stalin, Trotsky, Kamenev, Zinoviev, Rykov, and Tomsky—desperately anxious, no matter what their internal divisions, not to let power slip from their hands, reacted by defending their collective position, by maintaining a united front against everyone, including Lenin himself. As one tactic for dismantling this solidarity, Lenin began to work on Trotsky's vanity, but he soon realized he could never regain the physical strength to give Trotsky enough active support to allow him to break with his colleagues. Lenin then wrote to the forthcoming Twelfth Congress of the Communist Party a note in which he criticized every member of the Politburo in an attempt to discredit them with the Party and to create dissension among them. In this so-called testament, he made a last effort to destroy the apex of the disciplined hierarchy he had laboriously constructed, but he failed. The collective leadership of the Politburo survived him, and it remained for one of its members to complete Lenin's antibureaucratic mission by restoring the dominance of a single personality. Why Lenin did not recognize the rather high probability that the Politburo could not remain united and thus "bureaucratic" cannot be determined.

After the seizure of power in 1917, Lenin devoted all of his time and energy not required for surviving the Civil War to the construction of a proper "Soviet government." He destroyed all potential opposition to the rule of his Party, and he made it the disciplined and docile instrument of his will. He fought routinization in all aspects of life, struggling against "bureaucracy" until his very death. He retained his hatred of a "government of laws," he believed that true socialism was incompatible with freedom of assembly and of the press and with parliamentarism, and he fulminated against "the idea that laws, courts, and other rotten bourgeois concepts and institutions could ever fully replace terror and the 'revolutionary initiative of the masses.' "[18] His style of ruling was to try "to define and prescribe everything, give detailed orders and write detailed decrees and instructions on everything's execution,"[19] and he always avoided specifying his precise goals and spelling out the precise methods he intended to use.

Lenin's death in 1924 left the first stage of the revolution incomplete. He had not fully overcome "bureaucracy," and there was now no leader unhampered by rivals or commitments who could freely use the power of the movement to accomplish the second stage of the revolution. What happened during the next few years of Soviet Communism was not (as so many have believed) a simple struggle for power resulting in the triumph of the cleverest and least scrupulous of Lenin's lieutenants, but the reinstitution of the flexibility of the single revolutionary leader necessary for the construction of a "Soviet government." Although ideology was relatively neglected during this period because of the higher priorities of organization, Stalin soon decided—probably during 1927[20]—to initiate Soviet Communism's most revolutionary policy, the second-stage "collectivization" and "electrification" of the First Five-Year Plan.

Stalin's triumph over his rivals is often attributed to his concentrating on dull matters of administration and personnel while they spent their time considering high issues of revolutionary ideology. In the early 1920s, however, the most serious problems facing the Communist regime were those of organization. Every Communist was aware that his survival was absolutely dependent upon the apparatus of the Party, since popular attitudes toward Communism varied from indifference to hostility. Any attempts to go beyond the mere retention of power and to restructure society along communist lines unavoidably would evoke the strongest popular opposition. The movement had to be united and it had to appear to be united, and the only way to accomplish these goals was to concentrate power at the top. Trotsky's 1924 statement, "I know one cannot be right against the party," expressed his recognition that no member of the Party could challenge his superiors. Throughout this period, those who opposed Stalin had to be very careful not to appear to threaten the movement's unity. As Stalin's power increased, "The fear of factions . . . was almost pathological in all sections of the party."[21] The logic of the revolutionary vanguard was working itself out: to bring about total change in a society that does not (and cannot) want total change requires a movement that acts with a single will.

Stalin's attention to personnel is usually described as putting "his own men" in key positions, especially in the middle and lower ranks of the apparatus. He did this, of course, but "his men" were not time-servers who subsequently supported him out of gratitude for his patronage, but people who understood the necessity of revolutionary solidarity, as Stalin himself did, and who believed, as Lenin had before them, that Stalin had the organizational skill to create it. In the jockeying for position among Lenin's heirs, Stalin was always careful to identify himself with the Party as a whole and to appear as the most cautious and moderate leader preserving the Party from the recklessness of the Left and later from the shortsightedness of the Right. He even defended his surprising decision to institute the rapid collectivization of agriculture and the swift industrialization of the country as necessary to preserve the Party and the revolution, arguing that the movement could survive only if the economy were revolutionized immediately and the petty bourgeoisie destroyed once and for all. The Party may well have appreciated this argument and responded to Stalin as the Bolsheviks had earlier responded to Lenin when he demanded that they seize state power.

Stalin's behavior from the time of Lenin's incapacitation until the initiation of the First Five-Year Plan was the logical continuation of Lenin's seizure of unshared state power, defense of this power during the Civil War, and rationalization of it after 1920. Like Lenin before him, Stalin was ahead of his associates, and he had to threaten and bully them so that the concentration of power Lenin had created would not be dissipated. In retrospect, it appears that among those who survived Lenin only Stalin had the ruthlessness, single-mindedness, and power of will to carry on his work.

Stalin obviously sought personal power, just as Lenin had sought it, but, again like Lenin, he sought it for its usefulness. As soon as he had established his clear ascendancy within the Communist Party, he used his power for the impeccably Leninist revolutionary purpose of transforming the economy of the Soviet Union. Before 1928, however, he had a problem that the coup and the Civil War had solved for Lenin: his leadership of the revolution, his personal ascendancy within the revolutionary movement, had not been established. To establish it, he had not only to defeat his potential rivals but to discredit them as well, and hence he was obliged to attack their theoretical ideas and policy orientations. His wide-ranging assault upon the ideas and positions of everyone else made him appear an opportunist with no firm convictions of his own, but by at least as early as 1924 in his lectures at Sverdlov University he had demonstrated a clear understanding of and commitment to the basic principles of Leninism; and, once he had succeeded in destroying his rivals' claims to orthodoxy, he adopted policies that were logically implied by these principles. That some of these policies formerly had been advocated by his fallen competitors was and remains irrelevant.

By about 1928 the first or political stage of the revolution was essentially complete. "Soviet power" finally had been established and a "Soviet government" had acquired the ability to begin the second, economic stage. The first stage had begun when Lenin, relying upon the peculiar social ambiguity of the Russian workers and peasants, the fragmentation and ineptness of his opponents, and his own single-minded determination, had seized state power upon the collapse of the czarist autocracy. It had continued throughout the Civil War, when he was able to rely also upon police and military power. Following victory in the Civil War, he turned his full attention to the task of building an instrument of power capable of carrying out revolutionary policies in the face of unstructured but tenacious popular resistance. It was left to Stalin to complete this instrument, but in doing so he had also to raise himself as far above his associates as Lenin had been above his. Lenin had created the situation that led to Stalin's complete dominance of the Communist movement, but the luck of the revolution held once again when a man like Stalin was present to take full advantage of it.

Notes

1. V. I. Lenin, *What Is To Be Done?* (1902) (Oxford: Clarendon Press, 1963), p. 63. Stalin repeated this theory: "Problems of Leninism" (1926), in *Leninism* (New York: International Publishers, n.d.), 1:279.
2. V. I. Lenin, *Two Tactics of Social-Democracy in the Democratic Revolution* (1905) (New York: International Publishers, 1935), pp. 83, 84, 85, 95.
3. Lionel Kochan, *Russia in Revolution, 1890–1918* (London: Weidenfeld & Nicolson, 1966), pp. 177–81.
4. George F. Kennan, "The Breakdown of the Tsarist Autocracy," in Richard Pipes, ed., *Revolutionary Russia* (Cambridge, Mass.: Harvard University Press, 1968), p. 4.
5. Theodore H. Von Laue, *Why Lenin? Why Stalin?* (Philadelphia: J. B. Lippincott, 1964), p. 75.
6. John M. Thompson, in Pipes, p. 158.
7. Quoted by Bertram D. Wolfe, in Pipes, p. 133.
8. Adam B. Ulam, *The Bolsheviks* (New York: Macmillan, 1965), p. 335.
9. Robert V. Daniels, *Red October: The Bolshevik Revolution of 1917* (New York: Charles Scribners' Sons, 1967), p. 216.
10. John Keep, "Lenin as Tactician," in Leonard Schapiro et al., eds., *Lenin* (New York: Frederick A. Praeger, 1967), p. 153.
11. See John Erickson, "Lenin as Civil War Leader," in Schapiro et al., p. 163.
12. Ulam, p. 433.
13. See Jan M. Meijer, "Town and Country in the Civil War," in Pipes, pp. 264–65; and William Henry Chamberlin, *The Russian Revolution* (New York: Macmillan, 1935), 2:455.
14. Erickson, pp. 176–77.
15. Daniels, pp. 211, 225.
16. Ulam, p. 477.
17. See Ulam, pp. 554–62, for the basis of this account.
18. Ulam, p. 486.
19. Bertram D. Wolfe, *An Ideology in Power* (New York: Stein & Day, 1969), p. 176.
20. Leonard Schapiro, *The Communist Party of the Soviet Union* (New York: Random House, 1960), p. 361.
21. Schapiro, p. 299.

8

The Classless Society

For twenty-five years, Stalin tenaciously pursued the second stage of the revolution, the "economic" stage concerned with creating the forces and relations of production necessary for the "remolding of men's psychologies" and the advent of the communist society. Although he brought about radical and traumatic changes in many aspects of Soviet life, he failed in his effort to create a completely new pattern of beliefs and values. Toward the end of his life, he acknowledged that "bourgeois" modes of thought still persisted: the agricultural workers still viewed work solely as a means to their individual personal profit, and the intelligentsia were still influenced by the principles of capitalist expertise and rationality.

Nonetheless, in reviewing the history of Soviet Communism, Stalin found much to be thankful for. As a result of the regime's efforts, the relations of production in the Soviet Union had become socialist and "tremendous strides" had been made toward "electrifying" the forces of production. In addition, the former bitter divisions between the town and the countryside and between labor of the hand and labor of the brain had been eliminated.[1] As a result of these changes, the Soviet Union had become "classless" and had achieved "socialism." The condition of classlessness meant that there were no longer any insuperable impediments to the remolding of the Soviet people through further improvements in the forces and relations of production and through continuing attention to education in the area of culture. All that was needed was the persistent and long-term exercise of will by the revolutionary leadership.

The triumph of socialism, "the first or lower phase of communism," was a costly affair. The 1917 coup expended few material and human resources, but the Civil War, the First Five-Year Plan, the Great Purge of the 1930s, and the maintenance of so-called forced-labor establishments for counterrevolutionaries were extremely expensive. The economic costs of these policies cannot be measured, nor can the amount of human physical and mental suffering they caused be estimated. It is possible, however, to approximate the number of people who died so that socialism could be instituted and protected.

The process by which the Bolsheviks seized power from and then defended it against more or less organized opposition was relatively inexpensive. Deaths resulting from the coup of 1917 were negligible, and the confrontation between the Reds and the Whites during the Civil War, including battles, reprisals (the Red and White "terror"), and punitive actions by both sides against recalcitrant peasants, accounted for only a few hundred thousand deaths. The ferocity of both Reds and Whites against select groups of unarmed people was extraordinary, but the military engagements themselves were relatively mild, "largely as a result of the lack of will to fight on the part of the masses of peasant troops on both sides."[2]

The acute social disruption caused by the Civil War and by the severe treatment of peasants under War Communism, however, led to a large number of deaths from epidemics and famine. From 1918 through 1923, about three million people died from typhus, typhoid, dysentery, and cholera, and about nine million more disappeared, principally as a result of famine. There was a severe drought in 1920 and 1921, which would have resulted in many deaths had there been no Civil War and War Communism, but by itself it would not have cost twelve million lives.[3] For lack of any sure method of apportioning responsibility, half of the casualties can be attributed to nature and half to politics.

Once the Communist regime had destroyed its rivals, the cost of the revolution began to mount. The "collectivization" and "industrialization" policies associated with the First Five-Year Plan laid the basis for the socialist society and, according to Stalin himself, expended about ten million lives in doing so, although the politically inspired famines of the period by themselves could have claimed almost ten million victims.[4]

When Stalin had got his forces and relations of production into tolerable shape, he turned his attention once again to the problem of "Soviet power" and initiated the so-called Great Purge of the middle 1930s (to be discussed in the following chapter), which resulted in the outright execution of at least one million people and the death (by 1938) of another two million from conditions of imprisonment.[5] An additional nine million people were arrested during the Great Purge, and over the years they were joined in the prisons and labor camps by millions of others who were "removed from society" because they were carriers of nonproletarian ideas and attitudes. Perhaps twelve million of these prison and labor-camp inmates died as a result of their environment from 1938 until 1950.[6]

All the deaths resulting directly from Germany's invasion of the Soviet Union during World War II previously have been attributed to Hitler, but hundreds of thousands of Soviet soldiers lost their lives as a result of the disappearance of the professional officer corps in the Great Purge, and countless Soviet civilians, including entire "cultural minorities," were later liquidated for their real or presumed "anti-Soviet" behavior under German occupation.

These figures total about thirty-two million deaths. Although precision in these matters is impossible, this estimated total conveys at the very least the magnitude of the human cost of Soviet Communism; even admittedly modest estimates run into the tens of millions. Stalin and Lenin were deadly serious in their intent to transform an enormous society that by its size alone offered strong resistance to change. They did not have to conquer this society, and thus they caused relatively few deaths from military engagement. Their enemies were principally domestic and unarmed.

Once Stalin had brought the first or political stage of the revolution to the point where no one within the "Soviet government" could resist his political initiative, he boldly moved the Soviet Union into the second or economic stage with a logical and radical program designed to revolutionize the country's relations and forces of production. In the agrarian sector of the economy, according to Stalin, both the relations and the forces remained "capitalist." This situation could not be corrected all at once, but the first necessary step in the improvement of the relations of agricultural production was to destroy individual initiative. Simultaneously, the forces of agricultural production were to be improved—that is, "electrified"—by supplying the countryside with tractors and other types of agricultural machinery.[7] In the nonagrarian part of the economy, the relations of production were in reasonably good condition, because after Lenin's capture of state power the Communists had eliminated all sources of independent management. (Many small enterprises had arisen during the New Economic Policy, but they would be relatively easy to destroy.) The nonagrarian forces of production, however, were due for radical improvement by making very large-scale units involving a high degree of specialized and interdependent labor the predominant form of enterprise. In addition to bringing Soviet society closer to Stalin's model of communism, these forces of production were to create the tractors necessary for the "electrification" of the countryside.

Stalin's greatest effort in the economic stage of the revolution is associated with the period of the so-called First Five-Year Plan. Evidence suggests that his policies during this period were improvised and that he was never sure precisely how far the logic of his actions was to carry him. Nevertheless, his premises were always perfectly clear, and thus there was little ambiguity in his intentions. In retrospect, the neutral observer must agree with him that at this time the Soviet Union took gigantic strides in the direction of socialism.

From November 1929 until December 1932, Stalin subjected the Soviet Union to a cataclysmic revolution from above that Naum Jasny has called the "All-out Drive." One of the best-publicized goals of the drive was to double and even triple industrial output, with the emphasis on pig iron, steel, coal, electricity, and cement; to this end, investment in heavy industry was increased by 584 percent and the labor force by 89 percent. Increases in output, however, were not forthcoming: in Stalin's favorite area of steel, for example, total output during the drive rose by only 2 percent, and in all heavy industry output per worker declined by about 10 percent each year.[8]

The All-out Drive also included the forced destruction of private farming through the program of "collectivization." By the end of 1932, about fifteen million of the Soviet Union's twenty-five million peasant families were said to have been put into collective farms. One result of this program was a 22 percent decrease in gross farm output during a period when the population increased by about 7 percent. The peasants' resistance to collectivization led to the disappearance of 17 million horses, while Stalin's "electrification" policy was providing tractors of only 3.1 million horsepower.[9]

The fantastic impact of the All-out Drive on the Soviet peasants has been well publicized. The Black Repartition, the culmination of the dream of generations, was to be undone, and all were commanded, at gunpoint if necessary, to give up their land and animals and join a collective. The harsh treatment of the peasants—the "cruel civil war" that involved the machine-gunning of entire villages, the deportation under the severest conditions of at least ten million people, and the famines caused both by disruption of production and by the regime's deliberate withholding of grain as a means to shatter resistance—was not solely a response to peasant recalcitrance. Among these people who were shot, frozen, or starved were the kulaks, peasants incapable of changing their petty-bourgeois mentality and thus by definition ineligible for admission to the collectives. They were to be "liquidated as a class," despite the fact that there was no way in which this "class" could be defined.[10] The collectivization drive and the liquidation of the kulaks, as noted above, took about ten million lives.

Disruption in the urban and industrial parts of the Soviet Union during the All-out Drive was less drastic but still very severe. The real per capita income of the Soviet Union in 1932 dropped to about half its 1928 level, bringing it well below that of the depression-ridden capitalist countries. Stalin introduced a system of compulsory labor, his famous "elimination of unemployment," which relied on "work spreading" and thus lowered productivity. Working conditions were usually poor. Despite forced employment, there was a high rate of labor turnover, reaching 150 percent in all industry in 1930, as on an average half the workers changed jobs once and the other half twice in their search for less unpleasant work situations. The chaos in both the agrarian and the industrial sectors led to a drop in the growth of the Soviet population from 2.9 million in 1928 to 100,000 in 1933.[11]

It is now conventional wisdom that the All-out Drive was badly planned, overambitious, and not too rational. The classic and oft-quoted description is that of Isaac Deutscher, one of Stalin's most sympathetic biographers: "The whole experiment seemed to be a piece of prodigious insanity, in which all rules of logic and principles of economics were turned upside down."[12] By means of this madness, however, Stalin accomplished what he set out to accomplish: the forces and relations of Soviet production had been transformed and few who had survived the All-out Drive would ever doubt that capitalism had been expunged from the Soviet Union.

The All-out Drive established a pattern of economizing that has persisted well beyond Stalin's death. Its most important principles included these well-known items: the assumption that capital has no cost; the measurement of value by the amount of labor expended in the process of production; a relative indifference to the utility of products and to the efficiency of their production in relation to the total economy; the fixing of prices by decree rather than by supply and demand and the consequent elimination of money as a measure of value; an acceptance of lowered productivity in both industry and agriculture resulting from a low standard of living; an emphasis on ever-larger quantities of goods produced, to the detriment of quality, at the expense of overworking land, labor, and machinery, and often to the neglect of more efficient production methods; a piecemeal approach to the economy, with often economically arbitrary priorities, leading to overspecialization of agriculture, disregard of transportation and housing, periodic overproduction of certain industrial items, and frequent failures to provide sources of power for new factories; a fascination with size, prompting the construction of gigantic projects of at best questionable value;[13] a failure to provide incentives for agricultural workers, giving rise to an extremely inefficient use of agricultural labor, even in the area of "private" plots and livestock; the falsification of reports and other kinds of finagling by lower-level economic officials in response to unrealistic quantitative quotas; and the hoarding of labor and material by factory managers as a response to persistent shortages and arbitrary prices. The Stalinist economy functioned only by its reliance on *blat*, the highly irregular and normally proscribed allocation of supplies that depended principally upon a network of personal influence.

The net result of these principles was an economy with two striking characteristics. The first was a very low standard of living for the general population, with the incomes of the agrarian and nonagrarian sectors in 1952 estimated at, respectively, 60 percent and 78 percent of the incomes in 1928.[14] The second was the accumulation of vast amounts of investment capital that the regime could freely allocate according to its revolutionary purposes.

The preferred targets for investment were large "basic industries" utilizing technology that Stalin, from his nineteenth-century Marxist perspective, considered "advanced." Technology relying on computers, for example, was deliberately omitted because, as the *Great Soviet Encyclopedia* of 1955 put it, the use of computers increased "the exploitation of the working class by creating artificial redundancy and loosening the revolutionary tie between the worker and the means of production. . . ." The results of this availability of capital and of this theory of revolution were evident in Stalin's favorite area of steel production. Soviet blast and open-hearth techniques were superior to those used in the United States, but the Soviet steel industry, constrained by the need to produce in large quantities, could turn out only a rather limited range of sizes and shapes of steel. As Khrushchev himself once complained, moreover, this "advanced" steel industry occurred in an economy that did not produce plastics, fertilizers, and (of course) computers.[15] In short, the formation of large-scale industry was highly uneven, and little consideration was given to its cost in relation to other areas of investment. The All-out Drive set the pattern for an economy with a few islands of reasonably modern industry in an environment of a most unproductive agriculture, a no more than rudimentary consumer-goods sector, and a highly "irrational" allocation of investment. Although the drive did increase the Soviet Union's "heavy" industrial capacity, by no means can it be interpreted as a boot-strap operation in "economic development," since the Bolsheviks had inherited a rather well developed economy and Stalin benefited during the drive from a number of fortuitous circumstances.[16]

The All-out Drive was Stalin's first and principal contribution to the second or economic stage of the revolution. With devastating logic and thoroughness, he set out to destroy "capitalism" and to replace it with the forces and relations of production of "socialism," that is, large-scale mass production units and "collective" decision making. Although his policies were crude and hastily conceived—for he believed that the revolution had to advance in order to avoid retreating and he had more faith in willpower than in planning—their "irrationalities" were to him based on impreccable rules of logic and principles of economics. Lowered productivity, wasted resources, and countless human lives were entirely reasonable expenditures for a revolution in the forces and relations of production.

In the 1920s all leading Soviet Communists were aware that the country's economy was still very "capitalist" and that this situation was intolerable. The problem, as they saw it, was to obtain the capital necessary to construct the proper forces of production, that is, to "industrialize." The only source of such capital, as even the most zealous industrializers realized, was agriculture, but no one knew how to increase agricultural production without simultaneously strengthening the private sectors of the agrarian economy, without creating even more so-called kulaks.[17] Only Stalin had the command of revolutionary ideology necessary to resolve this dilemma. Capital for the proper forces of production could be obtained, and not only could capitalist relations of production in the countryside not be encouraged but socialist relations could be promoted—in other words, the *"kulaks* could be liquidated as a class." Unlike his comrades, Stalin had transcended the bourgeois presupposition that the living standards of the entire Soviet population could not be reduced by half, and he had understood that the willpower of the revolutionary regime was the logical replacement for the capitalist device of material incentives. Again, in plain language, the thing to do was not to rely on the capitalist device of bribing the peasants to produce more, but to kill two birds with one stone by socializing them and then taking a larger absolute amount of their (probably) reduced output.

Lowering the standard of living to get capital for heavy industry was not an interim measure of the All-out Drive, and the low return from this capital was not a temporary result of the hasty restructuring of the Soviet economy. The principal long-term goal of Stalin's economic revolution was the establishment of socialist forces and relations of production; his initial effort in this direction was the All-out Drive, "a determined *drive* of Socialism against the capitalist elements in town and country." The essence of agricultural "collectivization" was to create a "new form of *smychka*" (alliance) between the working class and the peasantry, and a reduction in agricultural output was a reasonable price to pay for this alliance.

It is not *any kind* of increase in the productivity of national labor that we need. We need a *specific* increase in the productivity of national labor, namely an increase that will guarantee the *systematic supremacy of the socialist sector of national economy over the capitalist sector*. That is the point, comrades.[18]

From the Stalinist point of view, only the human relationships involved in the process of economic production had any social significance; the products resulting from this process were of little interest and hence considerations of efficiency based upon optimal output had little relevance. The large-scale production unit was justified because it put many people in the proper social interrelationships, and what it happened to produce at what cost made little difference. Stalin had some difficulty in convincing the Party that the concepts of output and productivity of the economy as a whole were bourgeois concepts, and that only the performance of the socialist sector was of concern to socialist economics.[19] The most important element in this performance was the gross quantity of goods produced, for this amount measured the labor involved in large-scale operations and thus provided an index of the degree of socialization of the forces and relations of production. The larger the proportion of total output that came from large-scale operations, moreover, the higher the degree of economic socialization that had been attained, and hence an increase in this proportion, even if accompanied by a decrease in total production, constituted a social advance. Considerations of the cost, quality, and usefulness of the goods produced were all secondary matters.

The Stalinist theory of quantity as a measure of socialism also led to the phenomenon of economic "planning," which was not an attempt to coordinate the economy but an effort to command the highest possible total quantity of goods from the various enterprises in the socialist sector. "Overfulfilling a quota" at the expense of another enterprise did not necessarily disrupt a "plan," because the total output of the socialist sector was the overriding consideration.

For Stalin, consumption was more than an unavoidable nuisance; it was the cause of his greatest defeat, his inability to introduce full socialism in the countryside. In order to maintain agricultural production, not only could he not advance from the halfway device of the collective farm to the truly socialist agrarian factory, but he had to accept the "capitalist" institutions of private plots and livestock. At the Soviet economy's stage of progress, consumer goods, to Stalin's great distress, appeared in the form of commodities. Although the counterrevolutionary effect of commodity circulation could not be eliminated, it could be minimized by sharply restricting the quantity of available consumer goods and by emphasizing the consumption of organized services. The regime consequently gave its favored industrial workers few material goods but a fair amount of medical care, recreation, education, child care, and so forth. Only the living standard of workers in the socialist sector of the economy was of any importance, and it was considered perfectly adequate at a level that by bourgeois standards was only reasonably healthy subsistence. The life befitting human beings is determined by production and not by consumption, and thus when Stalin had accomplished his initial transformation of the forces and relations of production, he declared (in 1934) that poverty in the Soviet Union had been abolished. In his subsequent insistence that the Soviet people enjoyed material abundance, he expressed his opinion that the Spartan-like existence of his industrial workers came very close to the ideal of "to each according to his needs." Once the "alienation" of capitalist society had been overcome, all forms of human misery would disappear.

A final point regarding Stalin's motives for "industrializing" the Soviet economy is the relation between this policy and his capacity to wage war. An increased ability to produce military goods, perhaps not fully realized until after 1945, was a useful by-product of the All-out Drive's emphasis on heavy industry, but the purpose of the drive was hardly to effect such an increase. As Erlich has put it, "If Stalin's repeated warnings about the greatly increased danger of war were to be taken literally, the policy of the First Five Year Plan would look very much like a suicide prompted by a fear of death." Industry, said Stalin, is primarily for socialism and only secondarily for defense.[20]

Stalin's determined drive against the capitalist elements in the countryside took the form of "collectivization" and "dekulakization." These policies could not create truly socialist relations of production and genuine socialist attitudes, but they could destroy capitalist relations (that is, private farming) and initiate the remolding of the peasants' psychology. This drive had the highest priority, because as Lenin had said, the strength of capitalism lies "in the strength of *small production*, for unfortunately, small production still survives in a very, very large degree, and small production *gives birth* to capitalism and to bourgeoisie, constantly, daily, hourly, spontaneously and on a mass scale." Not only must small production be attacked, but (again following Lenin) there must be "a persistent struggle . . . against the forces and traditions of the old society. The force of habit of millions and tens of millions is a most terrible force."[21]

The collective farm was the interim solution to the problem of small production, but collectivization did not suffice to eliminate the old traditions. As Stalin drove the peasants into the collectives, he also launched a great offensive against the "last capitalist class" in the Soviet Union, that is, those people called kulaks. Prior to this time, the term "kulak" referred to a prosperous peasant who used specific methods of production, including the hiring of labor, but Stalin explicitly denied that there were any objective characteristics that defined a kulak and insisted that even a very poor man could be one. A kulak was identified by his attitudes, and his attitudes amounted to unalterable opposition to the revolutionary regime and to the collectivization movement. He could not be educated into acceptance of socialism—his psychology was immune to remolding —and hence he had to be liquidated "as a class."[22]

In Stalin's theory, the kulak personified the "psychology" of the peasant mode of production, and hence he was by definition a sworn enemy of socialism. In practice, the only was to identify a kulak was to observe his lack of enthusiasm for collectivization, and hence the de-kulakization program became extremely arbitrary. This arbitrariness, however, was a strength rather than a weakness of the program, because not only had the kulaks themselves to be eliminated (and dekulakization did not err on the side of leniency) but their elimination was an excellent method of teaching nonkulaks that the old ways of life were necessarily doomed and the new ways inevitable. Collectivization by itself could not teach this lesson. Stalin told his followers that it was a great error

> to believe that the members of the collective farms have already become socialists. No, considerable work has still to be done in order to transform the peasant members of the collective farm, to set right their individualistic psychology and to remold them into real toilers of a socialist society.[23]

Individualism among those "admitted" to the collectives could not avoid being at least dimmed by the knowledge of what was happening to those whom the regime had defined as enemies of the revolution, and the arbitrariness of the definition may well have helped drive home the message. Enemies were everywhere, even among those whose interests seemed to favor collectivization and those who had overtly accepted it, and none of them escaped the vigilance of the revolution. As Stalin said, dekulakization was not just an "administrative measure" but "an integral part of the formation and development of collective farms."[24] Everyone had to learn that social property was the sacred and inviolable basis of the existence of society.

The enormous initial cost of Stalin's agrarian policy, and its con-tinued cost in lost production, were reasonable prices to pay for the changing of the peasant psychology. Agricultural "inefficiency," like in-dustrial "irrationality," did not result from madness, inexperience, or stupidity; both were deliberately accepted as unavoidable by-products of the overriding revolutionary goal. Twenty years after the All-out Drive, Stalin once again explicitly rejected the principle of profitability and reaffirmed his intention to continue supporting heavy industry no matter how "unprofitable" it might be. (He always said that socialist forms of production would eventually be the most profitable and productive, but he never defined his terms or made any effort to prove his statement.) His last prescription for improving the Soviet economy was to increase its "irrationality" by further collectivization and centralization of control. The relations of production were ready for another revolution from above.[25]

Every type of society has its own special world view that corresponds to and reinforces its political and economic systems and, generally, its way of life; hence the attitudes, beliefs, and values of a classless society must be unique and unprecedented. Guidelines for the development of socialist science, history, and art cannot be precisely determined but will evolve gradually from the practical problems and experiences of the new society. Stalin, however, believed that the creation of theory through practice, like the changing of men's social attitudes, required the initiative of the revolutionary regime, and he gave much personal attention, especially after World War II, to this attempted revolution in culture.

Since every idea supports a specific type of society, no idea can be politically neutral and thus all bourgeois modes of thought, including the natural sciences, had to be restrained and eventually eliminated. There were early and sporadic attacks on bourgeois science in the Soviet Union, but the principal offensive against the physical and biological sciences came during Stalin's last and most autocratic years. From 1948 until 1952, "science for its own sake" was condemned, many scientists were accused of being idealists who did not maintain the unity of theory and practice, and a number of concepts and hypotheses basic to bourgeois physical science—including Einstein's theory of relativity, Bohr's complementary principle, and Pauling's theory of resonance— were declared reactionary. This intense offensive against physical science was relatively brief and shallow; no new socialist theories were presented as replacements, and only chemistry was seriously weakened.[26]

The biological sciences were subject to much greater revolutionary pressure when the famous T. D. Lysenko and his allies denounced the theory of genes as "formalistic, bourgeois, and metaphysical." As a result hundreds of the best-qualified biologists were dismissed or demoted, prominent scientists were charged with treason, laboratories were closed, books were destroyed and libraries weeded out, and public declarations of revolutionary allegiance were required. Every discipline from microbiology to veterinary medicine was affected.[27]

The Lysenkoists, moreover, produced a socialist replacement for this counterrevolutionary bourgeois biology. As Lysenko, who was a practical plant breeder rather than a laboratory scientist, put it, the new biology (which had its origins in the theories of the Russians Michurin and Timiryazev) was a materialist biology related to collective farm practice. It denied that plant chromosomes have genes, those idealist fictions with no more substance than caloric or phlogiston; instead, they have an independent hereditary substance that cannot be described but only comprehended, although it was described at least once as "living matter." The new biology, said its inventors, allowed for the mutations implied by the master science of dialectical materialism, and an understanding of the "given stage of development" of an organism made possible the alteration of its heredity. Materialistic biology, in addition, developed Stalin's theories that acquired characteristics are inherited and that gradual, small, quantitative changes can lead to rapid, radical, qualitative changes. All these statements of the Lysenkoists were purely deductive; they did not rely on accumulations of empirical data or upon controlled experiments.[28] After Stalin's death, the new theory gradually was abandoned, scientific biology was again pursued, and agriculture got a reprieve.

Since social science is concerned with current human relationships and what may develop from them in the future, it is of no use and interest to a society attempting to extricate itself from the past. The revolutionary society, however, contains people, and as individuals they had to meet the standard of the so-called new Soviet man, the "conscious, purposive builder of socialism, who is capable of change and modification to the ideals of the socialist state even as an adult."[29]

Stalin therefore encouraged the search for a set of new psychological principles that would provide logical support for the remolding of man to which he was committed. His psychologists obliged with the following principles: consciousness allows goal-directed action; the unconscious is unimportant; "training" and "self-training" are more important than "heredity" and "environment"; there are no limits to what training can accomplish; personality in a socialist society is no longer determined by socioeconomic factors; and the individual personality is indefinitely plastic. None of these principles was based on empirical data, and the hypothesis they were supposed to support, the linking of the new Soviet man to socialist society, led to no empirical research. Naturally, the presentation of the new theory was accompanied by a thorough exposé of Western psychology as a tool of the capitalist class.[30]

Artistic expression in Stalin's Soviet Union had to conform to the notorious criteria of "socialist realism." Every work of art had to be concrete and directly representational, optimistic and cheerful, social rather than private in content, laudatory of all revolutionary innovations, and "self-contained" in the sense that audiences were left with no questions and all problems raised were resolved. Only overt behavior was to be depicted or, at the most, open and obvious aspirations and emotions. These criteria were derived from Stalin's epistemological, psychological, and political postulates: since the unconscious is insignificant, everything about a work of art had to be obvious; since reality is completely knowable, no mysticism could be allowed; since theory and practice form a unity, all works of art had to be understandable to everyone; since art, like everything else, is a partisan matter incapable of political neutrality, nothing unfavorable to the regime or to its people was permitted; and, since man realized himself in interaction with other men, the representation of private experiences was forbidden.

Socialist realism involved more than standards of censorship; it also provided the general goals for artists in their capacity of "engineers of the human soul." Such engineering, related theoretically to the psychological principle of "training," was supposed to assist in the "ideological remolding and education of working people in the spirit of socialism." Since the "spirit of socialism" is oriented to the future rather than to the present, Soviet artists were enjoined to "glimpse our tomorrow," to put a "searchlight on the road ahead." The "realism" of socialist art was not concerned with "objective reality" but with depicting "reality in its revolutionary development"; indeed, socialist realism is "romanticism of a new type, revolutionary romanticism." It follows that Soviet art is the best, most advanced, and (since socialist society is free of conflict) the clearest and most understandable art in the world.[31] The happy peasants and the dedicated workers of Soviet literature and painting were glimpses of tomorrow and not intended to correspond to present reality. Unfortunately, however, since the perfect future cannot really be known, the best that Soviet artists could do was to extrapolate, earnestly but clumsily, from the imperfect present.

According to Stalin, the socialist historian was to deal with the past as the socialist artist dealt with the future. The first task of the historian, however, was to expose completely the "bourgeois falsification of history," otherwise known as "objectivism" or "value-free analysis," a historiography designed to "immortalize the capitalist system."[32] Like the socialist history that was to replace it, bourgeois history did not in any normal sense "justify" the society that engendered it: bourgeois society was "justified" by its very existence; its attempt to create a past in its own image was only a kind of buttress to its claim to current superiority. Its value-free objectivist method relied heavily on the technique of trying to determine whether or not specific past events "really happened."

Both the first and second stages of the socialist revolution were validated solely by their complete break with the past, by their very antihistoric nature, but the past had to be made consistent with the latest developments in this revolution. Since Stalin had proved his revolutionary superiority by succeeding Lenin, it followed that he had had similar superiority in the past and that everyone who was not his own creature was not a true revolutionary. The Bolshevik coup, consequently, had been accomplished by Lenin-Stalin, who also had won the Civil War. Since Trotsky, although he had been commissar for war, could not possibly have made any real contribution to military affairs, there was no reason even to mention his name in connection with this stage of the revolution.

As previously explained, the second task of historiography was to extend the logic of the socialist revolution to the time prior to the Bolshevik seizure of power. This was done principally by announcing that all past actions of the Great Russians, including political actions, were progressive and that all progress had occurred within the area currently occupied by the Soviet Union. As the famous Soviet historian, Anna Pankratova, put it, "Stalin has extended the limits of Soviet history by 1500 to 2000 years." That there is little evidence to support this view of the past is beside the point, for the so-called facts of history are only implications of a world view.

In addition to the creation of a new economic system, a new science, and a new art, Stalin's program to remold men's psychologies included an effort to change the moral consciousness of the Soviet people. The premise behind this moral reeducation was that, with the sole exception of the leader himself, every member of Soviet society, no matter what his intentions, was capable of counterrevolutionary activities and attitudes. Its working principle was that anyone engaging in such behavior was to be severely punished and usually removed, at least temporarily, from contact with the rest of society. This type of education became known as the Stalinist "terror."

The "terror" began in the mid-1930s with the initiation of Stalin's Great Purge. The Purge was initially an attack on those in positions of power, but it soon spread to the entire population of the Soviet Union until at least one in twenty persons was "no longer allowed to remain among the people"[33] and the labor camps were crowded with a cross-section of the Soviet Union's inhabitants. Arrests on this scale continued beyond the Great Purge, and by Stalin's death the labor camps contained from twelve to seventeen million persons.

These mass arrests established the principle that the Soviet Union, even after the advent of socialism, contained two types of human beings, "people" and "enemies of the people." The enemies included those persons who had been of some importance in prerevolutionary society, who at any time had been in active contact with foreigners, and who had committed an overt act against the Soviet regime, either intentionally as in complaining or spreading rumors or unintentionally as in breaking a piece of machinery. Most enemies of the people received fairly long but limited terms in the labor camps; the mortality rate in the camps was extremely high, however, and only very few who managed to complete their sentences were able to resume their previous lives. Like the kulaks before them, these enemies of the people were considered, in practice if not in theory, incapable of being educated. They were beyond the pale of revolutionary society.

The so-called terror demonstrated to everyone that only complete support of the revolutionary regime, support in both intention and deed, was acceptable social behavior, that any deviation, including any acknowledgment of the outside world or "bourgeois society" as something other than the mortal enemy of socialism, was the gravest breach of morality. For example, both the soldier who had patrolled the rubble of postwar Berlin and the civilian whose uncle had been a merchant under the czars had accepted a part of the nonsocialist world, even though they had been incapable of rejecting it. Socialist society could react to these deviations only with the most severe disapproval, and since the terrible force of prerevolutionary habits constituted a constant threat of mass recidivism, the deviants had to be quarantined. The scope of the terror clearly demonstrated that only the leader himself could hope to conform to the austere moral code of the revolution.

To implement the second stage of the revolution, Stalin attempted to destroy the preexisting ways of life and thought and to replace them with a socialist economy and a popular psychology that viewed work as life's prime want and socialist property as the sacred and inviolable basis of social existence. At the cost of tens of millions of lives, he appears to have been more successful in destroying than in creating.

Although the evidence regarding the beliefs and attitudes of the Soviet populace in the late Stalinist and post-Stalinist periods is rather sketchy, a number of generalizations can be stated with moderate confidence. Almost all the Soviet people have come to accept the Stalinist economic system as in the nature of things and they can hardly imagine an alternative to it; Stalin even may have convinced many of them that it is indeed a higher stage of human development through which everyone must pass. Virtually no one questions the principle of governmental control of heavy industry, considered "socialism" in contrast to the "capitalism" of the Western world, although some of the intelligentsia have suggested that consumer-goods industries be returned to private control, and most people perceive their low standard of living as unavoidable. The socialist economy is not challenged principally because everyone has lived with it for so long.[34]

The skilled industrial workers, the elite of Stalin's new society, are probably reasonably satisfied with their lot, having pride in their skills and consciousness of their indispensability, and, like nonmanual workers, they tend to see the relations among the various social strata in the Soviet Union as harmonious. Unskilled manual workers no doubt share the discontent of their counterparts in other countries, namely, that their jobs are uninteresting, their wages inadequate, and their esteem insufficient. It is probably true that, no matter what his individual grievances, the Soviet worker "questions hardly a single major aspect of the general organization of the Soviet factory system," and that he appreciates the "full employment" aspect of the Stalinist economy that provides him with a relatively low-paying but guaranteed job.[35]

Most Soviet administrators, specialists, and technicians seem to be satisfied with their jobs, standard of living, and opportunities for advancement, and they may even have become preoccupied with their work as a means of escape from the less pleasant aspects of Soviet life. The factory managers, who perform a critical role in the system of "socialist property," apparently accept the basic principles of the economy, although they believe they are given too few resources to meet their quotas and although most of them seem to be motivated in their daily decisions by the monetary bonuses that accompany the fulfilling of production norms.[36]

Reports on the agricultural workers, those people most affected by Stalin's economic revolution, are unanimous in stating that they are extremely discontented and hold the system of collectivization responsible for their unhappiness. Although some observers have concluded that the collective farmers want to return to a system of private farming, the more reasonable conclusion is that, two decades after Stalin's death, they have become resigned to the collective and are not committed to the reinstitution of private farming because they no longer understand the concept.[37] In the judgment of Andrei Amalrik, the "mentality" of the collective farmers has been "quite revolutionized by the fact of not being their own masters and the general precariousness of their situation." The collective farmers have the "dual psychology of the owners of tiny homesteads and of farm hands working on gigantic and anonymous farms," and, Amalrik concludes, no one really knows how this group views itself and what it wants.[38]

The available evidence strongly indicates that Stalin's intellectual and moral education led to an almost universal sense of anxiety. The Great Purge paralyzed the will of most people, forced at least those who had power to lie and dissimulate, encouraged maliciousness and treachery, favored the servile and the unprincipled, went far toward destroying the concept of objective truth, made sympathy a mark of weakness and mutual suspicion the principle of human relationships, and in general created an atmosphere of acute uncertainty and fear.

For the remainder of his life, Stalin's policy of harsh punishment for almost unavoidable counterrevolutionary behavior sustained the Soviet people's sense of anxiety and feeling of helplessness, and they continued to respond to his power by self-control and dissimulation.[39] According to Amalrik, Soviet morality in the post-Stalin period is a "class morality" that considers good to be "what at any given moment is required by authority." This orientation has "totally demoralized society and deprived it of any non-opportunistic moral criteria."[40]

It appears that the Soviet populace has tended to separate Stalin's program of education from the other aspects of his regime. They were and remain passively discontented in the sense that they dislike the concept of counterrevolutionary behavior but are incapable of imagining any replacement for the regime designed to execute the revolution. Among the probable reasons for their acquiescence is the belief that the only real alternative to "Soviet power" is anarchy. A group of former residents of the Soviet Union, when asked to state their political preferences, neatly separated power and policy by choosing law and order, freedom from arbitrary governmental power, and government-guaranteed cradle-to-grave security, under an enlightened (and thus un-Stalin-like) despot who would hold periodic plebiscites to test popular approval of his actions.[41]

All the preceding evidence supports the conclusion that Stalin was rather successful in weakening bourgeois attitudes and values but that he was unable to make most people understand that these attitudes and values were counterrevolutionary, decadent, and morally reprehensible. He seems to have undermined the normal relationships of trust, friendship, and so forth, but there is no evidence that he replaced them with a true sense of revolutionary dedication. The Soviet people, despite their traumatic experiences, did not come to understand Stalinism as did the delegate to the Eighteenth Congress of the Communist Party in 1939 who reported, "At that moment I saw our beloved father Stalin and I lost consciousness." Although Stalin failed to convince the Soviet people that material comfort in a well-ordered society had been condemned by history, he seems to have destroyed their sense of political reality and left them with, at best, the incredibly primitive aspiration to be ruled by an omnipotent party of benevolent Bolsheviks.

The lasting results of Stalin's revolution appear similar in the economic sphere. Certainly the populace was not educated to view social property as the sacred and inviolable basis of social life, but virtually no one can think of any other arrangement. As with the political system, those features of the economic system that were and are disliked are not seen as essential to the institution of social property; for example, the managers do not seem to connect the pressure on them to produce beyond the capacity of their allocated resources with the system's inability to measure value except by quantity of goods produced. Even granting that agricultural workers see collective farming as the cause of their discontent, if they can envision no replacement for it, Stalin's most revolutionary policy was a partial success.

Stalin's other goal in economic education was to raise work to the level of life's prime want. He failed completely to instill this attitude in the agricultural workers and unskilled laborers, but primarily because he could not "electrify" the entire economy and thus make their work more interesting. Skilled industrial workers at the end of the Stalinist period understood their importance to the economy and had pride in their work; they were no longer the half-peasants of 1917, although Stalin clearly was not really necessary for this transformation. Nonetheless, to the extent that the skilled laborer preferred job security to the full utilization of his technical ability, he fell short of Stalin's aspirations.

The intelligentsia seem to identify rather strongly with their jobs, if only because there has been little else in Soviet life to interest them. They no doubt have a reasonably firm commitment to production, but their interest in consumption, exemplified by the appeal of monetary bonuses and the suggestion that light industry be privately run, is not compatible with Stalin's goal of total commitment to work. The technological orientation resulting from the borrowing of "electrification" from capitalist society, as Stalin belatedly recognized, itself has a counterrevolutionary thrust; to the degree that it resembles "bourgeois expertise" it is incompatible both with the principles of socialist property and socialist value and with the Soviet Union's autocratic arrangement of power. Thus far, however, Stalin's successors have managed to use his methods of control and the results of his program of education to contain this fundamental contradiction of Bolshevism.

Notes

1. Joseph Stalin, *Economic Problems of Socialism in the U. S. S. R.* (Moscow: Foreign Languages Publishing House, 1952), pp. 30–31.
2. William Henry Chamberlin, *The Russian Revolution, 1917–1921* (New York: Macmillan, 1960), 2:75, 81.
3. See Frank Lorimer, *The Population of the Soviet Union* (Geneva: League of Nations, 1946), pp. 40, 41; and H. H. Fisher, *The Famine in Soviet Russia, 1919–1923* (New York: Macmillan, 1927), pp. 469, 497.
4. See Dana G. Dalrymple, "The Soviet Famine of 1932–1934," *Soviet Studies*, 15 (1963–64):259–60.
5. Robert Conquest, *The Great Terror: Stalin's Purge of the Thirties* (New York: Macmillan, 1968), pp. 529, 532.
6. I take ten million as the average annual population of the camps, with an annual death rate of 10 percent. This is a relatively low estimate. Conquest, p. 533, takes the even lower one of eight million. He says his figure of ten million deaths from the purge and the subsequent mass arrests "might require an increase of 50 percent or so . . . ," and my calculations so increase it.
7. Stalin, "Questions of Agrarian Policy in the Soviet Union" (1929), in *Leninism* (New York: International Publishers, n.d.), 2:198.
8. Naum Jasny, *Soviet Industrialization, 1928–1952* (Chicago: University of Chicago Press, 1961), pp. 77, 90, 99, 105–6.
9. Donald W. Treadgold, *Twentieth Century Russia*, 2d ed. (Chicago: Rand McNally, 1964), pp. 269–70; Jasny, pp. 96–97, 111.
10. M. Lewin, *Russian Peasants and Soviet Power* (Evanston, Ill.: Northwestern University Press, 1968), p. 494.
11. Jasny, pp. 72–73, 110; Alexander Erlich, *The Soviet Industrialization Debate, 1924–1928* (Cambridge, Mass.: Harvard University Press, 1960), p. 176; William Henry Chamberlin, *Russia's Iron Age* (Boston: Little, Brown, 1934), pp. 52, 55–56, 96, 103, 106, 116, 119; Alexander Baykov, *The Development of the Soviet Economic System* (Cambridge: Cambridge University Press, 1946), p. 215.
12. *Stalin: A Political Biography* (New York: Oxford University Press, 1949), p. 326.
13. See Marshall I. Goldman, *The Soviet Economy: Myth and Reality* (Englewood Cliffs, N. J.: Prentice-Hall, 1968), p. 96. "Reportedly," says Goldman, "Stalin also favored canals because he felt, in this way, his work could be appreciated on Mars."
14. Jasny, p. 446.
15. Goldman, pp. 94, 95.
16. N. de Basily, *Russia under Soviet Rule* (London: George Allen & Unwin, 1938), pp. 268–71; Erlich, p. 184.
17. Alec Nove, *Was Stalin Really Necessary?* (London: George Allen & Unwin, 1964), pp. 21–22; N. I. Bukharin, "Notes of an Economist," in Bertram D. Wolfe, ed., *Khrushchev and Stalin's Ghost* (New York: Frederick A. Praeger, 1957), pp. 295–315.
18. Stalin, "A Year of Great Change" (1929), in *Leninism*, 2:167; "Industrialization of the Country and the Right Deviation in the C.P.S.U." (1928),

in *Leninism*, 2:87; "The Right Deviation in the C.P.S.U." (1929), in *Leninism*, 2:155, 152.

19. "The Right Deviation in the C.P.S.U.," p. 152.
20. Erlich, pp. 167–68, and Nove agrees, p. 23; Stalin, "Industrialization of the Country," p. 73.
21. "The Right Danger in the C.P.S.U." (1928), in *Leninism*, 2:60; *Foundations of Leninism* (1924) (New York: International Publishers, 1939), p. 119; and "Problems of Leninism" (1926), in *Leninism*, 1:284.
22. "The Right Deviation in the C.P.S.U.," p. 129; "Editorial" (1930), in *Leninism*, 2:242.
23. "Questions of Agrarian Policy," p. 198.
24. "Questions of Agrarian Policy," p. 201.
25. *Economic Problems of Socialism*, pp. 27–28, 74.
26. Zhores A. Medvedev, *The Rise and Fall of T. D. Lysenko* (New York: Columbia University Press, 1969), pp. 44–47, 119, 133, 134, 147.
27. Medvedev, pp. 103, 72, 123–25.
28. Medvedev, pp. 318, 29, 145, 144, 31, 32, 135, 134, 37.
29. Raymond A. Bauer, *The New Man in Soviet Psychology* (Cambridge, Mass.: Harvard University Press, 1952), p. 163.
30. Bauer, pp. 132, 144, 146, 150, 151, 169, 152.
31. Andrei Zhdanov, *Essays on Literature, Philosophy, and Music* (New York: International Publishers, 1950), pp. 12, 13, 42, 43, 96.
32. An official Soviet statement quoted by C. E. Black, "History and Politics in the Soviet Union," in Black, ed., *Rewriting Russian History*, 2d ed. (New York: Vintage Books, 1962), p. 26.
33. Conquest, p. 315.
34. See Klaus Mehnert, *Soviet Man and His World* (New York: Frederick A. Praeger, 1961), pp. 196, 197; Raymond A. Bauer, Alex Inkeles, and Clyde Kluckhohn, *How the Soviet System Works* (New York: Vintage Books, 1960), pp. 120, 209; Alex Inkeles and Raymond A. Bauer, *The Soviet Citizen* (Cambridge, Mass.: Harvard University Press, 1961), pp. 242–43, 245; Andrei Amalrik, *Will the Soviet Union Survive until 1984?* (New York: Harper & Row, 1970), p. 19.
35. Mehnert, p.211; Bauer et al., pp. 123, 218, 220; Inkeles and Bauer, p. 126.
36. Bauer et al., pp. 122, 206–10, 268; Mehnert, pp. 212–13; Joseph S. Berliner, *Factory and Manager in the USSR* (Cambridge, Mass.: Harvard University Press, 1957), pp. 321–22.
37. Mehnert, p. 267.
38. Amalrik, *Involuntary Journey to Siberia* (New York: Harcourt, Brace, Jovanovich, 1970), pp. 168–69; and *Will the Soviet Union Survive until 1984?*, p. 36.
39. Bauer et al., pp. 116, 121, 134, 172, 252; Inkeles and Bauer, pp. 277, 287.
40. Amalrik, *Will the Soviet Union Survive until 1984?*, p. 37.
41. Amalrik, *Will the Soviet Union Survive until 1984?*, pp. 11, 12; Mehnert, pp. 214, 217; Bauer et al., pp. 134, 137–38, 138–39, 140, 142, 168; Inkeles and Bauer, pp. 242, 243, 246–47, 250, 251, 252–54.

9
The Antibureaucracy

$\mathbf{B}$y the end of 1929, Stalin had brought the first or political stage of the revolution to the point where he could overcome all opposition and all hesitation and launch the All-out Drive, his most ambitious effort in the economic phase of the revolution. Nonetheless, much remained to be done in the perfection of the "Soviet power" required to sustain the drive toward the ideal communist society. When the collectivization of agriculture was essentially completed, Stalin again gave his full attention to problems of power and by means of his Great Purge of the 1930s established the final form of his Soviet government.

The principal features of this government were an enormous concentration of power in the hands of Stalin himself, a high degree of confusion and inefficiency throughout the apparatus of power beneath him, and a strong tendency to rigidity in policy making and execution, marked by periodic radical changes in orientation. Stalin's personal power is well documented: although he could not do everything himself, his concern with and command of detail were extraordinary, and he could radically affect any area of Soviet life if he chose to do so. All his subordinates worked under great pressure and sense of urgency, duplication of effort was the rule, responsibility and authority were unclear, responses to practical problems were often inappropriate, and waste and poor quality were unavoidable, especially in the economy. Once the gigantic machine was set in motion—to produce copper tubing, or to revise a school curriculum, or to discover counterrevolutionaries—it almost always overfilled its quotas.

The standard account of Stalin's arrangement of power presents it as an overcentralized bureaucracy whose inefficiency and inertia resulted from his attempt to do too much, to regulate and to supervise every aspect of Soviet life. The essence of Stalin's system, however, was not bureaucratic ossification but organizational fluidity, and his great personal power came from his ability to innovate rather than to arbitrate among bureaucratic factions. Like Lenin before him, he detested and dreaded "bureaucracy"; considering his mammoth innovations in social structures, he was remarkably successful in avoiding it.

Since revolutionary progress depended upon the ability of the revolutionary vanguard to take unhampered action to bring about unprecedented change, no source of power outside the vanguard could be tolerated. The aristocracy and the bourgeoisie had been destroyed well before Stalin had established his mastery of the Communist Party, and all other potential opposition to the Party was eliminated as a result of the All-out Drive. As a preliminary to the drive's drastic reduction of real wages, the trade unions were stripped of their remaining power. The precipitate creation of heavy industry that followed so disrupted normal social relationships in the urban and industrial areas of Soviet life that there remained few constituency interests that the Party had to take into account. The peasants' ability and will to oppose the regime were wiped out by collectivization and dekulakization, and the revolution in the countryside also replaced the existing machinery of local government with a very large number of administrative agencies with overlapping functions and ambiguous responsibilities.[1]

At the conclusion of the All-out Drive, political power was the monopoly of the Party and other organizations under Stalin's direct control, but this arrangement still fell short of the ideal revolutionary instrument of power. In the first place, people with bourgeois expertise remained throughout the apparatus, especially in the military service. In the second place, many Communists in positions of power were "Old Bolsheviks," men whose standing in the movement predated Stalin's ascendancy and thus was to some extent independent of him, even though a number of them had helped him to succeed Lenin and to implement the All-out Drive. In the third place, the regime's power was in large measure organizational power, and it was especially dependent upon the tight network of relationships that constituted the Communist Party. With the disappearance of serious threats from outside the revolutionary movement, there was no longer any reason to tolerate such "bureaucracy." In brief, bourgeois experts, old Bolsheviks, and above all bureaucracy hampered the necessary spontaneity of the revolutionary movement, that is, they limited Stalin's own personal power. They had to be destroyed so that the political phase of the revolution could be advanced.

Stalin's method of eliminating these three impediments to true Soviet government has come to be known as the Great Purge of the 1930s. In the Great Purge he combined his attacks upon experts, Old Bolsheviks, and bureaucrats—and also his "moral education" of the general populace discussed above—into a single, vast campaign against what he said was a gigantic conspiracy to undermine the revolution and to restore capitalism in the Soviet Union. This charge of conspiracy was not mere propaganda designed to rationalize his actions, but a logical description of the counterrevolutionary force of the practices and attitudes he was determined to root out. In the normal sense of conspiracy—that a number of people consciously agree to pursue a certain policy—Stalin's charge was inaccurate, and Vyshinsky's attempts during the public trials to establish that his victims were conspirators greatly violated the "facts." According to revolutionary logic, however, the charge was accurate: anyone who was a bourgeois expert or a bureaucrat necessarily desired the defeat of the revolution and would have conspired to do so if he had had the opportunity; moreover, anyone who purported to be a revolutionary was responsible not only for his own revolutionary purity but for that of everyone else, and his tolerance of impurity amounted to a tacit conspiracy with the deviant. The assumption behind this reasoning is that holding a belief that in strict logic implies a given action is tantamount to performing the action.

Stalin carried his reasoning one step farther by accusing his victims of "acting on the instructions of the intelligence services of foreign states."

> Is it not clear that as long as capitalist encirclement exists, there will be wreckers, spies, diversionists and murderers in our country, sent behind our lines by the agents of foreign states?[2]

The leaders of the capitalist countries wish, at least unconsciously, to encourage the counterrevolutionary tendencies within the Soviet Union, and therefore they actively support the wreckers who in turn actively accept their support.

The counterrevolutionaries, said Stalin, were not linked together by an ideology but only by their conspiracy to reestablish capitalism.

> Trotskyism has ceased to be a political trend in the working class. . . . it has changed from a political trend in the working class which it was seven or eight years ago [c. 1930], into a frantic and unprincipled gang of wreckers, diversionists, spies and murderers. . . .[3]

They could have no ideology because the classless society of socialism allows only one ideology, that of the present Soviet leadership, a consideration (Stalin added) that many Party comrades had overlooked. The designation of his victims as "common criminals" was a logical extension of his belief in his own monopoly of political theory, and he charged them with specific but fictitious acts of sabotage and homicide and insisted that they substantiate the charges by "confessing" to these acts. In the midst of the purges, Stalin told the Soviet people that

> The further we advance, the greater the successes we achieve, the greater will be the fury of the remnants of the broken and exploiting classes, the sooner they will resort to sharper forms of struggle, the more they will seek to harm the Soviet state and the more they will clutch at the most desperate means of struggle, as the last resort of doomed people.[4]

As the revolution progresses, moreover, the discovery of counter-revolutionary tendencies becomes increasingly difficult and the leadership must constantly improve its vigilance. The closer both the society and the individual approach revolutionary perfection, the more critical it becomes to expose and root out their defects. As Vyshinsky pointed out during the public prosecutions, Stalin had predicted the occurrence of the kind of opposition he had now uncovered; and Stalin argued that the regime's admission that it had contained counterrevolutionaries would strengthen rather than weaken it.[5] Revolutionary progress depended upon reassuring the masses that the movement was at one with its leader.

Any bourgeois expert was an anomaly in a socialist society, but none was so dangerous as the professional military officer. During the period of the Great Purge, Stalin killed 3 of the 5 marshals of the Soviet Union (preserving the two "politicals," Voroshilov and Budenny); 14 of the 16 army commanders; all 8 admirals; 60 of the 67 corps commanders; 136 of the 199 divisional commanders; and 221 of the 397 brigade commanders. For good measure, he also purged the political commissars attached to military units: 17 of the 17 army commissars; 25 of the 28 corps commissars; and 34 of the 36 brigade commissars.[6] These men did not have to be brought to public trial, because as experts or associates of experts their counterrevolutionary orientation was perfectly obvious and thus required no "unmasking" as in the case of "Trotskyites with Party cards."

Although Stalin's destruction of his officer corps was fully justified by the logic of his revolution, he may well have had a more practical short-term motive. His pending Great Purge would unavoidably result in a high degree of confusion in the country's power-wielding organizations, a situation that might tempt the military to contemplate political action. Perhaps he believed it best for the top officers to go quickly and quietly.

The second special group to be purged were the Old Bolsheviks. Although most of them had at one time or another opposed some aspect of Stalin's policies or power, eventually all had accepted his predominance. Because of their long record of ineffectual resistance to Stalin, well-known men like Zinoviev, Kamenev, and Bukharin retained little political credit, but they were still willing, if the opportunity should arise, to replace him. Other prominent Old Bolsheviks, like Pyatakov, Ordzhonikidze, Rykov, and Krestinsky, had supported Stalin since the beginning of the All-out Drive and even had been instrumental in its implementation. They were possible, but not very likely, challengers to his position. Stalin's principal consideration, however, was not that any of these men might threaten his leadership but that each of them carried in himself revolutionary legitimacy, no matter how currently dissipated, acquired from his long association with the movement and especially from his personal association with Lenin. Revolutionary credentials could come only from the current leader; Stalin's de-Leninization campaign attacked not Lenin but all of Lenin's original community of revolutionaries who had survived him.

In order to establish his own monopoly of revolutionary legitimacy, Stalin had to prove that the Old Bolsheviks were impostors, that they had no revolutionary consciousness and indeed were no more than bourgeois reactionaries. The best way to do this, and simultaneously to demonstrate the absolute bankruptcy of all ideas other than his own, was to show that the Old Bolsheviks were merely "common criminals," and since they had not in fact committed common crimes, it was essential that they publicly confess to the criminal actions that Stalin's prosecutors had invented. (Whether they confessed voluntarily or under physical duress was irrelevant to Stalin.) The logic of his procedure, and the failure of his closest competitor to grasp this logic, can be clearly seen in the proceedings of the trial of Nicolai Bukharin.

Bukharin had not been tortured prior to his trial, but it seems that his family was used as hostage for his proper performance. He went much of the way with Stalin by admitting that he always had been ideologically incorrect—that is, he had opposed Stalin—and that this, although he did not at the time fully realize it, amounted to working for the restoration of capitalism. He accepted the principle of no neutrality, thus conceding that his failure to denounce deviationists constituted opposition, and he took personal responsibility for all the actions of the entire "counterrevolutionary bloc." Yet he denied that he was guilty of specific acts of murder, espionage, and spying and that he belonged to an organized group of conspirators.[7]

Bukharin confessed to being a counterrevolutionary because he had come to realize that his resistance to Stalinist proposals became opposition to the revolutionary movement once these proposals became the policy of the regime. In 1935 he said of Stalin, "It is not *him* we trust but the man in whom the Party has reposed its confidence. It just so happened that he has become a sort of symbol of the Party. . . ." In his final statement at his trial in 1938, he said, "For in reality the whole country stands behind Stalin; he is the hope of the world; he is a creator."[8] Bukharin thus acknowledged that the Party monopolized revolutionary consciousness and that Stalin personified the Party, and during his trial he went out of his way to detail his own departures from Stalinist orthodoxy. Yet he apparently failed to understand that if Stalin were "the symbol of the Party," no one else could share this symbolism with him and that anyone who, for whatever reason, did share it had to be absolutely discredited. Bukharin did not see that, once he had taken moral responsibility for general anti-Stalinist behavior, he had committed himself to confessing overt participation in specific acts of spying and assassination, although Vyshinsky tried very hard to show him he had made this commitment. Although Bukharin acknowledged that Stalin was the "hope of the world," he did not infer from this that the concept of a community of conscious revolutionaries was obsolete, and that, once the revolution had become the work of a single will, the leader had to be completely unencumbered, with his claim to revolutionary correctness shared by no one. As a consequence of this failure of logic, Bukharin refused to admit, and possibly did not understand, that he was indeed a common criminal. Stalin's reasoning was superior and, to say the same thing in another way, he closed the trial by making Bukharin an unperson.

The most significant part of the Great Purge of the 1930s, the part that constituted a major stage in the development of "Soviet power," was Stalin's liquidation, save for a few cronies, of all the men whom he himself had brought to power and standing in the revolutionary regime. By this move he dealt "bureaucracy" a colossal blow from which it never recovered during his lifetime.

The Seventeeth Congress of the Communist Party of the Soviet Union assembled in 1934 in a mood of "intra-party reconciliation, and of an attempt to rebuild the bridges between the Party and the people," after the traumatic experiences of the period of the All-out Drive.[9] As Stalin later pointed out, however,

> Among people who are not very skillful in politics, big successes and big achievements not infrequently give rise to carelessness, complacency, self-satisfaction, overweening self-confidence, swell-headedness and bragging.

Such attitudes "take the spring out of people," that is, they typify bureaucracy and hence counterrevolution. Moreover, said Stalin, in

1934 bourgeois elements were strong because they had Party membership cards and thus could penetrate all institutions and organizations.[10]

To remove bourgeois elements and to put the spring back into
people, Stalin purged his apparatus. There were 1,966 delegates to the
Seventeenth Congress; 1,108 (56 percent) of them were shot during the
next few years. Of the 1,827 rank and file delegates, only 35 (2 percent)
attended the Eighteenth Congress in 1939. In 1934, 139 members and
candidate members were elected to the Central Committee of the Party;
98 (70 percent) had been shot by 1938. The men who had made careers
by following Stalin prior to 1934 were purged, and then the men whom
he brought in as replacements after the first round of purges were themselves purged. In the last half of 1937, "the flower of Stalin's long-
nurtured administrative and political machine" was almost wiped out.[11]

In 1938, an entirely new group of men occupied positions of power
in the Soviet Union. The Stalinist cadres who had been educated by the
All-out Drive, by the succession struggle, and some even by the Civil
War, were replaced by new cadres educated by the purge. These new
men had learned that the will of the leader was supreme and that no one
but the leader was capable of attaining pure revolutionary consciousness.
This lesson was a logical continuation of what had been learned through
the destruction of overt and then passive resistance to the revolution,
and only a thorough purge could have taught it.

Stalin's weeding out of his apparatus unavoidably contained an element of arbitrariness, for strictly speaking no one but the leader can be
completely immune to bourgeois ideals, habits, and perspectives. Yet
not everyone could be purged, and the decision to end the Great Purge
may well have been based at least in part on this consideration.[12] Some
functionaries who had serious doubts about Stalinism may have survived,
and others who were highly enthusiastic may have perished, but these
errors were tolerable as long as most of the doubters were identified and
as long as the principle of the purge was fully understood. By means of
his so-called permanent purge, Stalin maintained this kind of attack upon
"bureaucracy" for the rest of his life, but the intensity of the Great Purge
was never repeated.

By the time that Stalin had completed his great offensive against the
bureaucratic mentality, he had established the pattern of revolutionary
power that would enable him henceforth to exercise completely unhin-
dered his leadership in virtually every aspect of Soviet life. The once
powerful Communist Party had become his docile instrument and the
agency that accomplished this task, the political police, had twice been
thoroughly purged. The leader alone had revolutionary legitimacy, and

the "cult of personality" reached its heights. In his official biography, which he edited himself, Stalin is called the "incomparable master of the Marxist dialectical method," the "teacher of the masses," and the "brilliant strategist of the proletarian revolution." He is characterized as a "genius" with "brilliant perspicacity," "crystal clarity of mind," and "invincible logic," yet without the "slightest hint of vanity, pride, or self-conceit." In peacetime, he developed a "complete theory of the socialist state" and produced the "pinnacle of Marxist-Leninist philosophical thought"; in wartime, he "foresaw the development of events and bent the course of the gigantic battle to his iron will."[13]

Not even a Marxist-Leninist genius, however, could rule the Soviet Union unaided, especially since his regime "sought to contain the whole life" of the country. Beneath the leader were numerous agencies of control, the recipients of endless directives from the center commanding one action or another and frequently specifying required procedures in minutest detail. So much was demanded of these agencies, and the shortage of capable personnel was so severe, that inefficiency and evasion were unavoidable and nepotism, bribery, embezzlement, and the like were widespread and often winked at. The pressure for accomplishment, and especially for fulfillment of production quotas, was enormous and unrelenting and the penalties for failure were severe. As Fainsod said, the apparatus charged with actual administration "lived in perpetual fear and in perpetual motion."[14]

Perpetual fear and perpetual motion were the distinctive characteristics of Stalin's antibureaucracy, maintained by his famous techniques of check and balance and deliberate ambiguity of responsibility. The most prominent elements of his perfected Soviet government were several enormous, formally hierarchical agencies, each with special political or economic functions to perform, but also with the responsibility of checking upon the behavior of all the others. Within the agencies, the principle of hierarchical responsibility was frequently ignored as high-level officials bypassed middle-level officials in their dealings with the lower levels. Individuals with great power in one of these functioning agencies often used personal relationships to establish their power in other agencies within a specific geographical area. There were also a number of centrally controlled agencies with no local operating responsibilities, such as the Ministry of Finance, the State Planning Commission *(Gosplan),* and the Ministry of State Control, that were used exclusively to check upon the operating agencies. At the top of all these functional hierarchies, special control agencies, and personal machines were Stalin and his personal staff, headed by A. N. Poskrebyeshev.[15]

The principal responsibility of the hierarchical apparatus of the Communist Party—the full-time functionaries assigned to geographical areas or to other agencies, such as economic ministries, youth organizations, and the military—was to obtain the desired kinds of public behavior, through education, propaganda, and the application of differential incentives for various kinds of work.[16] The main function of the economic ministries, of which the All-Union Ministries were the most important, was to oversee the operations of the economy, under the general guidance of the Party apparatus; in agricultural areas, the Machine Tractor Stations had especially significant supervisory powers. The "elected" Soviets were rather functionless at the top, but at the lowest levels they cooperated with the Party apparatus in a comprehensive surveillance of the people's lives.[17]

The so-called political police[18] was a very complex organization that maintained a permanent interest in the affairs of every member of the population, from the most to the least powerful, with an eye to counterrevolutionary behavior and attitudes. It was concerned with counterespionage and genuine subversion, but Stalin's very broad definition of counterrevolution meant that most of its attention was directed to people who were not consciously opposing the regime. For example, the political police kept extensive dossiers on "potential enemies," those people with certain social origins, outside contacts, and so forth. Its vast intelligence operations, incidentally, were matched by those of the Ministry of State Control, one of the agencies without policy-implementing responsibility.[19]

The political police was also charged with the disposition of the people who had committed counterrevolutionary acts. It administered the great forced-labor camps and thereby commanded a great reserve of labor utilized in large-scale economic enterprises. The police closely supervised the regular economy as well, for theft of material or breaking of equipment was a counterrevolutionary act; and it collected full information on the state of economic production, since the goals of production were a matter of basic revolutionary policy. Finally, it had a special responsibility for the activities of the revolutionary organizations such as the youth groups and artists' unions.[20]

The vast empire of the political police included a formidable concentration of physical power in the "internal army" of the Soviet Union, the Main Administration of Border Troops and the Main Administration of Internal Troops. These agencies had millions of fully armed men in peacetime and even more during World War II, and they were always completely independent of the Soviet Army command. The men of the internal army were drawn from the general body of regular military conscripts after a careful screening to ensure their perfect physical condition, unblemished political records, and family backgrounds free of counterrevolutionary associations, actions, and tendencies. The percentage of recruits of working-class origin was higher for the internal army than for the regular army; its equipment, pay, and living conditions were superior; and approximately 25 percent of its training time was devoted to political education. The internal army apparently was fully reliable from a revolutionary point of view; throughout the years it received, among others, these critical assignments: to suppress the popular uprisings that followed the famine of the All-out Drive, to guard against possible revolts in the regular army during the purge of the military in the 1930s, to remain stationed just behind front-line regular troops during World War II, and to carry out the postwar mass deportations of Soviet people who had been under German occupation.[21]

Stalin's well-known ability to control and change every aspect of Soviet life and to dispose of any of his subordinates depended upon the way he had distributed power among and within the separate agencies of his regime described above. By setting each of them against all the others and by allowing the lower levels of each to be highly independent of their formal superiors, he came close to eliminating the insulation, mutual protection, and inertia of the normal large administrative structure. From top to bottom, he sustained an "institutionalized mutual suspicion" and kept his functional and control agencies "in purposeful conflict."[22]

The political police was autonomous in the performance of its standard functions and it had full and secret control of its network of informers, but its regular appointments had to be approved by the Party apparatus and its personnel had to meet norms of behavior set by the Party. The police closely supervised the routine tasks of both the Party apparatus and the economic ministries, but these agencies could charge the police with interference in their work and with failure to maintain the proper ideological awareness.[23] The police could arrest Party officials for counterrevolutionary activity without clearance from their superiors, as the Great Purge amply demonstrated, but since the police was isolated from all other sources of power and unsure of its own pattern of internal authority, it was unable to resist being itself purged. The Party apparatus supervised the economic administration, but it was not allowed to intervene in the purely technical aspects of the economic process.[24] It had to be vigilant in assuring that production quotas were fulfilled, yet it had to avoid denunciation by the economic ministries for meddling in affairs beyond its technical competence.

In order to reduce mutual suspicion and purposeful conflict, the representatives of the functional agencies in specific units of operation frequently engaged in "familyness," that is, they agreed to refrain from denouncing one another, or at least to do so only moderately. Such

attempts to stabilize power at the lower levels of operation were naturally anathema to the regime, which fought the artifice by constant fulmi-
nation, by an insistence that lower-level authority not be delegated, by a
further weakening of the formal hierarchical pattern of authority, and by
fuller utilization of agencies like the Ministry of State Control that had
no local operating responsibilities.[25]

At the highest level of operation, the pattern of mistrust and competition was repeated. Directly under Stalin himself were a number of
prominent men, each of whom had attained great power as a result of a
high position in one of the regime's principal agencies or from having
made a specific area of policy, such as agriculture or cultural affairs, his
personal specialty. Occasionally one of these men established his control
over most of the normally competing agencies in specific geographical
regions—for example, Khrushchev in the Ukraine, Zhdanov in Lenin-
grad, and Beria in the Caucasus—and thus gained a territorial base of
power. Because their relationships with one another were completely
informal—that is to say, because each reported directly to Stalin and
because the agencies they headed had confused and overlapping areas of
responsibility—Stalin was able to use the standard technique of setting
them against one another, thereby retaining the ability to dispense with
any of them. For the lieutenants themselves, this arrangement meant
mutual distrust and constant contention.

The total lack of structured power at the top of Stalin's antibureaucracy was demonstrated by the struggle for succession following his
death. The power of the principal contenders, Beria, Khrushchev, and
Malenkov, came from their respective control of the political police, the
Party apparatus, and the government ministries. None of them, however,
had any claim to authority or legitimacy over the others, and none had
enough pure muscle to eliminate his rivals. They found themselves in, so
to speak, a perfect "state of nature."[26] The succession struggle was unavoidably an exercise in improvisation, for although the contestants
could rely upon past methods of infighting and temporary combinations,
there was no longer a leader to guarantee that their deadly contest would
not result in the disintegration of the entire regime. Stalin's heirs showed
their appreciation of this fact when, upon announcing his death, they
publicly warned the Soviet Union's myriad functionaries against "disor-
der and panic."

Stalin's final version of "Soviet power" was an instrument of rule highly
responsive to the leader's revolutionary initiative and thus necessarily
also highly flexible, confused, and inefficient. Although the working
principles of this instrumentality exerted a great autonomous force, so

that those people who comprised it had to conform to them or perish, the entire arrangement also depended upon the presence of enthusiastic revolutionaries at key points from top to bottom. Many, and perhaps even most, of those who operated the revolutionary machine were no more than cynics, but the absence of all overt opposition and natural dissenters and the stern education of the permanent purge undoubtedly created a climate well suited to the growth of convinced Stalinists.

There was no place in this arrangement of power for a political party of any type, and the Soviet Union was thus a "one-party state" only in the most trivial sense. The old Leninist idea of a community of conscious revolutionaries as a ruling "party" had been long abandoned. In the Stalinist era, the mass Party was a loose association of the successful and would-be successful; and the Party apparatus, although its functions of exhortation, example, and positive education were important, was only one among many control agencies and was clearly less powerful than the political police, the executor of Stalin's favorite revolutionary techniques of intelligence gathering and purging.[27] Yet when Stalin came to summarize the accomplishments of the revolution in his Constitution of 1936, Article 126 described the Communist Party of the Soviet Union as a voluntary organization of the "most active and politically conscious citizens in the ranks of the working class, working peasants, and working intelligentsia," as "the vanguard of the working people in their struggle to build communist society," and as "the leading core of all organizations of the working people, both public and state." The discrepancy between these descriptions and the actuality of the mass Party and the Party apparatus has puzzled many observers.

In discussing the 1936 Constitution, Stalin pointed out that under socialism, the lower stage of communism, there are no antagonistic classes and thus there is only one set of interests, those of the workers-peasants-intelligentsia, that must be defended; hence there can be only a single party.[28] This argument, however, cannot be taken at face value, because Stalin's theory of "Soviet power" could not admit the existence of an institution as bureaucratic and bourgeois as a political party. The 1936 Constitution was his summary of the progress made to that time by the revolutionary movement, and, from his point of view, the Great Purge's destruction of the Communist Party as an organization with a near monopoly of political power was a major revolutionary advance. Since he had no reason to obscure his evaluation of the situation, the answer to the discrepancy between his words and the actual distribution of power must be that the passages in Article 126, and other similar statements, are not to be taken literally. When Stalin used the word "party" he meant the revolutionary regime as a whole, not the Party apparatus or the mass Party or both. Consequently, Article 126 was intended to emphasize the solidarity between the regime and the masses.

A more important expression of Stalin's efforts to identify the masses and the regime was his resurrection of the old idea of elected Soviets. An entire chapter of the 1936 Constitution was devoted to a scheme of popular participation in the staffing of a large number of bodies, from the thousands of village Soviets to the Supreme Soviet of the USSR, which, save for a few minor functions performed by local Soviets, had virtually nothing to do with the regime's operation. According to Stalin, this popular participation constituted the world's "only truly free elections," although, from the bourgeois point of view, it served only to ratify "candidates" selected by the regime itself. Great amounts of energy and money went into the almost annual "campaigns" for one or another level of Soviets.

These "genuinely free elections" were important both theoretically and practically because they symbolized the classlessness of Soviet society and demonstrated the identification of the masses and the regime. Proof of this classlessness and solidarity was constantly furnished by the more than 99 percent of the votes received by the "candidates." The masses, however, had not progressed beyond the enthusiastic acceptance of socialism, and consequently they were incapable of understanding the policies required to move the society toward the higher stage of communism. This incapacity meant that their preferences regarding policy were not to be considered and that no power to determine policy was to be given to the men for whom they cast their ballots. Nevertheless, the masses' obligatory participation in staffing the Soviets helped them to understand the requirements of revolutionary progress, and it also counteracted bureaucracy by forcing the Party apparatus and other functionaries to go the masses.[29]

The 1936 Constitution also listed a number of obviously bourgeois democratic rights, the freedom of speech, the press, assembly and association, and religious belief and observance, and the inviolability of the person and the home. The inclusion of these "rights" clearly indicated the Constitution's status as an expression of a new way of viewing the relationship between a political regime and its subjects. No genuine member of the classless society could wish, for example, to say or print anything in opposition to a regime that truly represented his interests, but since he was not yet at the stage of development where he could understand the ultimate purposes of this regime, all speech and writing had to be subjected to strict censorship. According to this reasoning, there was nothing incongruous about the promulgation of these "rights" during the Great Purge and the subsequent liquidation of most of the men who wrote them. Both the rights and the electoral system were Stalin's adaptations of basic bourgeois-democratic political ideas and practices to the conditions of socialism. In this manner, he reinforced both his claim to have established the world's most advanced society and his argument that bourgeois democracy was not only undemocratic but obsolescent.

Stalin's antibureaucracy was the logical culmination of Lenin's concept of the "Soviet government" that would so arrange power that the socialist transformation of society could be accomplished with a minimum of counterrevolutionary interference. This arrangement amounted to a maximization of Stalin's personal power, and, quite understandably, he was personally affected by his own creation, taking on many of the attributes of the classic tyrant. His preoccupation with his own safety, harsh treatment of his associates, and suspicion of universal plotting and treason may have approached paranoia, but they resulted from a system set up for revolutionary purposes. At the supposed height of his insanity after World War II, he was able through his system of control to accomplish vast and careful policies: he reestablished his full control over the Soviet Union, deported and reeducated millions of people, launched a revolution in the arts and sciences, brought Communist rule to most of Eastern Europe, pursued an aggressive foreign policy, turned his attention once more to agriculture, and apparently was planning another thorough purge of his subordinates. In addition, in *Economic Problems of Socialism* he presented a cogent summary of his work since the All-out Drive, his tone being realistic to the point of mild pessimism, yet he retained his will to revolution and prescribed another great economic upheaval. Like all great leaders, he enjoyed power, but to say that he sought power for its own sake is to ignore completely what he did with his power and how, through his life-long protestations that he was working to establish a socialist and then a communist society, he himself accounted for its use.

According to bourgeois standards, Stalin's methods were criminal, but he did not subscribe to these standards. His methods (like his policies) were also inefficient and wasteful, but he did not measure human and material costs according to democratic and capitalist criteria. He could afford his own concept of cost because he ruled a vast land with a vast, unstructured population. In any event, no cost was too great for the remolding of the human psyche.

Notes

1. M. Lewin, *Russian Peasants and Soviet Power: A Study of Collectivization* (Evanston, Ill.: Northwestern University Press, 1968), pp. 426, 515.
2. Joseph Stalin, *Mastering Bolshevism* (1937) (New York: New Century Publishers, 1945), p. 9.
3. *Mastering Bolshevism*, p. 9.
4. *Mastering Bolshevism*, p. 22.
5. Robert Conquest, *The Great Terror: Stalin's Purge of the Thirties* (New York: Macmillan, 1968), pp. 115, 179; Stalin, *Mastering Bolshevism*, p. 40.
6. Conquest, pp. 485, 228.
7. Robert C. Tucker and Stephen F. Cohen, eds., *The Great Purge Trial* (New York: Grosset & Dunlap, 1965), pp. 328, 338, 339, 340, 341, 387, 388, 396, 656–58, 659, 660, 661, 665.
8. Conquest, p. 126; Tucker and Cohen, p. 667.
9. Conquest, p. 37.
10. *Mastering Bolshevism*, pp. 14–16.
11. Conquest, pp. 36, 38, 263, 265, 471.
12. Conquest, p. 317.
13. Marx-Engels-Lenin Institute, *Joseph Stalin: A Political Biography* (New York: International Publishers, 1949), pp. 57, 63, 64, 88, 91, 106, 123.
14. Merle Fainsod, *Smolensk under Soviet Rule* (Cambridge, Mass.: Harvard University Press, 1958), pp. 66–67, 77, 78, 83–85, 92, 107–8, 116, 145, 151.
15. See Bertram D. Wolfe, *Khrushchev and Stalin's Ghost* (New York: Frederick A. Praeger, 1957), pp. 219, 221; and A. Avtorkhanov, *Stalin and the Soviet Communist Party* (New York: Frederick A. Praeger, 1959), p. 190.
16. Barrington Moore, Jr., *Terror and Progress—USSR* (Cambridge, Mass.: Harvard University Press, 1954), pp. 9–10.
17. Fainsod, pp. 96, 145, 293.
18. The OGPU or Unified State Political Administration (1926–34), the NKVD or People's Commissariat of Internal Affairs (1934–38), and the MVD or Ministry of Internal Affairs (1939–53).
19. Moore, pp. 49–50.
20. E. A. Andreevich, "Structure and Functions of the Soviet Secret Police," in Simon Wolin and Robert M. Slusser, eds., *The Soviet Secret Police* (New York: Frederick A. Praeger, 1957), pp. 96–151.
21. V. P. Artemiev, "The Armed Forces of the Soviet Organs of State Security," in Wolin and Slusser, pp. 239–59. The critical assignments listed were given to the Troops of Special Purpose (OSNAZ) of the "internal army."
22. Fainsod, *How Russia Is Ruled* (Cambridge, Mass.: Harvard University Press, 1953), p. 109; Moore, pp. 13, 30.
23. Fainsod, *Smolensk under Soviet Rule*, pp. 73, 110, 160, 162, 167, 169, 281.
24. Moore, pp. 18–19.
25. Fainsod, *Smolensk under Soviet Rule*, pp. 86, 111, 378, 408; Moore, pp. 20–21, 23; Joseph S. Berliner, *Factory and Manager in the USSR* (Cambridge, Mass.: Harvard University Press, 1957), p. 324.
26. Myron Rush, *Political Succession in the USSR*, 2d ed. (New York: Columbia University Press, 1968), ch. 3.

27. Note Fainsod on the "one party state": The NKVD was guided by the Party "in a special sense," that is, "the Party was essentially a pseudonym for Stalin . . ."; and "It is a curious fact that even at the height of the [Great] purge, Stalin maintained the fiction of 'the leading role of the Party.' Still trumpeting this theme, Stalin proceeded in 1937 to use the NKVD to decimate the ranks of leading Party workers in the Western Oblast. This was the ultimate irony of Party control." *Smolensk under Soviet Rule*, pp. 171, 172.

28. *On the New Soviet Constitution* (1936) (New York: International Publishers, n.d.), p. 23.

29. Andrei Y. Vyshinsky, *The Law of the Soviet State* (New York: Macmillan, 1948), pp. 172–76, 479, 486, 665, 722.

IV
Mao's People's Republic of
China

I am alone with the masses.
Mao Tse-tung

10

The Thought of Chairman Mao

The revolution of Mao Tse-tung has been directed against what he calls twentieth-century imperialism and it has aimed at establishing a typically egalitarian utopia based, at least in the forseeable future, upon what can best be called "racial consciousness." For Mao the essence of the modern era is the opposition between the exploiting bourgeois imperialists, principally those of the white race, and the exploited, nonwhite people of the "colonial" or "semicolonial" areas. He has followed the Leninist thesis that imperialism has given rise to an "international proletariat" in the noncapitalist areas of the world, but his prescription for this proletariat is quite anti-Leninist. He has rejected the possibility of any borrowing from (or "synthesis" with) capitalist imperialism, and hence electrification, or the creation of capitalistlike work relationships, is quite unnecessary for, and possibly even incompatible with, the construction of the ideal society. His almost total theoretical unconcern with modern technology gives Mao's repudiation of bourgeois society a purity, and hence an appeal to certain contemporary Western intellectual romantics, that neither Soviet Communism nor National Socialism can match.

Imperialism will be overthrown and a new social order will arise from its ruins, and the power to do both is to be supplied by the people whom imperialism has most exploited and oppressed, the inhabitants of the world's colonial and semicolonial areas. The exploitation and oppression of imperialism, as Mao sees it, have been "cultural"; that is to say, imperialism has imposed upon colonial peoples potent modes of thought and behavior foreign to their true nature. This does not mean that he defends indigenous cultures, for traditional Chinese society also has been

151

an imposition on the Chinese "masses" and alien to their essence. For Mao the point is that the penetration of Western culture into China and similar areas has created a "contradiction" that will supply the energy for the exploited peoples to throw off both the new culture and their own traditional culture. Once these unnatural social fetters have been removed, the elemental force of the masses will be released, and this force will require only the proper leadership to bring into being the true culture of the masses, namely, the communist society.

Mao's theoretical presuppositions are basically similar to those of the other great revolutionary leaders examined above, although they are somewhat less sophisticated. Once he became committed to a revolution in human society and human nature, he realized that change of such magnitude could not occur without violence, and he understood that the Bolshevik coup of 1917 was an act consistent with this view of social development. The older order, whether Western imperialism or Chinese traditionalism, never voluntarily surrenders; there is no such thing as peaceful evolution from one kind of society to another.

Consistent with this interpretation of social change, Mao has seen struggle as the essence of human life: in the distant past, a struggle of men against nature, and in the recent past, as a result of the institution of private property, a struggle of men against men, opposing one another as "classes, nations, states, or political groups."[1] The interhuman struggle has taken a physical form, especially that of warfare. Early in his career, Mao seems to have expected this pattern of human conflict to culminate in a single great war of liberation by all the oppressed peoples against the united imperialists, but in later years, and with better logic, he has come to envision the end to imperialist exploitation as the result of many unconnected guerrilla actions. Whichever way imperialism will be destroyed, when struggle throughout history is interpreted as simple physical opposition, violence is indeed unavoidable. From his earliest years, Mao had been acquainted with violence, and he lived very much as a soldier from 1928 until 1949. He has always been impressed with martial virtues and the tempering effect of warfare upon the human personality; he was not unhappy at the prospect of a prolonged war with Japan because it would steel the Chinese people. When military action has accomplished its purposes, there remain many areas of struggle, against class enemies, of course, but also within the body of dedicated revolutionaries themselves.[2] Struggle is progress, and struggle is happiness.

The outcome of the prolonged contest with imperialism and its ally, traditionalism, is the inevitable destruction of both: "The great tide in the world is rolling ever more impetuously. . . . He who conforms to it shall survive, he who resists it shall perish. . . ."[3] When Mao wrote this in 1919, he only felt strongly that the great energy of the masses of the dominated areas could not long be contained; when he later came to Marxism, he added a veneer of historical determinism that postulated a constant movement from lower to higher social forms and attached a logical necessity to this development.[4] He remains, however, relatively indifferent to matters of "historical necessity" in the progression of mankind, possibly because the Chinese, unlike the Europeans, have never experienced a bourgeois revolution that indigenously supplanted and surpassed the traditional or "feudal" society. Mao's intellectual commitment has remained principally to the elemental force of the unnumbered masses.

Like all great leaders, Mao is more concerned with doing than with theorizing. Once again, his natural intellectual orientation seems to have been reinforced by his later exposure to the Marxist-Leninist concept of the unity of theory and practice. When he came to try some Marxist philosophy of his own, he recognized the unity of theory and practice as a key element in this philosophy, but he apparently has never completely comprehended it.[5] For Mao the issue is between abstract, theoretical knowledge and an understanding of the concrete circumstances in which the revolutionary must work. His so-called sinification of Marxism is the unexceptional recognition that whoever wishes to bring mankind to a higher stage of social development must gain the power to do so by using whatever local forces are available. As he has said, "There is no such thing as abstract Marxism, but only concrete Marxism. . . ."[6]

Although Mao apparently has never fully realized that the unity of theory and practice means that human knowledge is identical with human action, he has always been clearly aware that the whole point of comprehending man and society is to change them.[7] He grasped the essence of Stalinism: as he said, Marx and Lenin may have been clever theoreticians, but Stalin established socialism and made concrete the principle, "to rebel is justified," thus establishing himself as the "savior of all the oppressed" and the "greatest genius of the present age." Stalin was responsible for "epoch-making developments in the theories of Marxism-Leninism," and he understood the importance of putting politics in command.[8] Mao's own claim to philosophical and theoretical innovation is the claim to an unmatched understanding of how to make a revolution under the special circumstances of the era of imperialism, an understanding that he and others have considered the consummation of Marxism-Leninism, the most famous revolutionary tradition of all.

The human will is the supreme force in human affairs, and "Man's ability to know and change Nature is unlimited."[9] As a youth, Mao believed that people could be judged by the "energy" they possessed, and he admired Napoleon, Bismarck, and Kaiser Wilhelm II. In one of his earliest writings, in 1919, he followed Li Ta-Chao in stressing will and consciousness as the determinants of social change.[10] Throughout his life, says Schram, he has possessed "a single overriding priority; to the man who wills rather than to the man who knows."[11] The Long March of the 1930s symbolizes what iron will can accomplish against all odds; inevitably it has become one of the most important myths of Chinese Communism, and Mao never tires of recalling its various heroics. Willpower and voluntarism, however, are not merely prescriptions for revolutionary leadership, but the principal forces behind basic social change: "the epoch of world communism," Mao has said, "will be reached when all mankind voluntarily and consciously changes itself and the world."[12] Revolution is less concerned with creating new social arrangements than it is with getting people to desire a new mode of life and a new society.

Mao's unusually strong theoretical emphasis on the power of correct thoughts and revolutionary consciousness (especially his own) is qualified, however, by his belief that this power depends upon the existence of the true "mass society," which in turn depends upon the elimination of the social structures that in the past have contained the energy of the masses. His extreme voluntarism, in other words, presupposes certain objective social conditions, but his approach to the reordering of human interrelations is much more flexible than that of the Bolsheviks.

The goal of the forthcoming revolution is a perfectly egalitarian and thus perfectly selfless society, a concept originally suggested to Mao by his hatred of social stratification and his experience with the "unspoiled" peasantry, and reinforced and made more precise by his later understanding of Marxism. The first stage of the revolution will replace imperialism and traditionalism by socialism. Under socialism, says Mao in the lifeless manner characteristic of his (relatively infrequent) efforts to be a good Bolshevik, the relations of economic production will be "collective ownership" and each person will contribute "according to his ability" and receive "according to his work." Under communism, the second and higher stage of the revolution, the relations of production will be "ownership of the whole people"; differences between types of work and styles of life will disappear; and, as more products become available, commodities will be eliminated and each person can receive "according to his needs." In the era of world communism, there will be no classes, no capitalism, no exploitation, no states, and no war.[13]

Since the new order of communism is unprecedented, only its general principles can be sketched. There will be no social differentiations whatever; that is, the ideal society will be void of social systems as they are now understood. Communism will be based upon a type of interpersonal relationship completely free of "bourgeois sentimentality"; it will contain a new kind of person, an austere, dedicated pursuer of a common good that depends upon his own and everyone else's perfect selflessness.

Mao agrees with Stalin that, as socialism comes closer to realization, the "class struggle" becomes more intense, that is, the old individualist modes of thought become more tenacious and those who practice them more desperate; but he has gone beyond Stalin in his assertion that there will still be "contradictions" and hence struggle among the people after the advent of communism, "though its nature and form will be different from those in class societies." To believe in the eventual total elimination of struggle is to believe that mankind will cease to progress; humanity, however, "is still in its youth," and the communist era will contain many phases of development, each involving struggle. "The theory of the cessation of struggles is sheer metaphysics."[14]

Although this position suggests a concept of "permanent revolution," the meaninglessness of everything but struggle itself, Mao has only abandoned the unpersuasive idea that communism will mark the end of human history. He has retained the belief that a specific form of human social life, called "communism" and exhibiting the characteristics described above, will come into being as a form of human development higher than any achieved prior to its arrival. There will be even higher forms of development, however, and struggle is justified solely as a means to their realization; revolutionary leadership and revolutionary education, consequently, will always be needed.

Imperialism is the "exploitation" of the noncapitalist world by the capitalist powers. This exploitation had taken the form of Western domination of China's economic and political systems, a condition that most Chinese could understand, but it also had appeared in forms much more sophisticated than the use of gunboats and mercenary police and the establishment of business enterprises. The main thrust of imperialism, according to Mao, has been in the area of culture.

> The imperialist powers have never slackened their efforts to poison the minds of the Chinese people. This is their policy of cultural aggression. And it is carried out through missionary work, through establishing hospitals and schools, publishing newspapers and inducing Chinese students to study abroad. Their aim is to train intellectuals who will serve their interests and to dupe the people.[15]

It was very difficult for the Chinese people to recognize and to combat cultural aggression, for ideas like bourgeois democracy and liberal humanitarianism are subtle and insidious. Mao, however, had perceived the essence of the situation at least as early as 1923, when he identified the United States, the Western power least inclined to use crude force, as the leader of world imperialism. "America," he once said, "is the most murderous of hangmen."[16]

Even prior to his exposure to theoretical Marxism-Leninism, Mao had realized that cultural phenomena such as beliefs and values are invariably associated with specific political and economic systems.[17] Since all the ideas of liberal democracy necessarily support the inequalities of the bourgeois economic and political systems, imperialism is in total and comprehensive opposition to movements, such as Chinese Communism, dedicated to instituting a new social order. The Soviet Union has lost its revolutionary dynamism and become "revisionist" because its post-Stalin leaders have compromised with the bourgeois principles of expertise and technology. Their acceptance of capitalist encirclement has caused them to forget Stalin's dictum that socialism must be created "from scratch" and they speak of "peaceful evolution" of capitalism into socialism, thus in effect working toward the restoration of capitalism.[18] This Soviet experience has confirmed Mao's opinion that only the unspoiled (or undeveloped) areas, such as China, are capable of opposing imperialism.

Mao has always been adamantly opposed to liberalism, for it seeks peace (and thus is decadent and philistine), values friendship above ideological purity, and stresses tolerance of differing opinions. He has recognized that social systems are "the principal manifestations of the concept of bourgeois rights," and he has fought bourgeois individualism, insisting that the individual is secondary to the group and that the future takes precedence over the present.[19] He remains opposed to consumerism:

> You remember Kosygin at the Twenty-Third Congress: "Communism means the raising of living standards!" Of course! And swimming is a way of putting on a pair of trunks! Stalin had destroyed the kulaks. . . .[20]

Bourgeois technology and bourgeois art must be thoroughly rejected. Imperialism, in short, is a total way of life that seeks to dominate the world, and it can be frustrated only by an offensive along the whole cultural front.

The revolution that will overcome imperialism and establish communism can be based only upon those people least influenced by imperialism, namely, the "masses" of what imperialism calls the "underdeveloped areas." The masses are those hundreds of millions of materially and spiritually deprived people, found principally among the peasantry, whose "poorness and blankness" provide a clean sheet upon which can be put the newest and most beautiful words and pictures, yet whose innocence can provide a social force of extraordinary swiftness and violence, like a tornado or tempest or hurricane, a force that is irresistible. The masses have great willpower and great "energy." When the Chinese peasants arise against a social order, they completely shatter it, they arrest their enemies "at the slightest provocation," and their newly formed associations take autocratic control of all the details of life.[21] In sharp contrast to the Leninist fear of this elemental force of the peasantry, Mao saw it as a power to be harnessed for total revolution. The peasants' backwardness—their terrible force of habit—did not bother him, for he understood how easily the unthinking routine of traditional society could disintegrate into anarchy. The new society he aspired to create, moreover, did not depend upon the electrification of the countryside and thus did not require workers with capitalistlike discipline and rationality; he saw revolutionary capacity even in the outcasts of traditional society, the soldiers, bandits, robbers, beggars, and prostitutes. The faith in the revolutionary potential of the masses that Mao acquired from his observation of the Hunanese peasants in the 1920s underlay the Great Leap Forward and the Great Proletarian Cultural Revolution, his revolutionary experiments of three and four decades later.

In order to be usable for revolutionary purposes, however, the power of the masses needs cohesion and direction; random exercises of mass power against indiscriminate targets will bring about no lasting social change. The masses must act together, and against an identifiable enemy; they therefore need a sense of their own similarity and their difference from outsiders. The masses that will give their great energy to Mao's revolution are the Chinese masses.

Mao's preoccupation with China is well known. He tends to see it as the center of the world, and he is fascinated by its vast population and territory, both of which he usually exaggerates. There is nothing that "one-quarter of mankind" cannot do, from creating by their own unaided efforts a rich and strong socialist country to emerging as relatively powerful as ever from a nuclear war.[22] From his childhood, Mao has been concerned with the disintegration of the Chinese Empire, always defining it in the broadest possible geographical terms.[23]

The great masses of China not only possess the raw force to destroy imperialism and its ally, traditionalism, but in their Chineseness also have a principle of cohesion that can both shape this force and enable them to recognize the encroachments, especially on the cultural level, of Western imperialism. Mao's sinocentricity depends to some extent upon the tradition of the Middle Kingdom, but it goes well beyond this tradition, for his revolutionary hopes are based upon his belief that the Chinese people are aware of their uniqueness among, and possibly also their superiority to, the rest of humankind.

For Mao, as for virtually every other important Chinese politician who matured prior to World War II, being Chinese is a matter not of membership in a nation but of a consciousness that can best be described as "racial." Apparently there is nothing in Mao's writings and recorded speeches that deals with this issue of Chineseness, but his concept can be inferred from his other thoughts, from his intellectual milieu and the statements of other Chinese authors, and from official decisions by his regime.

When Chinese intellectuals were prompted to react to the challenge of imperialism, they tried to understand, among other things, the principle of political community underlying the strength of the Western powers. They knew, of course, that this community was called the "nation," but they had had no experience of a community made up of individuals sharing a common political interest and thus being equal among themselves and distinct from other human beings. Sun Yat-sen's response to this situation was typical: the English word "nation," he said, "has two meanings, race and state." Foreign countries have developed many states from one race and also included many "nationalities" (that is, races) within one state, but the Chinese way is to develop a single state out of a single race.[24] Sun uses the Chinese word *min-tsu*, which he translates as "nation," in a sense very close to that of the German word *Volk*.[25]

Even more revealing are the thoughts of Li Ta-chao, one of Mao's mentors and a founder of the Chinese Communist Party. In a lecture in 1924, Li defined a nation as all people who participate in a common history and culture, whether or not they are aware of their shared experience. A race, on the other hand, is a group based on biological characteristics and on the "racial instinct," the natural feeling of "being different." The white men, he continued, believe themselves culturally superior to the colored peoples and look on them as a lower class; thus, on the international scale, "the racial problem becomes a class problem." We Chinese, Li concluded, must once again "clearly manifest our national spirit! This has been my idea in dealing with this racial question. . . ."[26]

In 1962 an official conference in the People's Republic discussed the meaning of the word *min-tsu*, concluding that it was the equivalent of three words in English, Russian, and German: "people," *narod*, *Volk*; "nation," *natsiya*, *Nation*; and "nationality," *narodnost*, *Nationalität*. The conference went on to reject Lenin's contention that *narodnost* (nationality) was a phenomenon of capitalism and to affirm that the Chinese (strictly, the Han) were a nationality in their precapitalist period.[27]

Despite Mao's worry about imperialism, its culture had not penetrated China and the task of formulating a political community was the almost exclusive concern of the intellectuals. The Chinese bourgeoisie was, in Maoist terms, exceedingly flabby and it developed no sense of the bourgeois nationalism that the National Socialists and Bolsheviks found so restrictive.[28] It is clear that the intellectuals saw only the "racial instinct" as a possible base for the viability of a Chinese state, and there is no reason to suppose that Mao differed from them. Indeed, his revolutionary ideology is meaningful only when Chineseness in this sense is available to give form to the elemental energy of the masses in the drive to establish the true culture of the masses.

Chineseness for Mao is emphatically not dependent upon the great tradition of classical Chinese culture, for this culture (feudalism) suppresses the revolutionary potential of the masses, a relationship he has raised to the status of a Marxist contradiction.[29] In his youth, the overt humiliations China was suffering from foreign incursion led him to reject the imperial Chinese way, and after he had studied some Marxism-Leninism he said that the revolution must "liquidate the philosophical heritage of ancient China." In 1966 he criticized Stalin for having retained classical Russian art and art forms, and the "anti-Confucius" campaign of recent years has been the formalization of his own position.[30] Classical Chinese culture has always been only that of a small minority, maintained at the material and cultural expense of the masses.

Feudalism, moreover, is the ally of imperialism, because the wealthy (and thus cultured) stratum of traditional society profits from its connections with the imperialists and keeps the masses docile in the face of imperialist exploitation.[31] This cultural elite, called by Mao the "landlords," is so committed to the inherent inequality of feudalism and imperialism that its sense of Chineseness has been completely smothered. The inability of the landlord elements to realize their true racial instinct and to identify with the masses means that they are fundamentally antisocial, and all of them, including the Kuomintang, are consequently no better than common criminals.

The contradiction between the Chinese and imperialism, on the other hand, is less severe. Those people who have been contaminated by the insidious culture of imperialism, the bourgeoisie and the intellectuals of China, still retain the objective opposition of the true Chinese to this foreign invasion. They have, unlike the landlords, no commitment to feudalism, and they consciously desire the political and economic independence of China. Despite this orientation, they are incapable of taking the initiative against imperialism: they are so flabby that they must rely upon the Communist Party (the "proletarians") to lead the "bourgeois-democratic revolution," that is, the recapture by the Chinese of their own polity and economy.[32] Since the bourgeois-democratic revolution in China was directed against imperialism rather than against a society dominated by the bourgeoisie, Mao's "new democracy" announced in 1940 was not an alliance of "national" bourgeoisie, peasants, and workers but an alliance of all those who had a sense of Chineseness.[33] When, soon after 1949, China moved from the period of new democracy into the stage of the "transition to socialism," the cultural reform of the national bourgeoisie began at once.

At the beginning of the transition to socialism, or the "proletarian" in contrast to the bourgeois-democratic revolution, the Chinese bourgeoisie and intellectuals resist their own transformation, but their Chineseness eventually overcomes the foreign interests and attitudes they contracted from imperialism and they "enter the state of voluntary, conscious change." At first, of course, they "must go through a stage of compulsion," perhaps even being administered a "powerful shock," but then they become enthusiastic supporters of socialism.[34]

In addition to providing the principle of cohesion for their tremendous energy, the Chinese masses set the goal toward which this energy is to be directed. These hundreds of millions of unstructured and unspoiled souls desire nothing so much as a society of complete equality, where no one has more power, more knowledge, more wealth, more prestige, and even more beauty and more friends than anyone else. Said Mao in 1955, the masses are showing an "immense enthusiasm for socialism" and they are "dancing for joy" at the prospects of the further socialization of agriculture. After the initiation of the commune movement, a "new form of social organization" that "was entirely a creation of the masses" (and thus inevitable), "the masses of the Chinese peasantry rejoice over the people's communes from the bottom of their hearts. . . ."[35] The masses' only superficial integration into the traditional order and their relative freedom from imperialist influences enable them to take a detached and unbiased view of the true nature of man and society. Marx's attribution of this ability to the "proletariat" caught Mao's attention, and he adopted the word "proletarian" to describe it. His early use of guerrilla forces and of Communist-dominated rural areas became "the highest form of peasant struggle under the leadership of the proletariat," and more than thirty-five years later he named his revolutionary *opus magnum* the "Great Proletarian Cultural Revolution."[36]

Although the masses provide the goal of and the energy for revolutionary change, their aspirations must be articulated and their enthusiasm sustained, and hence revolutionary leadership is required. The true Maoist leader does not create new ideas and rely upon the sympathy of the masses for their support, for the masses "must educate themselves and liberate themselves" and no world outlook can be imposed on them. The leader must follow the principle of "from the masses, to the masses": he must study the views of the masses, distill and integrate them, and then get the masses to recognize these refined ideas as their own. This is the famous "mass line," neither "commandism," the departure from the ideas of the masses, nor "tailism," the failure to refine them. The leader resembles the midwife, making sure that delivery is neither premature nor delayed. Mao has said that he himself only wishes "to learn from the masses, to continue to be a school boy." He tries to avoid giving orders, preferring to ask his associates to consider the issue, to discuss it. He is a chairman rather than a leader: he does not march ahead blazing new revolutionary trails; he presides at a perpetual conference of the masses, articulating and summarizing their beliefs, ideas, and feelings.[37]

Revolutionary leadership is to be judged according to its clarity and consistency in understanding and expressing in words and actions the masses' innermost desire for the perfectly egalitarian society and, inferentially, for the truly selfless individual human being. Since the utopian revolutionary, like the creative artist, must bring out what is latent in his raw material, his principal qualification for leadership is his possession of imagination and insight, an ability to think and feel like the masses themselves, rather than an ability to organize and a knowledge of means-ends relationships.

The experiences of the Long March and the Yenan period apparently led Mao to believe in the possibility of the leadership of a select community of revolutionaries who could express as one person the true consciousness of the masses. The pre-1949 period, however, was concerned principally with the practical problems of survival and growth in an environment dominated by the forces of normalcy and even counterrevolution. The solidarity the Communist leadership demonstrated in responding to these problems was quite different from the solidarity required once the task of the Communist movement became the application of the mass line in order to construct a completely new society. Normal and previously useful political and military skills became manifestations of "bureaucracy" and bourgeois expertise in the new revolutionary environment, and Mao gradually came to consider most of his colleagues incapable of true leadership.

Reasoning, as well as experience, undermined the concept of collective leadership. The masses, and especially the Chinese masses, are so numerous that it is difficult for the individual to identify himself with them. To personify a regime by a single leader is, of course, a standard response to this kind of difficulty. The ordinary people of traditional society, moreover, always subconsciously have preferred the rule of a single benevolent autocrat, who guarantees not only their well-being but also their equality. Finally, and most significantly, since Mao's theory of leadership holds that the thoughts of the masses and the thoughts of the leadership ought to be identical, correct leadership can best be represented by a single mind perfectly attuned to the collective mind of the masses. Consequently, logic has supported experience in leading Mao to the theory of "Mao Tse-tung Thought," the theory that the true thought of the masses is precisely expressed in his own thought. The remarkable scope and power of Mao Tse-tung Thought are derived not from any individual—not even from a genius of a revolutionary leader, for the existence of genuis would deny the creativity of the masses—but from the inherent infallibility and breadth of the true mass mind. Mao Tse-tung Thought implies that personal cleanliness should be maintained, and recalcitrant machinery behaves once Mao Tse-tung Thought is applied to it. The Thought is selfless and autonomous; it is the mass line carried to its ultimate refinement; it is the acme of voluntarism. Mao's claim that he is "alone with the masses"[38] is deductively faultless.

Although Mao is not very interested in economics, he early recognized that private economic enterprise is inconsistent with the mass society,[39] and he has dutifully followed Stalin in analyzing society and social change in terms of the forces and relations of production. He tends to hold that, by and large, the relations of production take causal precedence over the forces of production. Under socialism, the relations take the form of "collective ownership": the communes exemplify collective ownership, but they are more than just collective farms because in them finance, commerce, industry, and government are merged with collective agriculture. This combination of functions in the communes "has opened up a way to reduce the differences between town and countryside and between worker and peasant." Under "advanced socialism," the relations of production will be "ownership by the whole people."

> The state, representing the whole people, can directly make a unified and rational distribution of the means of production and the products of enterprises owned by the whole people according to the requirements of the national economy as a whole. . . .

To change from collective ownership to ownership by the whole people, the communes must be combined in federations, thus further homogenizing the people and encouraging the development of "communist factors" and the raising of "the people's political understanding."

The relations of production under communism are ignored in official Chinese Communist literature.[40]

All this Marxist-Leninist-Stalinist verbiage is not very clear and not very persuasive. The genuine Maoist position is that politics always takes precedence over economics and that Stalin's concern with economic production as the very foundation of interpersonal relations is misplaced and perhaps slightly ridiculous. Mao has criticized the Soviet emphasis on heavy industry, for it "stresses administration and lacks the mass line." (He wants China to have only enough such industry to support his domestic and foreign policies of anti-imperialism.)[41] Finally, and most significantly, he has said that bourgeois attitudes can be destroyed prior to the destruction of bourgeois economic forms, such as commodities and market values. Indeed, to increase the "solidarity of hundreds of millions of peasants it is still necessary to vigorously develop commodity production and to increase currency."[42]

In any event, revolutionary consciousness is acquired much better on the land than in the factory,[43] and the power of one-quarter of mankind is so great that one need not worry too much about the specifics of economizing.

Mao's radical egalitarianism naturally is accompanied by a rejection of all expertise and specialization of function. At first he was routinely contemptuous of bourgeois and petty-bourgeois intellectuals and advocated the standard elimination of the distinction between manual labor and intellectual labor.[44] He later realized that expertise itself was a phenomenon of imperialism. "We do not have to open big tomes or small pamphlets; a bit of common sense will do." "Can philosophy, literature, and history not be taught down below? Must they be taught in tall, foreign-style buildings?" If one reads too much, he will become a bookworm, a dogmatist, and a revisionist. Intellectuals "deliberately turn simple things into mysteries." "The more you study, the more stupid you become." "In history it is always people with a low level of culture who triumphed over people with a high level of culture."[45] Most problems are manageable and have relatively obvious solutions, if one only will copy the masses and take the direct and simple approach.

Mao's belief that all good flows from the unstructured masses underlies not only his indifference to economics and his anti-intellectualism but also his appreciation of the Bolsheviks' theoretical hatred of "bureaucracy." In 1933 he said that "the ugly evil of bureaucracy . . . must be thrown into the cesspit," and in 1953 he pointed out that Stalin had "creatively developed Lenin's theory on Party-building." The true revolutionary leader is in continuous direct contact with the masses;

anyone who takes "routine paths" must necessarily fail. Mao's most forceful theoretical attack on bureaucracy came with his pronouncement that even in a "people's state" contradictions can develop between the leaders and the led, between the government and the masses, and of course the resolutions must always be in favor of the masses. Political leaders tend to acquire an "exclusive club" mentality; they must not forget that "China has a population of 600 million people," that is, that masses are more important by far than cadres.[46]

Mao has applied the famous Leninist principle of "democratic centralism," the arrival at absolute unity after free discussion, not to a limited vanguard of conscious revolutionaries but to the masses themselves. In 1942 he devised the formula, "unity-criticism-unity," as the operating code of his movement in its quest for power, but in 1957 he applied it to all the people of China.[47] Unity on revolutionary goals was to come from the masses themselves, and they thus in effect have come to comprise their own revolutionary vanguard. No other great revolutionary leader has so rigorously spelled out the premises of mass spontaneity and bureaucratic stultification. Mao's iron logic demonstrates most forcefully how total revolution is incompatible with any and all social systems: the withering away of the state, and indeed of every other normal interpersonal structure that provides some legality, ordering, and predictability, becomes quite understandable.

Notes

1. "Problems of Strategy in China's Revolutionary War" (1936), in *Selected Works of Mao Tse-tung* (Peking: Foreign Languages Press, 1965), 1:180; "On Protracted War" (1938), in Stuart R. Schram, *The Political Thought of Mao Tse-tung*, rev. ed. (New York: Frederick A. Praeger, 1969), p. 391.
2. This sense of struggle is beautifully conveyed by Mao's "Reading Notes on the Soviet Union's 'Political Economics'" (1961–62) and "Dialogues with Capital Red Guards" (1968), in *Miscellany of Mao Tse-tung Thought (1949–1968)* (Arlington, Va.: National Technical Information Service, 1974), pp. 247–313, 469–97.
3. Schram, p. 163.
4. "A Single Spark Can Start a Prairie Fire" (1930) and "On Contradiction" (1937), in *Selected Works*, 1:118, 334; "Dialectical Materialism" (1938), in Schram, p. 189.
5. "On Practice" (1937), in *Selected Works*, 1:296–97, 299; "Speeches at the Second Session of the Eighth Party Congress" (1958), in *Miscellany*, pp. 91, 117; "Where Do Correct Ideas Come From?" (1963), in K. H. Fan, ed.,

The Chinese Cultural Revolution: Selected Documents (New York: Monthly Review Press, 1968), p. 32.

6. "Report to the Sixth Plenum of the Sixth Central Committee" (1938), in Schram, p. 172.

7. "On Practice," p. 308.

8. "Speech on Stalin's Sixtieth Birthday" (1939) and "Tribute to Stalin" (1953), in Schram, pp. 426, 428, 429; "Concerning Mei Sheng's 'Chi Fa'" (1959), in *The Case of Peng Teh-huai, 1959-1968* (Hong Kong: Union Research Institute, 1968), p. 326.

9. "Critique of Stalin's *Economic Problems of Socialism in the U. S. S. R.*" (1959?), in *Miscellany*, p. 192.

10. Robert Payne, *Mao Tse-tung* (New York: Weybright & Talley, 1969), p. 41; Schram, p. 34.

11. Schram, p. 103.

12. "On Practice," p. 308.

13. "On Correcting Mistaken Ideas in the Party" (1939), in *Selected Works*, 1:111; "Resolution on Some Questions Concerning the People's Communes" (1958), by the Central Committee of the CCP, in *Communist China, 1955-1959; Policy Documents with Analysis* (Cambridge, Mass.: Harvard University Press, 1962), pp. 492, 493, 494, 497; "Problems of Strategy in China's Revolutionary War" (1936), in *Selected Works*, 1:183; "On Protracted War," p. 393; "The Draft Constitution of the CCP" (1968), in Schram, p. 328.

14. "On the Historical Experiences of the Dictatorship of the Proletariat" (Editorial, *People's Daily*, 1956), in *Communist China, 1955-1959*, p. 148; "On the Correct Handling of Contradictions among the People" (1957), in *Let a Hundred Flowers Bloom* (New York: Tamiment Institute, n.d.), p. 26; "Examples of Dialectics" (1959?), in *Miscellany*, pp. 204-5; untitled writing (1958), in Jerome Ch'en, ed., *Mao Papers: Anthology and Bibliography* (London: Oxford University Press, 1970), p. 65.

15. "The Chinese Revolution and the Chinese Communist Party" (1939), in *Selected Works*, 2:312.

16. "The Peking *Coup d'etat* and the Merchants" (1923), in Schram, p. 389.

17. *Report of an Investigation into the Peasant Movement in Hunan* (1927) (Peking: Foreign Languages Press, 1953), p. 59. His Marxist version is in "Dialectical Materialism," pp. 180-81.

18. "Reading Notes on the Soviet Union's 'Political Economics,'" p. 247; "The twenty-three point directive on the socialist education movement in the countryside" (1965), in Schram, p. 324. "The Soviet Union today is a dictatorship of the bourgeoisie, a dictatorship of the grand bourgeoisie, a fascist German dictatorship, a Hitlerite dictatorship. They are a bunch of rascals worse than de Gaulle." "Briefing" (1964), in *Miscellany*, p. 349.

19. "Combat Liberalism" (1937), in *Selected Works, 2:31*-33; "Comments" (ca. 1959), in *Miscellany*, p. 189.

20. Interview with André Malraux (1965), in Malraux, *Anti-Memoirs* (New York: Holt, Rinehart & Winston, 1968), p. 373.

21. "Article" (1958), in Schram, p. 352; *Report of an Investigation*, pp. 2, 4, 9; Payne, p. 41.

22. *Socialist Upsurge in China's Countryside* (Peking: Foreign Languages Press, 1957), with editorial comments by Mao, p. 14.

23. Schram, *Mao Tse-tung* (New York: Simon & Schuster, 1966), p. 236.

24. *San Min Chu I* (Shanghai: Institute of Pacific Relations, 1928), pp. 5–6.
25. James P. Harrison, *Modern Chinese Nationalism* (New York: Hunter College Research Institute on Modern Asia, n.d.), p. 24.
26. Quoted in Hélène Carrère d'Encausse and Stuart R. Schram, *Marxism and Asia* (London: Penguin Press, 1969), pp. 219–22.
27. George Moseley, "China's Fresh Approach to the National Minority Question," *China Quarterly* (Oct.–Dec. 1965):20, 21.
28. Harrison, p. 25.
29. "The Tasks of the Chinese Communist Party in the Period of Resistance to Japan" (1937), in *Selected Works*, 1:263.
30. "Dialectical Materialism," p. 186; "Instruction" (1963), in Schram, *Political Thought*, p. 368; "Summary of the Forum on the Work in Literature and Art in the Armed Forces" (1966), in Fan, p. 107.
31. "Analysis of the Classes in Chinese Society" (1926), in *Selected Works*, 1:13; "The Chinese Revolution and the Chinese Communist Party" (1939), in *Selected Works*, 2:319.
32. "The Tasks of the Chinese Communist Party in the Period of Resistance to Japan," p. 273; "The Chinese Revolution and the Chinese Communist Party," p. 321.
33. "On New Democracy" (1940), in *Selected Works*, 2:373.
34. "On Practice," p. 308; "Speech at the Hankow Conference" (1958), in *Miscellany*, p. 85.
35. *Socialist Upsurge*, pp. 41, 151; "Long Live the People's Communes!" (Editorial, *People's Daily*, 29 August 1959), in *Communist China, 1955–1959*, pp. 552, 554.
36. "On Practice," pp. 295–96; "A Single Spark Can Start a Prairie Fire," p. 118.
37. "Speech to the Albanian Military Delegation" (1967), in *Miscellany*, p. 459; "Some Questions Concerning Methods of Leadership" (1943), in *Selected Works*, 3:117–20; "On the Historical Experience of the Dictatorship of the Proletariat" (1956), in *Communist China, 1955–1959*, pp. 149–50; "Instruction" (1966), in Ch'en, p. 115.
38. Malraux, p. 375.
39. "Our Economic Policy" (1934), in *Selected Works*, 1:143–44.
40. "On the Correct Handling of Contradictions among the People," pp. 27, 28, 31–32; "The Question of Agricultural Cooperation" (1955), in *Communist China, 1955–1959*, p. 101; "Resolution on Some Questions Concerning the People's Communes" (1958), in *Communist China, 1955–1959*, p. 493.
41. "Speech on Economic Problems of Socialism" (1958), in *Miscellany*, p. 130; "On the Ten Great Relationships" (1956), in Ch'en, pp. 67, 68; "Speech" (1958), in *Miscellany*, p. 136; "On the People's Democratic Dictatorship" (1949), in *Selected Works*, 4:419; "On the Correct Handling of Contradictions among the People," pp. 55–57.
42. "Speech on Economic Problems of Socialism," p. 130; "Critique of Stalin's Economic Problems of Socialism," p. 195.
43. See Schram, *Political Thought*, pp. 110, 137.
44. "Talks at the Yenan Forum on Literature and Art" (1942), in *Selected Works*, 3:73; "Dialectical Materialism," p. 182.
45. "Talk in Hangchow" (1965), in Ch'en, *Mao and the Chinese Revolution* (New York: Oxford University Press, 1967), pp. 105, 107; "Mao's Remarks to

Students" (1964) and "An Instruction" (1966), in Ch'en, *Mao Papers*, pp. 96, 131; "Summary of the Forum on the Work in Literature and Art in the Armed Forces" (1966), in Fan, p. 121; "Reading Notes on the Soviet Union's 'Political Economics,'" p. 307.

46. "Pay Attention to Economic Work" (1933), in *Selected Works*, 1:134; "Tribute to Stalin" (1953), in Schram, *Political Thought*, p. 430; *Socialist Upsurge*, p. 44; "On the Correct Handling of Contradictions among the People," pp. 17, 43.

47. "On the Correct Handling of Contradictions among the People," pp. 19, 23.

11

The First Step in the Long March

$\mathbf{M}$ao Tse-tung and the Communist movement gained control of the Chinese mainland by a military victory in a civil war. Like Lenin, Mao triumphed because he defeated in armed action those who opposed his revolution, but, unlike Lenin, he was unable to support this action with the mechanisms and prestige of a governmental apparatus previously seized in a coup. Since at least 1916, there had been no central administration in China that anyone could seize; even Chiang Kai-shek's partial unification of the country in the late 1920s had been destroyed by the Japanese invasion.

Early in his career Mao recognized that, in order to capture a China so politically fragmented, the Communist movement had to have an army of its own. Although he always has emphasized the power that grows out of a gunbarrel and has given it credit for his victory in 1949, he also has said that the Communists' military power ultimately depended upon their unique ability to "mobilize the masses." Mobilization of the masses included recruiting and retaining an army and getting the populace to accept it; but Mao believes that it included something more, that the Communists mobilized the masses prior to 1949 in the same way they have mobilized them since, by expressing in their revolutionary goals the fundamental but probably unconscious aspirations of the great majority of the Chinese people. In seeking the reasons for the birth, persistence, and eventual triumph of Chinese Communism, the Chairman's theory of mass mobilization must not be entirely discounted.

By the end of the nineteenth century, the traditional Chinese political order had proved itself incapable of resisting imperialism, the impact of

169

Western economic technology supported by the physical force of the foreign powers. The Chinese Empire, like all such political societies, was predicated upon its own self-sufficiency and immutability. During the long period of its isolation from the world political system, the empire's stabilizing mechanisms had been so perfected that they could not adjust to the new threat from outside. The traditional regime could only repress administrative and ideological innovations and hope that the imperialists would go away. Imperialism, however, was persistent, especially in its cultural form, and in 1911 the last Chinese dynasty, the Ch'ing or Manchu, collapsed principally from sheer inappropriateness.

A group of intellectuals, who had been affected by cultural imperialism and who thus assumed that the strength of the Western powers was at least in part dependent upon their political systems, managed to promulgate a constitution for a Republic of China to be governed by elected assemblies. Ideologically, this constitution was designed to replace the traditional principle of political hierarchy; practically, it was a challenge to the dominance of indigenous military forces. Since China had been a "semicolonial" country, imperialism had implanted no concept of popular legitimacy nor even any appreciation of bourgeois administrative efficiency. Most Chinese consequently "felt instinctively that a surrender of power to [the central and provincial elected assemblies] by the military strongmen would only bring confusion."[1] For their part, these strongmen, whose power had kept China from complete disintegration upon the collapse of the empire, had no intention of abdicating. General Yüan Shih-k'ai, the commander of the Peking area; easily attained the presidency of the new republic, and he by and large ignored the National Assembly, finally dissolving it in 1913. Some of the leaders of Sun Yat-sen's movement—the T'ung-meng-hui, later the Kuomintang—tried to save the parliamentary principle, but most political activists, including Sun himself, were at least indifferent to its fate. Bourgeois democracy had been proved totally inappropriate, at least for the foreseeable future.[2]

General Yüan's nullification of the constitution suggested a return to the autocracy of the empire, and he subsequently tried to set up a new dynasty. Even the most conservative Chinese objected to this move,[3] and an attempt after Yüan's death in 1916 to restore the Manchu dynasty was also signally unsuccessful. By 1920 at the latest, the traditional principle of empire was no longer a feasible method of Chinese political unification.[4] Another principle had to be found, and in the meantime the Chinese policy, society, and economy further disintegrated. From about 1916 until about 1928, local military leaders, or "warlords," tried to provide government on a decentralized basis, but this approach was a conspicuous failure.[5] Independent armies proliferated,[6] warfare was continuous, finance was chaotic, agricultural output shrank, wealth and the wealthy fled the countryside, opium production (for revenue) was encouraged, inland trade was virtually destroyed, flood-control systems fell into disrepair, food shortages could not be relieved, and the poor suffered from extortionate "taxes," unemployment, and high rents and rates of interest. The old order had indeed collapsed, imperialism had provided nothing to serve as a replacement, and the politically minded intellectuals were well aware of this situation.

The Bolshevik coup of 1917 greatly impressed those Chinese, including Sun Yat-sen, who were seeking a political theory that was neither traditional nor bourgeois-democratic. Even more interesting was the Bolsheviks' method of organizing political power, a method that prevailed over both tradition, in the form of the White counterrevolution, and bourgeois modernity, in the form of Western intervention in the Russian Civil War. A Chinese Communist Party, closely associated with the Comintern, was founded in 1920, and by 1927 it had almost 58,000 members.

During this initial period of its existence, the strategy of the Party was to support the "national revolutionaries," of whom the Kuomintang appeared to be the most promising, rather than to develop an independent organization openly challenging this force for political unity as well as the warlords and the imperialists. The Communists thus established an alliance with the Kuomintang, with the aim of capturing it from within, and the Soviet Union provided it with material and organizational assistance. This strategy committed the Communists to working for the capture of China principally in the urban areas, the home of three nontraditional groups, the "national bourgeoisie," the intellectuals, and the industrial workers. The countryside was, to say the least, peripheral to their plans.

This strategy failed because the Communists were unable to appeal both to the workers and to the bourgeoisie and intellectuals. The desire for independence from the West was the primary political motive of the businessmen and the intellectuals, and the Kuomintang at this time was an adequate vehicle for its expression. The Communists, for their part, were somewhat too closely linked with a foreign country, even though this country's regime had denounced imperialism.[7] Although they were successful in organizing a strong following among the industrial workers, there were just too few such workers to provide an independent source of power. About half of China's industrial workers were in Shanghai, with most of the remainder in Canton and Hankow, where they were almost lost among the vast numbers of traditional artisans and coolies.[8] Even if this element of Communist power had been much stronger,

China had no central governmental apparatus that could be seized in a coup. The only urban political phenomenon of any importance was the Kuomintang, another movement aspiring to control all of China. In 1927, Chiang Kai-shek, unhampered by bourgeois rules of constitutionality, purged the Communists from his movement, destroyed their trade-union power, and eventually drove them from the cities. The businessmen and the intellectuals were not especially concerned about the Communists' defeat.

Although powerful elements in the Communist Party retained the belief that their revolution could succeed only with an urban base, the Party's expulsion from the cities, as can be seen in retrospect, confirmed the opinion of those Communists, among them of course Mao Tse-tung, who held that China's political decentralization would allow the establishment of rural areas under the control of Communists from which an attack upon the cities could successfully be launched. For more than twenty years, the intra-Party strength of those Communists who sought an urban base and the entire Party's dependence upon the Soviet Union obliged Mao to qualify his position, but he never wavered from his conviction that the sole revolutionary potential in China was the elemental energy of the rural masses. This thesis was correct, but the power of a rural-based movement would not have sufficed for the capture of China if the Japanese invasion had not weakened the Kuomintang's military force and allowed Mao to neutralize the "national bourgeoisie" and the intellectuals of the cities.

Although Mao did not gain full control of Chinese Communism until at least the early 1940s, an account of the 1949 victory in the Civil War must focus on what he and his associates had been doing since 1927, even when they were isolated from their own movement and at the mercy of the armies of Chiang Kai-shek.

During Mao's early years in the countryside, his "Marxism" was little more than a superficial identification with a world view he understood as radically egalitarian and violently opposed to both traditionalism and imperialism, combined with a confidence derived from the successes of Lenin and Stalin. He fully understood, however, that to survive in rural areas and eventually to capture China required a military force.[9] When, in 1927, Chu Teh and his soldiers joined Mao and his followers in the inaccessible mountains of Chingkangshan in east-central China, this military force got its modest start with an army of perhaps 5,000 men.

By 1930, Mao and Chu were strong enough to set up the famous Kiangsi Soviet, their first formal attempt to base military power on a peasant society by "mobilizing the masses." They succeeded in building an army of more than 100,000 men by 1933 in an area containing from 12 to 15 million people,[10] and they were driven from their stronghold a year later only by a huge effort on the part of Chiang Kai-shek, who overwhelmed them with troops for attack and with fortifications and political organizers for retrieving captured territory and people. Despite his progress toward solving the problem of using the rural base in a limited area, Mao was still subject to the power of the Kuomintang and the cities.

In the Kiangsi Soviet the "masses" were "mobilized" by organizing "poor peasants" into a poor-peasant corps and a farm-labor union,[11] and by pursuing a radical and thorough elimination of "landlords" and "rich peasants." Since in this locale the quality of the land varied greatly and many different types of crops were grown, these representatives of the old order were identified according to their use of hired labor and status as creditors rather than by the extent of their land holdings.[12] Communist methods included mass meetings, public trials, bureaus of political security to search for counterrevolutionaries, and "selective terror." The property of the condemned was turned over to the "poor peasants," and their cash was given to the new units of local government.[13] In these proceedings in his own enclave, Mao was not out of line with the programs of other (and rival) sectors of the Chinese Communist Party, but he clearly found the policy congenial and he appears to have shown unusual enthusiasm in purging his subordinates for their failure to pursue it.[14]

This radicalism allowed Mao to base an armed force on a peasant society, at least for a limited period in a limited area, because it removed all sources of resistance to Communist power. With the disappearance of all potential patrons, the traditional patron-client relationship, the only form of social cohesion known to the countryside, could no longer exist. The "poor" peasants who remained could only support the Communists' radical egalitarianism and acquiesce in their impressment into the Red Army, or flee to the mountains.[15] These peasants, moreover, were undoubtedly less than happy with Mao's principal military tactic, to "lure the enemy in deep," a means of preserving his armed forces at the expense of the local population that would be overrun and probably punished by this enemy.

Throughout this period, Mao also was engaged in a struggle for power within the Communist movement, and consequently, like Stalin before him, he had to vary his policy pronouncements to attack those of his rivals who were most threatening and to compromise when he could not attack. Nonetheless, the policy of the Kiangsi Soviet was fully consistent with his earlier views expressed in *The Peasant Movement in Hunan* and with his later activities, from the Yenan period until the present time. When in 1935, Chang Kuo-t'ao, one of Mao's principal rivals within the Party, argued that the Communists in the future should set up governments "acceptable" to the people of the area they were occupying—thus implicitly criticizing the Kiangsi Soviet—Mao insisted that the Kiangsi variety of popular mobilization was the only acceptable form of government.[16] Here Mao's tactical position almost certainly corresponded to his fundamental theory of revolution.

In 1934 the forces of Mao and Chu, now numbering only 30,000, left Kiangsi by breaking out of a Kuomintang military encirclement and fled to the west. Some two years later, after the famous Long March of about 6,000 miles around the area of Kuomintang strength and after many (recounted) acts of desperate heroism, about 10,000 of them arrived at the sparsely populated, desert region of Shensi in north-central China. This unpromising territory had the great advantage of being even more inaccessible than Chingkangshan to Kuomintang military penetration, a situation confirmed by the Kuomintang's subsequent involvement with the Japanese invasion. The Yenan period, the most curious in the history of Chinese Communism, had begun.

Mao's rise to the leadership of the Chinese Communist movement was slow and difficult. Just prior to the Long March, he was in definite eclipse, but he began to regain his power when the Kuomintang drove the Communists to the north and west, "when the movement itself was in its apparent death throes," and by the end of 1935 he was in control of the central organs of both the military forces and the apparatus of the Soviet government. This control, especially of the army, proved decisive in the contest for leadership.[17] In addition, as the Japanese fortuitously undercut the position of the Kuomintang, Mao's strategy was confirmed, and he gained the aura of correctness so important to a revolutionary leader. Finally, and of equal importance, he had proved himself a skilled and ruthless infighter and a master of the purge and the methods of secret-police work. By 1945 Chinese Communism had become Maoism.

Under the more favorable circumstances of the Yenan period, Mao resumed his effort to build an army—his goal was one million men—by mobilizing the rural masses. In addition, he now had devised a method of neutralizing the urban areas of China and thus the Kuomintang. His strategy, it should be noted, was precisely the reverse of that of Lenin.

As in Kiangsi, Mao pursued a policy of eliminating "landlords" and redistributing their property, but his techniques had changed. Instead of outright liquidation of the local notables, he followed a program of sharply reducing rents and rates of interest and of virtually abolishing taxes for the majority of the population. With the backing of mobilized "poor peasants" and the troops of the Red Army, the more wealthy peasants were "confiscated by installment."[18] Perhaps 10 to 20 percent of the land in Mao's area was redistributed after 1937, most of it taken from absent "landlords" branded as "traitors" to the anti-Japanese resistance. Those who remained in the Communist areas were protected if they supported the so-called war effort, although an undetermined number of "class enemies" were liquidated under accusation of treason.[19]

During this period Communist territorial bases, in the Yenan area and throughout China, were selected according to military and political considerations that had no connection with the social and economic conditions of those who inhabited them. It thus happened that the distribution of neither wealth nor land was a problem in north China prior to Mao's arrival, and the Communists had to manufacture dissention from the modest differentials that did exist.[20] This "mobilization of the masses," of course, was possible only because Mao's military forces and civilian cadres, although much reduced after the Long March, were nonetheless the only organized power in this area.

Faced with organized Communists willing and able to challenge the existing order, the "poor peasants" reacted like the good traditionals that they were and went along with what seemed to be a winner. Naturally, when the Communists abandoned an area to the Kuomintang, the peasants lost their attachment to radical egalitarianism, and in places where the Japanese later established themselves the natives were not at all reluctant to support them. When the peasants could not satisfy their first preference of being left alone, they cooperated with whatever power was present and appeared to be the lesser evil.[21]

Mao's immediate purpose in gaining the cooperation of the local peasantry was to provide financial and other support for the million-man army that was to capture all of China for him. This army was gradually and painfully put together over the years in Yenan, growing in numbers under favorable circumstances and suffering heavy losses when conditions deteriorated. Recruitment was not left to chance: men were enlisted under intense public pressure manufactured by the Party's cadres, a process that came close to press-ganging.[22] As the army was constantly increased by such methods, it was constantly losing men through desertion. During times when Communist governmental power was unimpeded, the desertion rate was about 20 percent; when in 1941 and 1942 the Japanese put great pressure on the Communists, the rate increased to about 40 percent.[23]

In the wake of the Japanese invasion of north China, many villages created their own armed defense organizations, a customary response to the disintegration of governmental power dating back at least to the T'aip'ing Rebellion. The peasants understood that, in the last analysis, every village and perhaps every family had to rely on its own resources, and ultimately on its own physical force, for self-defense. The extreme parochialism of these defense organizations allowed the Communists considerable freedom of action, but more significantly it provided them with semiprocessed material for their army. Their structure of disciplined civilian and military cadres enabled them to incorporate these basically apolitical organizations for self-defense into the framework of the Red Army.[24]

The localism of these defense organizations made it possible for Mao and his cadres to manipulate them for the purpose of stopping and then defeating the Kuomintang. On the other hand, their lack of commitment to anything but their villages often led them to refuse to help defend other areas and made them vulnerable to persuasion and pressure by the Kuomintang and the Japanese.[25] Things went the Communists' way when, in the winter of 1940, the Japanese army began its "pacification campaign," an operation designed to eliminate all sources of resistance as quickly as possible so that troops could be transferred from north China to a corridor leading to the raw material of southeast Asia necessary for the anticipated war with the United States. The brutality of the campaign allowed the Communists to argue most reasonably that the local self-help paramilitary groups, some of which had recently sought Japanese protection against the Communists, could turn to no one but the Communists for protection from the Japanese pacifiers. The Communists also began to expand their militia after the initial impact of this campaign.[26]

To overcome the parochialism of the local defense association, which often enough led to looting and other similar behavior when the troops were away from their home areas, the Maoists made a rather large investment in what they called the education of the Red Army. Although this program was an innovation in the Chinese military practice of the time and no doubt helpful to the Communist cause, the education dealt only with the most elementary human relationships and was quite without political content. Officers, for example, were told not to beat their men, and the men were told not to mistreat civilians.[27]

A similar lack of political sophistication characterized the leading military and civilian cadres who provided the political muscle for mobilizing the masses and the framework that made a Red Army out of innumerable local defense units. Their ideology was little more than "take from the rich to give to the poor," and their primary sentiment was a hostility to everything, both traditional and modern, that suggested social superiority.[28] These were the "old guerrilla fighters," who proved useful also after 1949 in the campaigns to eliminate landlords and to rectify bourgeoisie.

During these years, in addition to acquiring and supplying an army in his north China base, Mao had to protect his movement from his more powerful rival for control of China, the Kuomintang, and once again the Japanese offered him his opportunity. He could accomplish his goal if the Japanese army neutralized Chiang Kai-shek's military force and if he could use the Japanese presence to neutralize Chiang's urban supporters by getting them to see the Communists as stalwart patriots and untiring fighters for China's freedom from foreign domination. Japan's determination to confront the United States allowed both of these aims to be realized.

Although Mao's approach to the non-Communist part of China throughout this period varied according to the interest of the Soviet Union in "united fronts" against Hitler and according to the military strength of the Kuomintang and the Japanese,[29] he made a consistent effort to present the goals of his movement as no different in essence from those of the urban intellectuals and businessmen. The Communist "suppression of hostile elements," mostly labeled "traitors," was muted, a departure from the practice during the Kiangsi period when information regarding the elimination of the rural gentry had disturbed the cities. Mao also made a virtue of necessity by advertising as "moderation" a relaxation of his radical social and economic policies designed to increase production for his military effort. He instituted a political system based on "universal suffrage" that gave the impression that power was "shared" with local non-Communists, in contrast (of course) to the "dictatorship" of the Kuomintang. He described his program to increase rudimentary literacy as "universal education" and succeeded in convincing a number of outsiders that free intellectual investigation was encouraged in Yenan. This propaganda image came to be known as the New Democracy, although the principal message of his pamphlet, "On New Democracy," was a perfectly clear statement that the Kuomintang, the cities, and the bourgeoisie were to play no role whatever in building the new China. Perhaps the most ironical feature of this period was that in 1942 Mao initiated the Rectification Movement, a thorough purge of Communist cadres to eliminate nonradicals and non-Maoists.

At no time prior to 1945 was the Communist army able to cope with the forces of the Kuomintang, and hence Mao had to use the Japanese army to protect his own. Since he was also no match for the Japanese, their defeat of the Kuomintang would have eliminated his chance for ultimate victory. His object was to keep them fighting one another while leaving him in relative freedom to build his power. At the same time he had to appear, for the benefit of the urban areas, as if he were actively participating in the patriotic war, even though there was little he could do against the Japanese. The only real aid he could provide the anti-Japanese war effort was to combine his forces with those of the Kuomintang, a step he refused to take because this combination would lead to his absorption and then destruction by Chiang's movement, which was stronger militarily and recognized by the outside world, including the Soviet Union, as the official government of China.

The Communists therefore remained behind the Japanese lines where the Kuomintang could not get at them and where they could build their movement from those people seeking protection against the Japanese. They avoided military contact with the Japanese until 1940, although they managed to publicize their attack on a Japanese platoon during the Kuomintang's successful action at P'ingshin Pass in 1937 as a major action resulting in thousands of Japanese casualties.[30] In 1940, the Communists initiated the Hundred Regiments Offensive against the Japanese in an attempt, for which Mao himself apparently had little enthusiasm,[31] to divert the Japanese army's attention from the Kuomintang and to raise the Kuomintang's morale. The offensive was not very productive: it did little damage to the Japanese, had little effect upon the possibility of peace talks between Tokyo and Chungking, and resulted in severe losses for the Communists. Never again did the Red Army engage the Japanese in other than guerrilla actions, and these had virtually no influence on any military operation the Japanese wished to conduct.[32]

The entry of the United States into the war against Japan assured that the Kuomintang would continue fighting the Japanese and that the Communists could continue their buildup of power behind the Japanese lines. The most serious danger for Mao was that the United States would reinforce the Kuomintang to the point where it could engage both the Japanese and the Communists, but this danger disappeared when the Americans decided to concentrate on the Pacific islands rather than on the Asian mainland. The stalemate between the Kuomintang and the Japanese continued until 1945, time enough for Mao to acquire the military strength he considered necessary to challenge Chiang for all of China.

In the spring of 1945, Mao claimed to have an army of 910,000 men, a militia of 2.22 million, and a "self-defense corps" of 10 million.[33] He was close to his goal of a one-million-man army, having succeeded in putting under arms about 0.9 percent of the approximately 95.5 million people under his political control.[34] At the beginning of the Civil War, the

Kuomintang armies had about 3 million men, and the number of combatants remained constant throughout the war at about 4 million, with the Communists gradually increasing their share. There were limitations to the military establishment the Chinese economy could support, but, in proportion to "one quarter of mankind," the Civil War resembled warlord armies skirmishing for booty. In this case, however, the booty happened to be China itself.

The military side of the Civil War from 1945 until 1949 is difficult to describe and explain because both the United States and the Soviet Union were involved and because accounts of the period seem to lack scholarly objectivity. The critical battles were for Manchuria and the northern Chinese plain, and there is no doubt that the physical access of Mao's armies to this area was better than that of Chiang's and that the Soviets were better placed than were the Americans to give military and material aid to their favorites. The United States, moreover, was clearly more reluctant than the Soviet Union to risk a major war in China.[35] Since the involvement of both in the struggle for power in China was part of the whole episode of Japanese military expansion, it was also a part of Mao's environment that he could not control. He could only take advantage of opportunities created by extraneous forces.

Mao's military and civilian cadres brought to the Civil War the old guerrilla fighter's determination not to be denied the destruction of the existing order. Chiang Kai-shek had nothing to match this, and his officers and troops tended to behave in the traditional fashion of fighting when they were winning and quitting or defecting when they were losing. During the war, 105 of 869 Kuomintang generals defected to the Communists, an instance of a more general bandwagon effect.[36]

More important, as soon as the Communists gained military control of a new area, they "mobilized the masses" precisely as they had done since the days of the Kiangsi Soviet. In this way, they were able to dominate the local population, to ignore resistance to military service, and to create an opposition to the return of the "landlords" with the Kuomintang armies. During the period from 1946 until 1948, the Communist armies recruited 1.6 million Manchurian and north Chinese peasants.[37]

The Japanese invasion was disastrous to Chiang Kai-shek's attempt to destroy the Communists and to unite China. Throughout the period of the Japanese presence, his military force was superior to that of the Communists, but he was prevented from bringing it to bear upon them. He could not get to Mao's forces, carefully placed behind the Japanese lines, and he could not afford to alienate those urban patriots who saw the Japanese as the principal enemy. His ideal strategy was to attack the Japanese, thereby proving his patriotism and exposing the Communists, but he lacked the military power to follow it. He thus was obliged to adopt a Maoist strategy of husbanding his strength for the civil war that would follow the American defeat of Japan.[38] Unlike Mao, however, he was under constant pressure from the United States and his own constituency to expend his forces in action against the Japanese.

The intellectuals, students, and enlightened businessmen of China's eastern cities were a principal source of Chiang's difficulties, especially after 1945. They had been infected by the imperialist ideas of individual freedom while retaining the traditional presumption of a right to pronounce on the mandate of heaven. They were, consequently, extremely critical of the Kuomintang's effort to secure itself against Communist penetration. Although they did not support the full claims of Communists, they opposed Chiang and favored the incorporation of the Communists in a "coalition" government, an attitude that Communist propaganda naturally took full advantage of.[39] The cities gave Chiang additional trouble, for their relatively complex economies were severely dislocated, especially by inflation, during the period of the Civil War.[40]

The American entry into the Japanese war gave Chiang badly needed military assistance, but it forced him to cooperate with the Western powers and hence to compromise his claim to represent the rebirth of an independent, imperialist-free China, whose destiny was once again to lead the world in culture and civilization. His difficulty was symbolized by the uproar in late 1946 over the alleged rape of a Peking University girl by an American marine. On the other side, Mao's physical isolation assisted him once again by allowing the Communists to appear free of foreign associations.

The principal irony of Chiang's position relative to the urban areas was that he had little sympathy for the bourgeois-liberal values they expressed, albeit in a semitraditional or flabby way. He was determined to revive the glorious tradition of Chinese culture, adding only a few devices of modern technology as a concession to the world political system.[41] His commitment to Chinese tradition, and his political dependence on the large landholders of the interior, meant that he could have no policy of "mobilizing the masses." Although these "masses" were far from rising in elemental fury to strike down the traditional social order, the average peasant was completely indifferent to its restoration. If the Japanese had not intervened, Chiang no doubt could have defeated the Communist armies, ignored the peasants, suppressed the intellectuals, and pursued for at least a generation his ambiguous program of reconstruction.

The vast and amorphous Chinese environment and the paucity of accurate information make it unusually difficult to explain the triumph of Mao and his Communist movement. His eventual success clearly depended, as he always has said that it did, upon his ability to maintain a tightly knit organization of activists leading a disciplined army that could sustain itself among the Chinese peasantry. This accomplishment can be accounted for as follows. The activists of the movement were motivated by a rejection of both traditionalism and imperialism and by a vague vision of an egalitarian society. The army recruited men who could not resist what amounted to impressment or who saw enlistment as the only way to protect their families and property. The military force so constituted was able to survive physically because China's political disunity and later dismemberment prevented the creation of a force superior to it. The peasants initially accepted Communist power because peasants always accept power, and they continued to support it because it was the only force that could provide them with physical security. The Communist armies won the Civil War because their initiative, superior leadership, and favorable location gave them a momentum that could not be overcome. Beneath all this lay the military shrewdness, personal ruthlessness, organizational skill, and political acumen of Mao Tse-tung, who, moreover, gave the movement an air of dynamism and assuredness that strongly attracted not only the peasants but also those more sophisticated Chinese who desired only a credible object for their political loyalty.

This straightforward explanation of Mao's victory in 1949 is persuasive in view of the evidence, but it nonetheless appears rather superficial. In the first place, it implies that the reasons for his victory had very little to do with the reasons why he desired it; and, in the second place, it ignores his own belief that the peasants supported him because they wanted him to revolutionize Chinese society and move toward true communism. A more fundamental explanation seems desirable, and a tolerably acceptable one is available to those willing to entertain hypotheses regarding fundamental social forces for which there is little direct evidence. The primary hypothesis of this explanation is that the impact of Western imperialism separated China's cities from its countryside.

The Chinese cities were unable to resist the intrusion of bourgeois ideas and techniques and, as a consequence, their traditional ideology and organization collapsed. Since, however, the penetration of imperialism was only superficial—China was a "semicolonial" country—the cities did not take on a bourgeois orientation. This development left the vast countryside without its customary source of political and ideological guidance and, therefore, without a principle of social integration. The clash of basic cultures resulted, in short, in a social formlessness for

China as a whole, a system-free period when the great rhythm of life of the unnumbered peasants alone ruled the hour. In willfully destroying the traditional social structure of rural China, Mao was only helping history spell out the logic of the situation. Once society had disappeared, the enormous energy of the peasantry became available to whoever understood how to harness it. Mao's hatred of and contempt for those Chinese revolutionaries, from the Bolshevized Communists of the 1920s to the "bureaucrats" and "revisionists" of the 1960s and 1970s, who have sought power and inspiration from the cities, has had a strong theoretical foundation.

The unleashed energy of the "masses," however, was not a neutral force applicable to any social goal; it could be used only for purposes that corresponded to the basic aspirations of China's hundreds of millions of villagers. Throughout the centuries, whenever the Chinese peasantry had come into temporary possession of political power, it had sought to establish a social equality of varying degrees of comprehensiveness and sophistication. Although from 1911 until 1949, as in all previous periods, the peasant consciously and outwardly supported any power that promised peace and stability, in his heart of hearts he longed for the perfect social equality that is incompatible with the imperialist division of labor as well as with the Confucian hierarchy of status. The peasant's longing for such a utopia, moreover, was reinforced by the only political theory he even dimly understood, namely, the Chinese imperial tradition of the omnipotent, benevolent autocrat who takes perfect care of and maintains perfect harmony among his equally beloved and thus equally privileged children.

Although circumstances often forced Mao to engage in tailism and to send soothing messages to the cities, he always was careful to maintain his ideological and organizational independence and hence to keep himself free of commitment to a structured, and therefore inegalitarian, society of the future. Chiang Kai-shek, on the other hand, was doubly compromised: he consciously chose to retain a large measure of tradition, and his dependence on military and other aid from the United States prevented him from making a clean break with imperialism. Even though Japan's military invasion may have been in one sense a fortuitous event that gave Mao his only opportunity to capture China, the disintegration of Chinese society as outlined above created a vacuum that naturally and predictably invited the penetration of a neighboring state. The presence of the Japanese, and the resulting presence of the Americans, it might be added, could have reminded the Chinese of their Chineseness. Mao's projected revolution, after all, had a specific geographical and demographic scope, and its success may have depended in part upon the Chinese people's sense of their own identity, that is, upon their "racial instinct."

The political genius of Mao Tse-tung took advantage of China's almost complete lack of social structure and political orientation to move the Chinese people in a direction that, according to all the evidence, few of them consciously desired to go. His own theory of this operation, that his revolutionary goals represented the authentic ideals of the ordinary Chinese, may be unverifiable in principle. Dismissing it, however, eliminates any connection between the way he came to power and what he has done with his power. It may well be that the utopian egalitarianism of Maoism was the political theory most congenial to the amorphous body of the poor and blank Chinese masses.

Notes

1. George Moseley, *China Since 1911* (New York: Harper & Row, 1968), p. 24.
2. Jerome Ch'en, in Jack Grey, ed., *Modern China's Search for a Political Form* (London: Oxford University Press, 1969), p. 16.
3. Moseley, p. 29.
4. See Harold R. Isaacs, *The Tragedy of the Chinese Revolution,* 2d ed. (Stanford, Calif.: Stanford University Press, 1961), p. 10.
5. Lucian W. Pye, *Warlord Politics* (New York: Praeger, 1971), pp. 167–70.
6. By 1928 there were 82 armies in China, only 9 of which were under the direct control of Chiang Kai-shek. Ch'en, p. 26.
7. Jacques Guillermaz, *A History of the Chinese Communist Party, 1921–1949* (New York: Random House, 1972), p. 139.
8. Guillermaz, p. 140.
9. "Why is it that Red Political Power can exist in China?" (1928), and "The Struggle in the Chingkang Mountains" (1928), in *Selected Works of Mao Tse-tung* (Peking: Foreign Languages Press, 1965), 1:66, 99.
10. James Pinckney Harrison, *The Long March to Power* (New York: Praeger, 1972), p. 200.
11. Ilpyong J. Kim, *The Politics of Chinese Communism: Kiangsi under the Soviets* (Berkeley: University of California Press, 1973), pp. 126–35.
12. Guillermaz, p. 210.
13. Harrison, p. 207.
14. Harrison, pp. 215–17.
15. Richard C. Thornton, *China: The Struggle for Power, 1917–1972* (Bloomington: Indiana University Press, 1973), pp. 66, 67.
16. Thornton, p. 84.
17. Thornton, pp. 49, 53, 79, 88.
18. Tetsuya Kataoka, *Resistance and Revolution in China* (Berkeley: University of California Press, 1974), pp. 124, 129–30, 132.
19. Harrison, p. 318, Kataoka, pp. 134–35.
20. Kataoka, pp. 295, 310; Roy Hofheinz, Jr., "The Ecology of Chinese Communist Success: Rural Influence Patterns, 1923–45," in A. Doak Barnett,

ed., *Chinese Communist Politics in Action* (Seattle: University of Washington Press, 1969), pp. 48, 49, 76.

21. Kataoka, pp. 14, 286; Harrison, p. 319; Chalmers Johnson, *Peasant Nationalism and Communist Power* (Stanford, Calif.: Stanford University Press, 1962), pp. 59, 66–67.

22. Kataoka, p. 283.

23. Kataoka, p. 281.

24. Kataoka, pp. 106, 301, 311.

25. Kataoka, pp. 113, 116, 282, 292.

26. Kataoka, pp. 112–13, 200, 264, 268, 279.

27. Samuel B. Griffith, *The Chinese People's Liberation Army* (New York: McGraw-Hill, 1967), p. 31; Kataoka, pp. 300–301; Guillermaz, p. 188.

28. Michel Oksenberg, "Local Leaders in Rural China," in Barnett, pp. 160–61; Kataoka, p. 230.

29. Thornton, pp. 118, 121.

30. Kataoka, p. 63.

31. Kataoka, p. 216. In his self-criticism in 1959, P'eng Teh-huai said that the One Hundred Regiments Offensive was a mistake because it was a case of "nationalistic indignation blurring the class stand"—*The Case of Peng Teh-huai, 1959–1968* (Hong Kong: Union Research Institute, 1968), p. 34.

32. Griffith, *Peking and People's War* (New York: Frederick A. Praeger, 1966), p. 23.

33. Harrison, p. 372.

34. Compare these figures for 1959: 2.02 percent for Iraq, 11.11 percent for Taiwan, 2.52 percent for Greece, and 1.51 percent for Finland. Bruce Russett, "Measures of Military Effort," *American Behavioral Scientist* 7 (February 1964): 26–29.

35. Thornton, chs. 7, 8.

36. Harrison, p. 424; Johnson, p. 10.

37. Harrison, p. 406; John Gittings, *The Role of the Chinese Army* (London: Oxford University Press, 1967), pp. 62–63.

38. Kataoka, pp. 54, 148, 227.

39. Harrison, pp. 404–6.

40. See Michael Lindsay, F. F. Liu, and John Leighton Stuart, in Pichon P. Y. Loh, ed., *The Kuomintang Debacle of 1949: Collapse or Conquest?* (Boston: D. C. Heath, 1965), pp. 7–13, 15–16, 19.

41. See Philip Jaffe's introduction to Chiang Kai-shek, *China's Destiny and Chinese Economic Theory* (New York: Roy Publishers, 1947).

12
A Revolution in Culture

When Mao established the People's Republic in 1949, he announced that the Communist conquest of China was only the first step in a long march of 10,000 miles. For almost a generation now, he has spared no effort to keep hundreds of millions of Chinese stepping briskly along the road toward a new society and a new human nature. In effecting this trek, he has utilized a remarkably close blending of policy, methods, and power. Both Hitler and Stalin intended that their functionaries and their people gain revolutionary understanding from following the proper methods of implementing revolutionary policy, but Mao's concept of the "mass line," that all such policies are both conceived and carried out by the "masses" themselves, has taken this technique of revolutionary education well beyond its development under his two predecessors. In Communist China, methods and policy often have been virtually indistinguishable.

In order to create a society of perfect equality among perfectly selfless people, Mao has relied principally upon a device that might be called "voluntary thought reform." Although he has realized that social, economic, and political systems shape human attitudes and therefore has introduced important structural innovations, he has been more concerned with getting directly at the mind of the individual by means of mass-mobilization campaigns and small-group interactions. As a result of this approach, Mao's China has been the most structureless of the great revolutionary regimes and its people have surpassed all others in participating in the attempt at their own transformation.

Mao has never hesitated to destroy his enemies—rival Communists, Kuomintang activists, and "landlords"—and now and then he has expressed great satisfaction with his record.[1] Although his social policy occasionally requires that people be killed,[2] his concept of the Chinese masses and his emphasis upon psychological remolding have tempered the normal revolutionary urge to liquidate those classified as counter-revolutionaries. Nonetheless, the cost in human lives of the march to communism has been large enough in absolute terms.

The absence of hard information and the reluctance of outside observers to judge according to the logic of revolution in the absence of such information mean that only the roughest estimates can be made of the number of people who have died in the name of the true mass society. Even the most modest estimates, however, indicate beyond doubt that Mao, like his predecessors in the business of total revolution, has taken his historical mission quite seriously.

From 1927 until 1949, there were about 2,500,000 deaths. This figure includes 150,000 (a very low estimate) from 1927 until 1934; 100,000 during the Long March, 50,000 during the Japanese war, and 1,250,000 from 1945 to 1949 (all three standard estimates); and 1,000,000 "landlords" and "rich peasants" liquidated in the areas that came under Communist control from 1945 until 1949 (a very high estimate).[3]

From 1949 until the Great Leap Forward in 1958, a number of sustained programs were followed in order to remove the influence, but not necessarily the persons, of various "counterrevolutionary elements." The land-reform program of 1949 to 1952 undoubtedly cost the lives of several million "landlords" and similar types; the 1951–52 campaign against counterrevolutionaries cost another million and a half; the bandit-suppression campaigns, ostensibly to eliminate remaining pockets of overt physical resistance, disposed of many people from 1949 until 1956; the "three anti" and "five anti" campaigns of 1951–53 and the antirightist campaign of 1958–59 resulted in killings and other deaths; and, finally, the collectivization of agriculture from 1953 until 1957 was accompanied by a significant number of casualties. Accurate information is not available—and often even informed guesses are lacking—on the cost of the first decade of the People's Republic. An estimate of twelve million lives is modest but reasonable.

The Great Leap Forward from 1958 to 1960 forced the peasants to give up much of the property they had retained after collectivization and, through its disruption of the economy, caused severe shortages of food and other essentials. The regime said that the lives of more than 500 million peasants were affected by the Great Leap, and Mao himself in

1958 said that there were probably 30 million people in the exploiting class;[4] it is hence not unreasonable to suppose that one million people, or 0.2 percent of this total, were eliminated for resisting communization. The guess that the shortages of food caused by the Great Leap resulted in the starvation of an additional one million brings the total to two million, a relatively high estimate.

Since the Great Proletarian Cultural Revolution of 1966 to 1969 was a very disorganized and decentralized operation, it cost fewer lives than its scope might suggest. In 1967 Mao said that there were at most 35 million "bad elements" among the masses,[5] and we can here assume that 20 million were subject to some kind of struggle. The early unrestrained skirmishing among students, workers, and other groups undoubtedly caused many casualties. The aftermath of the Cultural Revolution, including the forced relocation of 25 million youth to the countryside and the outright execution of those impeding the restoration of order, also must have involved many deaths. The structureless nature of the Revolution and its extemporized conclusion make estimates even more like guesswork, but it would be surprising if fewer than a million people died during this period, a figure somewhat higher than those usually given.

Labor-reform camps are a standard institution in Communist China, but as yet much less is known about them than about their Stalinist counterparts. Estimates of the normal annual population of these camps range from 10 million to over 30 million; 20 million, that is, about 3 percent of a population of 600 million, is a reasonable figure. The death rate in the more severe of these camps is high, but again no one knows how high. Since the firsthand accounts of life in the camps appear at the present time to be less hair-raising than those that came from the Soviet Union, an annual death rate of 3 percent (compared to the 10 percent for the Soviet camps) appears acceptable. This implies that in twenty-five years about 15 million people have perished as a direct result of forced labor, another modest estimate.

If another million deaths from miscellaneous causes, such as the suppression of the Tibetans and Uighurs and the killing of people trying to flee China, are added to the preceding figures, the human cost of Communism in China becomes about 33.5 million. For a total revolution, this number is relatively small; in terms of percentage of the total population, it is less than one-third the human cost of Bolshevism in the Soviet Union. It must be remembered, however, that with one-quarter of mankind at one's disposal, one might become careless of human life and thoughtlessly rather than deliberately double the figure presented above.

Although Mao has considered "education" the principal technique of revolution, he has always realized that at least some rudimentary changes in social systems are prerequisite to the changing of people's beliefs and attitudes. In the first eight years of the People's Republic, he severely reduced individualism in the economy by means of the programs of land reform, agricultural collectivization, and the socialization of business. When he went beyond these relatively routine measures and attempted a thorough restructuring of Chinese society in the Great Leap Forward, he failed to achieve his primary aim. Since the conclusion of the Great Leap, he has refrained from trying to remake society according to any preconceived pattern. Even when the highest priority in a specific campaign has been given to structural innovation, he has made sure that the business of directly influencing the "thoughts" of as many people as possible has not been neglected.

The land-reform program for all of China was instituted shortly after the Communist victory in the Civil War, and its completion was proclaimed in 1952. This program was a continuation of the type of "mobilization of the masses" Mao had pursued since the time of the Kiangsi Soviet. It was a regime-controlled version of "all land to the tillers," a manipulated and directed "tornado" of a peasant uprising. It succeeded in eliminating all remaining traditional forms of political and economic power in China's countryside by expropriating and then liquidating "landlords," "rich peasants," and other local notables. Its principal method was also that of prepower days, namely, to take advantage of any and all sources of rivalry in the villages, including those among sublineages of clans. The whole operation was carried out by the old reliable former guerrilla fighters, with their hatred of and contempt for privilege, backed when necessary by military force.[6] The masses' education in the criminality of individualism was intensified by subjecting many of the millions of counterrevolutionaries to "people's trials."

Concurrently with land reform, the "three anti" and "five anti" movements against private businessmen were conducted and completed, with the result that private economic power virtually disappeared from the urban areas. Although these movements were confused and not well organized, they met little resistance: businessmen were too weak even to protest; when their demoralization did not lead to suicide, their most typical attitude was resignation. Throughout the attack on private business, the regime was careful to stress that even capitalists—Chinese capitalists, that is—at the bottom of their hearts welcomed the new collectivist society.[7]

As a side effect of land reform and the socialization of business, and continuing a trend begun during the Civil War, mainland China acquired a centralization of political control unprecedented in the twentieth century. Mao had no interest in such centralization, although it proved useful for the subsequent collectivization of agriculture and the Great Leap Forward, for centralization is, in the long run, incompatible with the mass society. During the Cultural Revolution, he moved vigorously against this bourgeois, bureaucratic phenomenon.

Because the Chinese Communist regime had controlled its domestic version of the Russian Black Repartition, it was in a relatively strong position to follow land reform by agricultural collectivization. Nonetheless, land reform had created new vested interests, among formerly poor peasants who now had their own land and among cadres who saw a division of the spoils as the highest goal of revolution. Apart from the new vested interests, the peasantry, in both the old and the newly "liberated" areas, clearly disliked collectivization, but it could not resist the regime's ubiquitous and constant pressure. By 1957 collectivization had established an agriculture at least as socialized as that resulting from Stalin's All-out Drive and at a lesser (although still significant) cost.[8] Collectivization for Stalin was the first step toward the goal of factorylike production in agriculture, but for Mao it was a preliminary to the self-contained commune that was much more than an economic unit. Stalin had no sympathy whatever for rural life, but Mao saw in the simple virtues of the unspoiled yokel the raw material for a new society. As a consequence, he had to collectivize less ruthlessly and to be more solicitous of the well-being of the resulting collectives, and more than once he has criticized Stalin's hamhandedness and failure to follow the mass line in the agrarian sector.

The Great Leap Forward of 1958 to 1960 was Mao's most ambitious attempt to change the structure of China's society in order to create a set of objective conditions conducive to his ultimate goal of a genuine community. His ideal was to put the entire rural population into communes of about 25,000 to 30,000 persons, each to be highly self-sufficient and to contain only a minimum of specialization of function and other sources of social differentials. This great plan, however, failed to establish a new form for society, since the commune proved incompatible under the circumstances with the production of economic goods essential for normal life. Although the short-lived policies of the Great Leap provided valuable experience and education for everyone, Mao's next effort at fundamental revolutionary change—the Great Proletarian Cultural Revolution—carefully avoided anticipating any new social forms.

In September 1957, a directive from the Central Committee of the Communist Party authorized the continuing consolidation of agricultural cooperatives, and by the spring of 1958 Mao had decided to amalgamate the cooperatives into what were to become the communes. In July, communes began to appear, and in August the enlarged Politburo formally announced the policy of communization. The regime claimed that, by September 1958, 90.4 percent of the peasant households in China had been organized into 23,384 communes, with an average of 4,797 households (24,000 to 29,000 people) per commune. Each commune was intended to be a self-contained administrative, political, economic, cultural, and military unit; every member was to sleep in dormitories and eat in mess halls (when, that is, not eating and sleeping at the work site); virtually all private possessions, including cooking and eating utensils, were to be turned over to the commune; children were to be cared for in nurseries and old people in "happiness homes"; payment for work was to be on an individual rather than a household basis, so that housewives, children, and the aged could no longer be supported by relatives; when not at work everyone was to engage in military drill "when the cock crows and the sun sets"; and in their spare time the peasants were to produce iron and steel in their famous backyard furnaces.[9] The move to create this kind of life was, according to the regime, "precisely an expression of the consciousness of the Chinese peasants"; "the masses of the Chinese peasantry," it said, "rejoice over the people's communes from the bottom of their hearts. . . ."[10] The peasants, for their part, bitterly opposed communization, and many cadres were physically abused.[11]

During the latter half of 1958, a brief effort was made to establish urban communes, usually based on factories, mines, schools, and offices, but sometimes on residential areas. The urban movement never really gained momentum, and the regime's maximum claim (as late as June 1960) was that 52 million city dwellers were organized in 1,027 communes.

The communes and other devices of the Great Leap Forward did not have a chance to prove their ability to create true proletarian consciousness because the dislocations in the processes of economizing they caused, or at least contributed to, forced a reluctant regime to abandon them in practice, although it kept insisting on their ideological flawlessness. During the Great Leap, almost everything that could have gone wrong from an economic point of view in fact did go wrong. The regime began the campaign by assuming in its revolutionary fervor the accuracy of reports that the 1958 harvest had been incredibly high, and hence it cut the sown acreage for 1959.[12] The commune system rested on the premise that the peasants would work hard without concrete incentives and after being relieved of their personal possessions. The agricultural work force was badly allocated and seriously depleted by the disregard for technical expertise, the absence of planning, and the use of labor on enterprises such as earthworks and miniature smelters. In both 1960 and

1961, the harvests were very poor and the shortage of food led to widespread and severe malnutrition,[13] the stagnation of light industry, and a precipitous fall in exports. Contributing to this fiasco were the continually decreasing number of draft animals, the overworking of those that remained, and the absence of long-promised farm machinery.

The enterprises into which labor was directed from agriculture fared no better. The great mass-labor projects, in addition to expending valuable manpower, were often counterproductive. Construction of canals and irrigation works frequently led to deterioration of the soil, floods, and droughts, and often enough the dams and dikes failed to hold. "Reclaimed" land was not always seeded and not always worth seeding. The small manufacturing enterprises set up to achieve local self-sufficiency took scarce raw materials from larger, more efficient plants, and their products were often so defective they had to be scrapped. These local industries also used so much fuel that timber was seriously depleted. Labor suffered severely from overwork; the efficiency of the tired people dropped sharply and the rate of accidents rose sharply.[14] The People's Republic during the period from 1960 until 1962 experienced an economic depression on the scale of the capitalist depression of the early 1930s.

Mao's essay in restructuring society during the Great Leap foundered on the economic realities he had hoped revolutionary enthusiasm would make irrelevant. Although he once had said, in an incidental way, that the Great Leap Forward was to include a "technological revolution so that we may overtake Britain in fifteen or more years,"[15] his principal purpose was not industrialization, modernization, increases in productivity, or raised living standards, but a brand-new set of social relationships. Economism and revisionism—the concern with economic incentives and price mechanisms, the belief that forces of production are more important than relations of production, and the desire for higher consumption and better working conditions—are crimes in the eyes of the Maoist leadership. For decades, Mao has had to suffer the carping of the post-Stalin Soviet leaders on the inadvisability of agricultural collectives and communes and, much worse, the deviations of his own lieutenants on such matters as economic productivity and military efficiency.

The retreat from the Great Leap involved the division and even disintegration of many of the communes, often to a level below that of the pre-Leap collective farms. The free market in agriculture was expanded, the production of consumer goods was increased, and some new capital was invested in agriculture. The normal principles of the Chinese Communist economy—to be disrupted again but not as severely during the Cultural Revolution—reasserted themselves, and their resemblance to those of the Stalinist economy is striking.

To repeat a familiar list, the economy of the People's Republic has been characterized by the fulfilling of quantitative quotas at the expense of quality and of the proper allocation of resources; the weakening of labor by overwork and lack of incentives; the expectation of results without corresponding investment; the hoarding of material, energy, and information; the absence of consumer goods and parts for capital goods; the presence of a ubiquitous black market; the use of mass labor, unsupported by capital, to perform tasks of dubious value at the expense of more economically rational projects; the forced and completely unstructured emigration of great numbers of people to barren lands where they can barely support themselves; the very low standard of living of the general population, accompanied by a rudimentary social welfare program for industrial workers; and, finally, a number of modest accomplishments in highly technical fields principally related to military power. As Mao has said, the economy is regulated not by the law of value but by putting politics in command.[16]

The radical policies of the Great Leap were formally abandoned by the Ninth Plenum of the Eighth Party Congress in January 1961, but the regime insisted that this retreat did not imply any deficiencies in ideology. The responsibility for failure was placed solely and squarely on the lower-level cadres; Lin Piao proclaimed that the solution to the post–Great Leap difficulties was to improve political and ideological work; and by January 1962, official editorials were calling for revivals of "revolutionary enthusiasm" and the "subjective initiative and creativity" of the masses.[17] Although another major revolution in the economy has not been attempted, sporadic efforts have been made to revive the principles of the Great Leap Forward. Despite his indifference to economics, Mao recognizes that free markets and rational planning are "economist" measures that unavoidably encourage the essentially urban pursuits of industry and commerce.

The typical Maoist method of revolutionary change is to try to get directly at people's beliefs and attitudes rather than to seek to influence them indirectly by experimenting with new social systems, and the great mass campaigns of the People's Republic have been a major expression of this method. These campaigns have been "struggles" against counterrevolutionary beliefs and values, struggles in which everyone is to be set against himself and against everyone else, from the lowest to the highest—excepting, as always, Mao himself, for to accuse the Chairman of counterrevolutionary thoughts is to contradict the very principle upon which thought reform is based. The true spirit of the masses, undiluted selflessness and egalitarianism, is to be instilled in everyone's consciousness by criticism and self-criticism and generally by the participation of hundreds of millions of people in the effort to stamp out selected bourgeois or traditional attitudes or to emulate someone who has learned to see himself exclusively as part of the collectivity.

In addition to land reform, the socialization of business, collectivization, and the Great Leap—movements concerned with structures as well as with education—there have been constant campaigns designed almost exclusively to change the attitudes of the population and to "rectify" the cadres. Among these were the thought reform of writers in 1951; various counterrevolutionary movements during 1954 and 1955; another socialist reform of private business, 1955–56; the antirightist movement and the rural socialist education movement, in 1957; and the People's Liberation Army rectification movement, 1957–60. During the depression years of 1960 to 1962, no campaigns were initiated. In 1962 the intellectuals were once again attacked, and the very comprehensive Socialist Education Movement combatted capitalist tendencies in the countryside and "cleansed" the rural cadres. In 1963 came the four-cleanups campaign and in 1964 the Learn from the PLA Movement, when everyone was exhorted to model himself on the selfless soldiers and when political departments staffed by army political officers were attached to civilian industrial and commercial organizations throughout the country. In 1965 all ranks in the army were abolished, and in November of that year Mao renewed his attack upon the intellectuals. By May 1966, the Great Proletarian Cultural Revolution, the greatest of all thought-reform campaigns, but one quite different from its predecessors, had begun in earnest.

Prior to the Cultural Revolution, the campaigns were conducted according to a standard format.[18] The decision to initiate a campaign was made by the principal leaders in Peking, who then set up an *ad hoc* organization to conduct it. So-called work teams were trained to carry out the campaign and especially to struggle against whatever unhealthy tendency among the regular cadres had been associated with the campaign. The media of mass communication then took up the themes of the campaign. When these preparations were completed, the work teams were divided into small groups and assigned to geographical areas where they first attacked their target groups and then organized meetings to involve as many ordinary people as possible in these attacks. At the conclusion of the campaign, the entire apparatus was dissolved. In addition to educating the masses, the campaigns trained or disclosed new activists and increased the supply of potential cadres.

This type of campaign was always difficult for the regular lower-level cadres, because the grass-roots approach of the work teams prevented the cadres from seeking protection from their superiors and because what was to be reformed was either their own attitudes or those of the people for whom they were responsible. Over the years they had learned how to adjust to these periodic challenges, but each year perhaps 5 percent of them got into real trouble.

In 1966 Mao decided that the time had come for a "revolution in culture" to complete the work of the "democratic revolution" prior to 1949 and the "socialist revolution" from 1949 to 1966.[19] The constant campaigns prior to this time had not provided a solution to the problem of destroying the culture of feudalism and imperialism because, in a quite contradictory way, they had depended upon devices central to this culture. The culture of the revolutionary masses, the "proletarian" culture, can be established (as everyone knows) only by the masses themselves. Both the cadres who usually operated the People's Republic and the work teams that periodically checked on the cadres were in essence bureaucratic, and hence their efforts to forward the revolution could succeed only in impeding it. The goal of the Cultural Revolution—to eliminate all bourgeois, economist, and revisionist ideas and practices and also the "four olds" of traditional ideas, culture, customs, and habits—necessarily included the elimination of the institutions that had conducted the Chinese democratic and socialist revolutions.

All this was something unprecedented: said Mao, "I have not experienced cultural revolution before. . . ."[20] There will be other cultural revolutions in the future, he said, but only two or three can be conducted in a century; the first one "should consolidate things for a decade at least."[21] The positive results of this initial experiment in the unprecedented were, of course, difficult to predict. The masses' destruction of feudalist and bourgeois social systems and institutions would be accompanied by their spontaneous creation of new arrangements regarding interpersonal behavior, presumably to resemble those of the Hunanese peasantry and of the Paris Commune. In sharp contrast to the Bolsheviks, Mao has not seen his revolution as divided into political and economic stages.

The actual conduct of the Cultural Revolution had to be extemporaneous and "spontaneous," but its origin and general goals required some planning. For the initial and principally destructive phase of the Revolution, Mao utilized a device brilliant in its simplicity and obviousness: he released China's youth from their schools and set them against everybody and everything that represented power, stability, and continuity. The famous Red Guards probably were first organized by some of Mao's "leftist" supporters, and probably without the knowledge of the regular Party and governmental officials. By the early summer of 1966 they were active in Peking, where they were officially constituted on August 18 at the renowned mass rally attended by Mao and his then alter ego, Lin Piao. For about one year, perhaps as many as twenty-five million of these uncommitted, but not necessarily mass-minded, youths brought the message of cultural revolution to those people whose discontents made them mobilizable, and they attacked government, academic, and Party dignitaries, harassed industrial managers and workers, invaded private homes to destroy nonproletarian artifacts, and generally terrorized the country.[22]

This negative phase of the Cultural Revolution was remarkably successful. Mao, the Red Guards, and the masses smashed most of the Republic's bureaucratic institutions and invalidated their authority and expertise. The Chinese Communist Party, the epitome of bureaucracy, was in ruins. Virtually everyone associated with bureaucracy, from county-level officials to the president of the Republic, had been discredited. By January 1967, almost all Party secretaries and propaganda officials from the center to the counties had been dismissed. By the spring of 1968, more than three-quarters of the members of the Politburo who were active before the Cultural Revolution had been dismissed and the Central Committee Secretariat had been stripped of power. Ninety percent of the directors of Central Committee departments had disappeared; more than two-thirds of the members and alternate members of the Central Committee had been seriously criticized; three-quarters of the first and second secretaries of Provincial Party Committees were no longer in evidence; and all first secretaries of the regional party bureaus were seriously criticized and probably lost their power.[23] The leading military personnel purged were three of seven vice-ministers of national defense; the director and two of five vice-directors of the army's General Political Department; the chief of the general staff and four of his eight deputies; three of eight vice-commanders of the air force; the first political commissar of the navy; the commanders of the armored force, the artillery, and the railway corps; four of thirteen military area commanders; nine of thirteen military area first political commissars; thirteen of twenty-five military district commanders; and seventeen of twenty-five military district first political commissars.[24]

Capitalism and revisionism—that is, expertise, hierarchy, and inequality—were inseparably linked with the bureaucracy, and the bureaucrats themselves, whether or not they agreed with Mao's route to communism, had to be discredited in order to discredit the positions they had held. The inability of office-holders to understand a true mass movement, to transcend bourgeois presuppositions, and to avoid revisionist backsliding was demonstrated by their reaction to the Chairman's original call for a great cultural revolution. The Politburo, presumably under the influence of Liu Shao-ch'i—subsequently labeled the "number one party person in a position of authority taking the capitalist road" and "China's Khrushchev"—decided to send out work teams from the center to shake up the local power structures. Mao quickly repudiated this direction from above.

The cultural revolution had to come from below; the masses had to learn proletarian culture by acting as proletarians. The clearest example of such self-instruction was the famous wall-poster campaign, the public display of posters containing revolutionary slogans and, more important, attacks upon people in positions of power. Mao himself joined the campaign. He invited the revolutionaries to "bombard the headquarters" in order to root out the leading comrades, "from the central down to the local levels," who were frustrating the Cultural Revolution. These posters were truly Marxist-Leninist because they came directly from the masses and they "concentrate in a single day twenty years' education of the masses."[25]

In addition to its negative task of destroying bureaucracy, the Cultural Revolution was supposed to create its replacement. In December 1966, Mao began his effort to bring about the positive phase of the Revolution by calling for the "seizure of power from below," the spontaneous creation of decision-making institutions by the masses themselves after the fashion of the Hunanese peasants of an earlier generation. A month later Ch'en Po-ta, one of the most enthusiastic supporters of the Revolution, recommended the establishment of soviets modeled on the Paris Commune of 1871.[26] It seems that certain "revolutionary rebels" did take over in the province of Shansi in January 1967, and in February of the same year a Shanghai Commune was proclaimed. These apparently were reasonably genuine seizures of power from below, but they were very short-lived. Both were soon transformed into "three-way alliances" in which former cadres and representatives of the army shared power with the revolutionary rebels.[27] The alliances were a clear indication that the masses had failed to generate a replacement for bureaucracy. The Red Guards, for example, proved themselves incapable of anything other than destruction, for they almost immediately divided into factions that fought one another at least as enthusiastically as they fought counter-revolutionaries.

Mao's principal supporters in Peking, led by the Central Cultural Revolution Group, vigorously resisted the three-way alliances as a betrayal of the Revolution, but the anarchy in China spread and intensified and frequently developed into outright warfare, with engagements using machine guns and resulting in thousands of casualties. In September

1967, Mao was obliged to condemn the radicals and support the reestablishment of order.[28] Rebellion is justified and chaos should be tolerated,[29] but only when they enable the masses to act creatively. The Red Guards were sent to the countryside, and the most radical Cultural Revolutionists were purged as counterrevolutionaries. At the close of the Cultural Revolution, in July 1968, Mao told the representatives of five leading revolutionary mass organizations: "You have let me down and disappointed the workers, peasants, and the army men of China."[30]

Mao's retreat from the Cultural Revolution's variety of mass mobilization was another at least partial defeat in his continuing struggle against the cities. The Cultural Revolution was an urban phenomenon; throughout its course the people of the rural areas experienced very little of its disruption, unless they lived in close proximity to a city.[31] Although Mao and his associates had little faith in the rural cadres, they understood that the heart and the source of bureaucracy were in the cities.

The cities also contained another primary target of the Cultural Revolution: economism, the presumptions that production must follow bourgeois rationality and that a high living standard is desirable. (As one revolutionary group announced in Shanghai: the counterrevolutionaries seek to "corrupt the revolutionary will of the masses with material interests, to bring about peaceful evolution, and to let middle class ideas run amok.")[32] The urban workers were supposed to be the force to destroy economism, but they failed to respond properly. Indeed, save for the participation of some of them to avoid getting into political trouble and of others to enjoy embarrassing their superiors, their principal response was to oppose, often violently, what they perceived as a move to undermine their jobs.[33] Seizures of power from below were impossible under these circumstances, and the three-way alliances had to be instituted.

The Cultural Revolution's attack upon bureaucracy and economism led to serious disruptions in the Chinese economy, but they were mild compared to the effects of the Great Leap Forward. The Cultural Revolution's concentration upon the cities meant that the basic processes of the agrarian economy remained intact, and hence the economy as a whole was less affected. It also proved relatively simple, once the workers had rejected their opportunity to make history, to revive industry and commerce.

The Great Proletarian Cultural Revolution fell far short of Mao's maximum aspirations, but it was by no means a complete failure. Bureaucracy in the form of the Chinese Communist Party had been dealt a mighty blow from which it probably will not recover during the Chairman's lifetime. Although the institutionalization of power soon had to be reestablished, among its principal participants was Mao's most trusted association, the People's Liberation Army, whose repressive and "law and order" orientation during the Revolution, incidentally, has been greatly exaggerated. And no one who experienced these years would ever again question the potency of mass action and proletarian culture.

Economism and bureaucracy are logically connected with science, technology, and expertise in general. According to Mao, ideology and politics are the soul of technology, and the number of (bourgeois) technicians in the People's Republic has been carefully restricted.[34] He has not sought the emergence of a new breed of "revolutionary experts" but has been determined to dispense entirely with experts and to rely upon "collective entrepreneurship" based upon collective incentives, another example of his confidence in the creativity of the masses. The successor to expertise is redness, the understanding that "politics must take command" in the sense that all the canons of bourgeois expertise, including the distinction between the generalist and the specialist, must be discarded in favor of the principle of the basic creativity of mass action. Formal education in Communist China, with its work-study programs, thus has been designed for the masses rather than for any elite.

In pure science, too, politics must be put in command.[35] Bourgeois science ("a pile of garbage") must be replaced by proletarian science, a science to be created not by the "intellectualism" and "individualism" of pure theory and laboratory research but through the cooperative and nonhierarchical action of the masses. Scientists trained according to bourgeois principles must study the thought of Mao, devote themselves to solving practical problems, and engage in the class struggle, that is, do manual labor at the work site. During the Cultural Revolution, "a grave, acute, complex class struggle" took place in the natural sciences and "proletarian science and technology rebels" purged the National Academy of Sciences. Many purged scientists were reinstated after the Cultural Revolution, but their reeducation has continued. In 1970, for example, the Revolutionary Great Criticism Writing Team of the Academy of Sciences denounced the idea that science requires specialized knowledge and asserted that "science is created by the laboring people," and "aid-left" men from the PLA were assigned to various scientific institutes.[36] As under other revolutionary regimes, the attacks upon bourgeois natural science have been sporadic.

The most interesting example of the creation of science by the masses is in the field of medicine.[37] That "medicine is a scientific art, something for a small number of authorities," is a bourgeois prejudice; true medicine "comes from the masses' experience and hence can undergo a movement developing the broadest mass participation. . . ."[38] Modern doctors, poisoned by their bourgeois orientation, must be ideologically reformed so that they can understand the "medical legacy of the mother-land." Various folk remedies, such as medicinal herbs, assorted charms, and acupuncture, constitute this legacy, and the peasants' faith in them is a genuine manifestation of mass culture. The efficacy of these trusted remedies has been widely extolled, they have been clearly described as replacements for, not supplements to, bourgeois medicine, and expensive schools and clinics for their practitioners have been constructed. During the Great Leap there was a "frantic drive to collect from among the people enormous numbers of herbals and secret remedies as the popular essence of the nation's medical wisdom. . . ." The post-Cultural Revolution policy of sending "barefooted doctors" to the countryside is less a practical matter than an affirmation that bourgeois expertise is unnecessary as well as counterrevolutionary.

Elsewhere in the realm of ideas, the new historiography of the People's Republic has been concerned less with rewriting the past from the proletarian point of view—although, as Mao has said, "All things that occurred in history must be liquidated"[39]—than with using selected past events to aid in thought reform. The peasant wars, for example, have been used to teach the necessity of struggle and to help the intellectuals overcome their objectivism. The most typically Maoist development in historiography, however, has been the virtual dismissal of history writing as a matter even for proletarian experts and the subsequent dispatch of literate people to the grass roots to consult with ordinary people, to collect the stories of villages, communes, factories, and poor families, and to compile "vast collections of folklore and songs and ethnic tales . . . as repositories of the most primary data of popular history."[40] Ideally, the masses are to be their own historians.

At the Yenan Forum on Art and Literature in 1942, Mao said that the level of literature and art in China had to be raised "in the direction in which the workers, soldiers, and peasants are themselves advancing. . . ." Artists were to follow the mass line by producing works of art corresponding to the true desires and aspirations of the masses; their points of departure were to be wall newspapers, popular songs, and plays of army troups. On the substantive level, all emotions, feelings, and values are class-oriented: there is no such thing as human nature in general,[41] a theme that has been strongly emphasized in the anti-Confucius campaign since 1973. The task of the artist was to see and reflect "what is new, revolutionary, and vital in life."[42]

In 1966 the Forum on Literature and Art in the Armed Forces carried Maoism a step farther by announcing that no intellectual—that is, someone with more than a high school education—can be trusted to produce proletarian art and, more generally, to accept the values of the masses. Specialization, even in following the mass artistic line, is counterrevolution. Since art is of and for the masses, it is only logical that it should be by them as well. Everyone was encouraged to contribute to wall newspapers, produce big-character posters and political cartoons, engage in amateur theatricals, and redecorate traditional buildings and parks with red flags and pictures of and quotations from Chairman Mao, and a campaign to collect millions of poems from the masses was instituted. This emphasis on proper proletarian art has made a vigorous reappearance as another principal theme of a recent anti-Confucius campaign.

In the past, the experts or intellectuals, the scientists, scholars, and artists, have constituted a privileged group that has monopolized knowledge and culture. As Chen Yi, then foreign minister, said during the Cultural Revolution: it was not important that Stalin killed many people and encouraged a personality cult; these were small mistakes. His serious error was to encourage technology and to tolerate "the capitalist evils of intellectuality," for after his death the intellectuals were used by the Khrushchev regime to restore capitalism. In China, " we are attempting to eliminate the intellectual class."[43]

Mao's bias against all kinds of bourgeois expertise and his commitment to mass spontaneity have strongly influenced the concrete response of the People's Republic to the force of international imperialism. Communist China has bitterly denounced everyone—not only the United States and the Soviet Union—who has supported in any way the imperialist pattern of world power, but it has done very little to challenge this pattern.

One of Mao's highest priorities has been to establish his control over that territory he considers historically Chinese. His regime has gone to great pains, and several times has resorted to arms, to make good its claims to insignificant border areas and offshore islands, and it has vigorously repressed separatist movements. His greatest frustration here has been Taiwan, an integral part of his concept of the empire, and this situation is ironical because his military intervention in Korea, which he felt obliged to take in order to protect the northeast part of his precious domain, probably guaranteed the inaccessibility of Taiwan during his lifetime.

All true revolutionary movements that seek to establish a genuine communal mass society are impeded by their sworn enemy, imperialism, but these movements can occur only as spontaneous actions by the indigenous masses. An organized worldwide revolutionary effort against imperialism, after the fashion of the Comintern, is thus inconceivable in Maoist terms. The People's Republic can give limited material and unlimited spiritual aid to revolutionaries outside of China, but the "liberation of the masses is accomplished by the masses themselves"[44] and accomplished without the aid of technically complicated weapons and the economy that can produce and support them. Mao's indifference to so-called economic development and his hostility to expertise have done much to deprive China of the economic and military power necessary to confront imperialism, but this limiting domestic policy is part of a larger theory of revolution that allows for the exportation of only exhortation and example.

The Maoist scorn for all aspects of bourgeois society and its transplants in colonial areas has had the additional effect that the foreign policy of the People's Republic during most of its life has been unusually inflexible and incapable of compromise. The Soviet Union's acceptance of certain fundamental principles of the nonrevolutionary order, in the hope that time will be on the side of Communism, has been a leading element in its perfidious revisionism.

Imperialism is an urban phenomenon and North America and Western Europe are the "cities of the world." The triumph of the world's countryside, Africa, Latin America, and Asia (definitely excluding the Soviet Union), principally by means of guerrilla warfare, is inevitable. Imperialists and revisionists "will be swept like dust from the stage of history by the mighty broom of the revolutionary people."[45] Although Chinese Communism avoids direct references to racial differences, the division between the cities and the countryside is also the division between the white and the nonwhite people of the world.[46] Thus far, however, the racial consciousness that undoubtedly exists has had very little practical effect, for the doctrine of spontaneous revolution has prevented any international action in the name of racial differences or of racial superiority

All of the great twentieth-century revolutionaries have understood that the "education" of their people is an absolutely critical matter. The National Socialists and Bolsheviks paid careful attention to science, technology, and art, and they utilized devices not unlike the Chinese campaigns, but neither of them developed anything comparable to the Maoist technique of education in revolutionary consciousness by means of face-to-face pressure in small peer groups. In this environment, individualism can be proved highly vulnerable and an identification with the collectivity eminently secure.

The small group (hsiao-tsu) consists of from eight to fifteen people, drawn from factory units, offices, schools, urban neighborhoods, and the like, who engage in periodic sessions of criticism and self-criticism in a collective and mutually supportive effort to transform themselves. These groups are designed to cut across normal primary groups, and thus their members have no ties other than their membership. Although small groups are supposed to exist in all areas of society, in practice they are concentrated in schools, offices, and generally among cadres and future cadres. Apparently they have been rare in the countryside.[47]

The small group is an ideal vehicle for a direct and systematic attack upon the most intimate forms of individualism. Friendship, loyalty, sincerity, trustworthiness, and love all create special and therefore selfish associations that necessarily conflict with everyone's commitment to the community. Instead of counterrevolutionary friendship, there is "comradeship," a cordial, helpful, but basically impersonal relationship resembling that between bourgeois professional colleagues.[48] Instead of love, there is the common experience of serving the collective. Happiness, that most selfish of concepts, is dismissed as superstition.

Mao's theory that the masses in their hearts oppose individualism and welcome the perfect community means that everyone "voluntarily" participates in his own de-individualization. On the level of the country-wide campaign, the concept of voluntarism refers to the relationship between Mao and the masses, but in the small group it has a more concrete meaning. To practice voluntarism there is to volunteer to do things, usually but not always suggested by those in power, that are inconsistent with one's selfish interests.[49] Each person is supposed to volunteer to give up his private property and his leisure time, to have his standard of living reduced, and to take an undesirable job in an unfavorable location. If he does not volunteer, he may be publicly criticized by his associates in an effort to discover the flaws in his character that have prompted such antisocial behavior. Even if he is not criticized, he knows that his failure to volunteer will be held against him and that some day, in some unpredictable way, the regime will penalize him. By applying concentrated social pressure, the regime has attempted to get everyone to act against his "own" interests, in the name, of course, of the good of the whole community. The comprehensive use of this kind of psychological pressure appears to have created a general feeling of guilt: no one is free of attitudes and thoughts that are counterrevolutionary and thus everyone is destined to be publicly exposed and treated. Safety, however, resides in the recognition that one demonstrates his selflessness by being constantly alert to the selfishness of others.

An estimate of the impact of Maoism upon the people of China can be only most general and tentative. More than two decades after Stalin's death, we still cannot judge with any precision his success in remolding the psychology of the Soviet people, and in Mao's case direct evidence is even more scarce and Mao himself still exists to maintain the momentum of his revolution.

On the credit side of Mao's ledger, his voluntary thought reform may have created a collective consciousness among the regime's cadres and activists. Former cadres report that their lives were indeed collectivized by the "general atmosphere of restrictive security-consciousness" and the close and intense scrutiny and pressure from both superiors and colleagues.[50] Secondly, comradeship, that nonpersonal relationship of mutual concern (rather as if everyone were a social worker), may have been to some extent internalized among a people who have never experienced bourgeois individualism with its need for close personal ties to augment the personality.[51] Third, the youth and the intellectuals (in the Western sense), people with relatively few commitments to things, localities, and other human beings, may have been captured by the regime's idealistic collectivism. In Hong Kong, Dai Hsiao-ai, the former Red Guard, badly missed the movement's "sense of cooperation in seeking to attain some higher and ultimately more worthwhile goals," and a schoolteacher in Shanghai considered the excesses of the Cultural Revolution a reasonable cost for overcoming the "indifference of officials to the people they served."[52] Fourth, and with reference to structural changes, the regime's economic policy of discouraging individual acquisition and attempting to provide minimal security for everyone may have encouraged a sense of collective survival.[53] Finally, the decades of experience with the lifestyle and education of the Communists' military establishments must have contributed something to the strength of comradeship and the individual's identification with the masses.

The debit side of Mao's ledger appears to have more and larger entries. The changes in behavior that undoubtedly have occurred may not come from new basic attitudes, or at least not from the proper kinds of attitudes. Conformity to the new communal ethic may consist only in the routine playing of expected roles, and there may be widespread awareness that others, as well as oneself, are practicing only duplicity and hypocrisy.[54] The new attitudes, moreover, do not seem to be self-sustaining and thus appear to require constant stimulation from above.

The selflessness of the new kind of human being is virtually impossible to obtain in a normal environment requiring the solution of normal problems by the use of normal methods of human interaction. Work has to be done and "politics taking command" can only interfere with it. All organizations and associations, even the small study groups, give rise to differentiation of their members, if only on the grounds of political purity or selflessness themselves. Competition for the things honored by bourgeois or traditional society may be sharply reduced, but competition for proletarian honors remains.[55]

As the urbanites remain under the influence of bourgeois culture, the peasants continue to exhibit their traditional mentality. Family and clan ties remain strong, traditional status differentials are still observed, and the traditional style of compromise and superficial harmony continues to shape interpersonal relations.[56] The members of the collectives are always trying to engage in "side production," that is, to pursue small business enterprises and to tend to their private plots and animals. Even the soldiers of the PLA follow the old practice of petty crime and retain a high degree of concern with their own careers and the fortunes of their families.

On balance, it appears that the short-term interests of the "masses" and their desire for social stability and predictability have outweighed any subconscious urge they may have toward a perfectly egalitarian society. Mao's plan to recast humankind may well have succumbed to the terrible force of habit of hundreds of millions.

Notes

1. E.g., "Speech at the Expanded Meeting of the CCP Political Bureau" (1956), and "Speech at the Second Session of the Eighth Party Congress" (1958), in Miscellany of Mao Tse-tung Thought (1949–1968) (Arlington, Va.: National Technical Information Service, 1974), pp. 34, 98.
2. "Speech at Hangchow Conference" (1963), in Miscellany, p. 322; "On the Ten Great Relationships" (1956), in Jerome Ch'en, ed., Mao (Englewood Cliffs, N.J.: Prentice-Hall, 1969), p. 79; Stuart R. Schram, Mao Tse-tung (New York: Simon & Schuster, 1966), p. 119.
3. A useful summary of the estimates of deaths through 1970 is given in Richard L. Walker, The Human Cost of Communism in China (Washington, D.C.: U.S. Government Printing Office, 1971), p. 16.
4. "Speech at the Hankow Conference" (1958), in Miscellany, p. 85.
5. "Speech to the Albanian Military Delegation" (1967), in Miscellany, p. 460.
6. See Ezra F. Vogel, Canton under Communism (Cambridge, Mass.: Harvard University Press, 1969), pp. 101–6.
7. See Vogel, pp. 156–64, 168; and Robert Loh, Escape from Red China (New York: Coward-McCann, 1962).
8. Thomas P. Bernstein, "Cadre and Peasant Behavior under Conditions of Insecurity and Deprivation," in A. Doak Barnett, ed., Chinese Communist Politics in Action (Seattle: University of Washington Press, 1969), pp. 365–99, and "Keeping the Revolution Going," in John Wilson Lewis, ed., Party Leadership and Revolutionary Power in China (Cambridge: Cambridge University Press, 1970), 239–67.
9. Cheng Chu-yuan, The People's Communes (Hong Kong: Union Press, 1959), pp. 10, 94, 106.
10. See Arthur A. Cohen, The Communism of Mao Tse-tung (Chicago: University of Chicago Press, 1964), p. 185; and Communist China, 1955–1959; Policy Documents with Analysis (Cambridge, Mass.: Harvard University Press, 1962), p. 552.

11. R. J. Birrell, "The Centralized Control of the Communes in the Post-'Great Leap' Period," in Barnett, pp. 400–433; Vogel, p. 255.
12. K. C. Yeh, "Soviet and Communist Chinese Industrialization Strategies," in Donald W. Treadgold, ed., *Soviet and Chinese Communism: Similarities and Differences* (Seattle: University of Washington Press, 1967), p. 358.
13. Vogel, pp. 254–55, 273.
14. Yeh, pp. 359–60; Vogel, pp. 243, 251, 254, 272; Cheng, pp. 118–21.
15. Untitled writing (1958), in Ch'en, ed., *Mao Papers: Anthology and Bibliography* (London: Oxford University Press, 1970), p. 63.
16. "Critique of Stalin's *Economic Problems of Socialism in the U.S.S.R.*" (1959?), in *Miscellany,* p. 199.
17. Philip Bridgham, "Factionalism in the Central Committee," in Lewis, p. 224.
18. This discussion follows Alan P. L. Liu, *Communication and National Integration in Communist China* (Berkeley: University of California Press, 1971), pp. 87–97.
19. "Talk" (1966), in Ch'en, *Mao Papers,* p. 44.
20. "Dialogues with Capital Red Guards" (1968), in *Miscellany,* p. 485.
21. "Speech to the Albanian Military Delegation," p. 459.
22. Gordon A. Bennett and Ronald N. Montaperto, *Red Guard: The Political Biography of Dai Hsiao-ai* (Garden City, N.Y.: Doubleday, 1971), pp. 79–83.
23. Charles Neuhauser, "The Impact of the Cultural Revolution on the Chinese Communist Party Machine," *Asian Survey* 8 (1968):465–88; and Parris H. Chang, "Mao's Great Purge: A Political Balance Sheet," *Problems of Communism,* 18:2 (1969):1–10.
24. Jürgen Domes, "The Cultural Revolution and the Army," *Asian Survey* 8 (1968):362.
25. *Peking Review,* 11 August 1967, p. 5; *People's Daily,* 20 June 1966, in K. H. Fan, ed., *The Chinese Cultural Revolution: Selected Documents* (New York: Monthly Review Press, 1968), p. 309.
26. Domes, *The Internal Politics of China, 1949–1972* (New York: Praeger, 1973), p. 179.
27. Domes, *The Internal Politics of China,* p. 180; D. W. Fokkema, *Report from Peking* (Montreal: McGill-Queen's University Press, 1972), pp. 93–94; Neale Hunter, *Shanghai Journal* (New York: Frederick A. Praeger, 1969), ch. 12.
28. Jean Daubier, *A History of the Chinese Cultural Revolution* (New York: Random House, 1974), p. 213.
29. Mao, "Talk" (23 August 1966), in Ch'en, *Mao Papers,* p. 35.
30. Chang, p. 3.
31. Richard Baum, "The Cultural Revolution in the Countryside," in Thomas W. Robinson, ed., *The Cultural Revolution in China* (Berkeley: University of California Press, 1971), pp. 453–54.
32. Louis Barcata, *China in the Throes of the Cultural Revolution* (New York: Hart Publishing Co., 1968), p. 132.
33. Domes, *The Internal Politics of China,* pp. 176–77.
34. Mao, "Instruction" (1958), in Ch'en, *Mao Papers,* p. 82; Ying-mao Kau, "The Urban Bureaucratic Elite in Communist China: A Case Study of Wuhan, 1949–65," in Barnett, p. 264.
35. Mao, "Instruction" (1968), in Ch'en, *Mao Papers,* p. 154.
36. *China News Analysis,* no. 696 (16 February 1968), pp. 4–7, and no. 843

(4 June 1971), pp. 4–5.

37. See Mao, "Directive on Work in Traditional Chinese Medicine" (1954), in *Miscellany*, pp. 12–13. "Traditional" medicine is not the medicine of feudalism but of the masses.

38. This discussion follows and quotes from Ralph C. Croizier, *Traditional Medicine in Modern China* (Cambridge, Mass.: Harvard University Press, 1968), pp. 167–69, 175–88.

39. "Speech" (1954), in *Miscellany*, p. 16.

40. Harold Kahn and Albert Feuerwerker, "The Ideology of Scholarship: China's New Historiography," in Feuerwerker, ed., *History in Communist China* (Cambridge, Mass.: M.I.T. Press, 1968), p. 9.

41. "Talks at the Yenan Forum on Literature and Art" (1942), in *Selected Works of Mao Tse-tung* (Peking: Foreign Languages Press, 1965), 3:77–78, 80, 84, 90.

42. Lin Mo-han, *Raise Higher the Banner of Mao Tse-tung's Thought on Art and Literature* (Peking: Foreign Languages Press, 1961), p. 27.

43. Reported in W. A. C. Adie, "China's 'Second Liberation' in Perspective," in *China after the Cultural Revolution: A Selection from the Bulletin of the Atomic Scientists* (New York: Random House, 1969), p. 29.

44. Lin Piao, "Long Live the Victory of the People's War!" (1965), in Samuel B. Griffith, *Peking and People's Wars* (New York: Frederick A. Praeger, 1966), p. 85.

45. Lin Piao, pp. 95, 110.

46. See Ishwer C. Ojha, *Chinese Foreign Policy in an Age of Transition* (Boston: Beacon Press, 1969), p. 215; and Barcata, pp. 193, 194, 279.

47. Martin King Whyte, *Small Groups and Political Rituals in China* (Berkeley: University of California Press, 1974), pp. 3, 10, 15, 39, 155, 186.

48. Vogel, "From Friendship to Comradeship," in Roderick MacFarquhar, ed., *China under Mao: Politics Takes Command* (Cambridge, Mass.: M.I.T. Press, 1966), p. 420.

49. This discussion follows Vogel, "Voluntarism and Social Control," in Treadgold, pp. 168–84.

50. Barnett, *Cadres, Bureaucracy, and Political Power in Communist China* (New York: Columbia University Press, 1967), p. 435.

51. Vogel, "From Friendship to Comradeship," p. 416.

52. Bennett and Montaperto, p. 236; Hunter, p. 287.

53. Birrell, p. 414.

54. Whyte, pp. 86, 93, 232; Michel Oksenberg, "Getting Ahead and Along in Communist China," in Lewis, p. 323.

55. Whyte, p. 219.

56. Barnett, *Uncertain Passage: China's Transition to the Post-Mao Era* (Washington, D.C.: Brookings Institution, 1974), pp. 33–34; Richard H. Solomon, *Mao's Revolution and the Chinese Political Culture* (Berkeley: University of California Press, 1971), p. 515.

13

To Follow the Mass Line

According to Chairman Mao, the masses themselves determine the broad goals of the revolution, decide upon its concrete policies, and put these policies into effect. In the area of execution, however, pure spontaneity is rare indeed, and hence there must be some kind of select group to take the initiative. Mao Tse-tung Thought, expressed by the suggestions and advice of Mao Tse-tung, can provide a general direction, but somehow it must be supplemented. Since 1949, Mao has been struggling with the problem of how to obtain this unavoidable supplement without contaminating his revolution with bureaucracy.

Neither Stalin's solution of retaining formal hierarchies kept fluid by constantly purging their personnel as enemies of the people nor Hitler's technique of relying on extremely vague and shifting authorization was suitable for the Chinese revolution, for both imply and by and large admit that some people are better revolutionaries than others. Mao's radical egalitarianism, in strict logic, cannot acknowledge that any cadre has special revolutionary ability or deserves special privileges. In the drive toward the communist society, only Mao and the masses are progressive; all bourgeois experts, intellectuals, and generally people with unusual characteristics—a classification that definitely includes cadres—are counterrevolutionary. As Mao said just prior to the Cultural Revolution, in the battle to create the true society, "we are alone . . . I am alone with the masses. Waiting."[1]

In capturing the Chinese Communist Party and then using it to capture China, Mao demonstrated an unmatched command of the techniques of group struggle. He was a master of organizational invention and manipulation, the principles of divide and rule and of tactical alliance, the methods of secret police and of security forces, and the strategy and tactics of guerrilla warfare.[2] In 1942 and in 1955, he conducted standard purges of his apparatus that significantly concentrated power, first in the Communist movement and then in the People's Republic, in his own hands, but purging is a most inappropriate style for one who is chairman of the perpetual meeting of the masses.

By about 1956, Mao had eliminated all real opposition to his dominance of the People's Republic, and his style of rule became more casual and his power more muted. He came to rely, as it has been said, more upon his ideological preeminence than upon his organizational muscle. He began a withdrawal from day-to-day administrative matters, and his senior lieutenants gained an impression of their own independence, many apparently quite openly opposing his positions and formally voting against him. These lieutenants—and also many outsiders—were falling farther and farther behind the reasoning of the revolution's leader, whose superior insight gained from his having made a revolution was supplemented by the logic of his relationship to the people he wanted to change. Mao, like Stalin before him, could see what others could not; but, unlike Stalin, he did not march out to capture his opposition. His ideological terrain at this time, like his geographical and demographic terrains of earlier years, favored the guerrilla strategy, and in a real sense he drew his bureaucratic enemies in deep.

It has frequently been suggested that Mao's neglect of the burgeoning bureaucracy within China was brought sharply to his attention in 1956 by Khrushchev's speech denouncing Stalin and by the Hungarian revolt against communism. Both of these backslidings, from the Maoist point of view, resulted from Stalin's compromise with bureaucracy and expertise, and the Chinese revolution could not afford to repeat this error.

Early in 1957, Mao essayed his first and badly conceived attack on bureaucracy in general and the cadres of Communist China in particular. His speech in February, "On the Correct Handling of Contradictions among the People," stressed the "contradictions between those in positions of leadership and the led, and contradictions arising from the bureaucratic practices of certain state functionaries in their relations with the masses." In April, the regime initiated the so-called Hundred Flowers Campaign against "bureaucratism, subjectivism, and sectarianism" within its own ranks and insisted on the participation of the intellectuals, who had declined a similar invitation a year earlier. For about a month during May, the intellectuals complied, but they went somewhat beyond their charge by criticizing the prevailing methods of thought reform and by explicitly attacking Party "despotism." An anti-rightist campaign was then directed against them.

The Hundred Flowers Campaign was an attempt to involve the masses in evaluating the course of the revolution by exposing the cadres to the criticisms of the intellectuals.[3] Even if by 1957 the intellectuals had been cured of their capitalist outlook, and there was really very little reason to expect that they had, they could involve the masses only most indirectly. This feeble version of the mass line, however, was speedily terminated.

The apparatus of revolutionary power in the People's Republic prior to 1966 and the Great Proletarian Cultural Revolution was an antibureaucracy on the Stalinist model. It was extremely complex, with an extended inspection system and an enormous volume of reports; the work loads imposed on the lowest levels were often overwhelming; the division between political and technical work was highly confused; orders from the center always took precedence over usual procedures and rules; and the position of the average functionary was so precarious that he had to expend a great amount of energy just to maintain it. The net result was an overcentralized, overdeveloped, ponderous administrative system, confusing to insiders and outsiders alike and periodically on the brink of complete collapse.[4] The most significant power groups during this period were the central agencies for propaganda and education, the offices in charge of Communist Party structure and personnel, a number of regional groupings under prominent leaders, governmental ministries such as the Ministry of Public Security, and the People's Liberation Army.

The Chinese Communist Party apparatus, from the Central Committee to the local committees or "basic level" units, was a formidable force prior to 1966. The CCP, and especially its propaganda department, were responsible for carrying out all the principal campaigns from 1949 through the period of the Great Leap Forward. The People's Republic during this period came close to experiencing "rule by the Party,"[5] but in the early 1960s Mao put the Socialist Education Movement under the control of the People's Liberation Army, thereby depriving the Party of its propaganda function and the basis of its power. Even at the lowest levels, militia units replaced Party groups as the leaders of the important study sessions. When the revolution against the Party itself began during the Cultural Revolution, the Party had no physical force to counteract the army's, it could not take a public position opposed to Chairman Mao, and it did not control the media of communication.[6] It could resist its own destruction only by delaying and temporizing. At the Ninth National Congress of the CCP in April 1969, although "the idea of a

Chinese Communist Party" was preserved, "the last rites for the national organization that had brought the revolutionary movement to victory in 1949" were pronounced.[7]

The Ministry of Public Security was another important, but less well known, agency of control in the pre-1966 People's Republic. Its structure and operations were kept secret, but it seems to have had a considerable amount of reasonably independent force: it controlled the police throughout the country; it maintained close surveillance of and dossiers on a large proportion of the population; and it directed the "security forces" that had charge of prisons and labor camps and that also served as an "internal army" guarding frontiers and internal communications. In 1961 it commanded a total of perhaps 1.7 million men, and its influence on the general population was strong and extensive but not perceived as especially threatening. Local Public Security agencies probably were responsible to local Party branches regarding investigations and related functions, but the Party apparatus as a whole could not command the physical force at the disposal of the Ministry.[8]

During its first decade, the Ministry of Public Security was headed by Lo Jui-ch'ing, and Lo's ties with P'eng Chen suggest that at this time the Ministry cooperated with the Party apparatus. In 1959, Lo was replaced by Hsieh Fu-chih, who was then presumably an ally of Lin Piao and thus associated with the military. During the Cultural Revolution, Hsieh presided over the dismantling of his own agency; the Ministry, and also the courts and the Procuracy, were attacked as "conservative" and apparently almost completely undermined. Normal public-security functions seem to have been taken over by the military.

The People's Liberation Army was the final leading agency of power prior to 1966. In sharp contrast to the situations in the Third Reich and the Soviet Union, the army of Communist China always had been used by the leader as an instrument of revolutionary change. Since the PLA was not inherently bureaucratic, it survived the Cultural Revolution, a story to be told below.

These pre-1966 mechanisms (and others not covered here) enabled Mao to carry out the great campaigns and structural changes of the early years of the People's Republic. They also made it possible for him to create, by means of an enormous propaganda operation that penetrated to grass-roots study groups and "struggle meetings," his own godlike image that eventually allowed him to eliminate them. When, during these early years, he wished to carry out really radical policies, such as collectivization and communization, he went directly to the local level and let all the higher officials, including the Politburo, ratify the changes after the country was committed to them.

Following his failure to involve the masses in the business of the cadres in the Hundred Flowers episode, Mao decided to change the entire social structure of China by means of the Great Leap Forward. The Great Leap was completely dependent upon the various administrative apparatuses, despite the theory that its innovations sprang from the masses; but once again the cadres proved incapable of translating the Maoist vision into reality. The Great Leap, moreover, was followed by a severe economic depression lasting until 1962, and disaffection was widespread among both cadres and ordinary people. The issue of bureaucracy came to a head when Marshal P'eng Teh-huai, a self-styled blunt and outspoken man, criticized the Great Leap as "commandism" that ignored practicality, and when Mao found it difficult to get a majority of his senior colleagues to support his own position that the Great Leap was a (barely qualified) success.[9] The existing administrative apparatus was clearly incompatible with following the mass line, especially since this apparatus had proved impervious to standard methods of purging, even including the purge of P'eng himself, a very old comrade-in-arms and a military hero as well.

Mao's initial move was to resign, in December 1958, from the presidency of the Republic, the epitome of bureaucratic positions and one he had obtained apparently in a fit of revolutionary absent-mindedness. Upon resigning, he announced, quite logically and almost prophetically, that he was going to devote himself to "theoretical work."[10] His reasoning, once again, was not understood. The apparatus continued in its bureaucratic ways, and in 1961 and 1962 a number of intellectuals, presumably supported by high political figures, produced some satirical criticisms of the leader. This subtle attack came to nothing, for it reached only other intellectuals and Mao soon put a stop to it,[11] but the incident did reaffirm the total inadequacy of the existing methods of revolution making.

Mao's next move was to construct his so-called cult of personality, the identification of himself with the masses and especially the identification of Mao Tse-tung Thought with the *Volksgeist*. Since the true spirit of the masses is infallible, Mao Tse-tung Thought cannot be incorrect and its oracle cannot be opposed. Mao had understood rather early that a revolutionary leader must be accepted by his own movement as completely free of error,[12] but he did not realize until the late 1950s that establishing his infallibility, not only as a political principle but as an epistemological premise, was an excellent way to destroy bureaucracy. By about 1966, he had succeeded in transforming Mao Tse-tung, the top man in the People's Republic, into Chairman Mao, the personification of the Chinese people. To quote two prominent outside observers: "He has encouraged and elevated adulation of his own person to a level as mentally deadening and morally outrageous as any previous idol-worship has ever been"; and he has gone "further than anyone else in the infusion of his man-word corpus into every psychological cranny of Chinese existence."[13]

Although the cult of Mao certainly has not affected everyone in China, indoctrination in the schools led the youth to believe the Chairman when he told them in 1966 that both the social system, which they had accepted as just, and their rulers, whom they had considered to be good men doing their best, were rotten and counterrevolutionary, and to wait for his instructions on how to destroy them.[14] According to at least one intellectual during the Cultural Revolution, Mao is "an all-knowing, all-powerful god, a higher being who now dwells upon this earth and encompasses in his person the feelings, cares, ambitions, hopes, expectations, and possibilities of the proudest people in the world."[15] In any event, by the time of the Cultural Revolution, no one in China could use any ideological appeal or theoretical argument against any position that Mao had taken or presumably taken. In "The Constitution of the Communist Party of China" adopted in 1969, Mao Tse-tung Thought was enshrined as the "Marxism-Leninism of the era in which imperialism is heading for total collapse and socialism is advancing to world wide victory."

By the spring of 1966, Mao had decided to begin the third or cultural phase of his revolution, again without consulting his lieutenants, whose pro forma approval he obtained some months later. The negative aspect of this third phase was to get rid of bureaucracy and revisionism by instructing ordinary people how to detect and then how to demolish them. Mao did not plan to purge anyone after the Stalinist fashion but to eliminate completely the structure of positions that bred counterrevolution. The logic of his attack, however, led to the purge of specific officeholders as personifications of the evil he wished to stamp out, and he found many Stalinist techniques, such as postulative counterrevolutionary conspiracies, virtually irresistible.

Upon Mao's call for a cultural revolution, the apparatus, almost by reflex, responded by sending out work teams from the center to supervise the replacement of the old culture by the new and to purge some cadres in the process. For "fifty days" Mao waited for someone in the apparatus to point out its errors, but he was disappointed and finally had to do it himself. Upon Mao's criticism, Liu Shao-ch'i, the person formally responsible for the work teams, submitted a self-criticism; when it was not accepted, he presumably submitted his resignation,[16] but that too was not accepted. For the next two years, until he was formally dismissed in October 1968, Liu was "the number one party person taking the capitalist road" and "China's Khrushchev," and he was charged with every conceivable opposition to the revolution, including common criminality.

Liu Shao-ch'i always had been much more impressed than Mao with the utility of structural changes as methods of revolutionary progress, a reflection perhaps of his early urban, semi-Bolshevik orientation. He had always cooperated fully with Mao, and he was a fervent champion of the Great Leap Forward.[17] His writings were second only to Mao's, and he was assumed by all to be Mao's successor. Whether or not he ever realized the true meaning of his admission that he had failed to understand that the new stage of the revolution required the masses to liberate themselves,[18] he soon recognized that he was through as a leader of the Maoist revolution.

The opposition to the Cultural Revolution's assault against bureaucracy came not from the planned resistance of a number of highly placed leaders but from the enormous inertial force of the myriad cadres.[19] These hordes of functionaries were not opposed to Maoism or even to Liu's work teams,[20] but they were prepared, quite spontaneously, to act in concert to preserve the concept of functionary. They made their point before too long, but only because Mao's revolutionary rebels failed him.

The novelty of this attack on the apparatus and the almost instinctive resistance it met obliged Mao to clarify the issue of revisionism by personifying it. Liu Shao-ch'i, appropriately the president of the People's Republic, was accused in a vast propaganda campaign of possessing the characteristics of a normal administrative functionary: he wanted efficiency, expected subordinates to comply with the directives of superiors, and selected personnel on the basis of their technical qualifications. Since opposition to the current stage of the revolution implies opposition to all former stages, he also was accused of, among other things, compromising with the Kuomintang and the Japanese, opposing the Great Leap Forward, and favoring the private economy—all, by the way, (objectively) false accusations. To complete the package of counterrevolution by proving that Liuism was not a political trend in the working class, Liu was branded a common criminal. Cadres are unavoidably counterrevolutionary, now and at all previous times; they persist, moreover, as Liu Shao-ch'i himself persists in the office of the president.

The need to rehabilitate some of the cadres for the three-way alliances obviously diluted the attack on bureaucracy, and it brought a new and disparate element to the campaign against the person of Liu Shao-ch'i.[21] In addition to being a symbol of revisionism, he became a scapegoat for everyone who was to participate in the stabilization of the Cultural Revolution. All factions of the radicals could be united in their hatred for him, and former cadres could regain their revolutionary credentials by repudiating him. The attack of the radicals upon the "good cadres," whom Liu was accused of persecuting, could be deflected by interposing this incarnation of evil.

The dissolution of the Communist Party and the Ministry of Public Security during the Cultural Revolution left the People's Liberation Army in possession of the only concentration of political power in the country. From Mao's point of view, this situation was not without its advantages, for over the years the PLA has been his favorite revolutionary association, a far from normal army charged more with education than with fighting or administering.

Although Mao has seen his military forces as primarily an instrument of revolution, over the years in response to the exigencies of the moment he has used them for a number of normal and unrevolutionary purposes. Prior to 1945, the Communist armies provided protection for the movement against the Kuomintang and the Japanese; from 1945 until 1949, they were employed to conquer the Chinese mainland; from 1950 until 1953, they fought a more or less conventional war in Korea; and, during the later stages of the Cultural Revolution and beyond, they have supplied most of the administrative framework that has held the People's Republic together. With the exception of guerrilla action in the pre-1945 period, these tasks have been inconsistent with Mao's concept of a true people's army.

Since the liberation of the masses must be by the masses, whenever revolution requires military force, as during the period prior to 1949, this force must somehow be applied by the people as a whole. In such situations, power means guns, but only guns in the hands of the revolutionary masses and guns suited for unstructured guerrilla action in a rural environment. In the final analysis, men always take precedence over weaponry, and reliance on military methods is only a variety of reliance on the elemental force of the masses. Even when military action is necessary, liberation is more than just dealing physically with armed counterrevolutionaries; it also includes an attack upon counterrevolutionary habits, institutions, and modes of thought. The job of the People's Liberation Army prior to 1949 was not solely to achieve military victory, and with its military victory its task of liberation was far from complete.

Whenever military action must be taken against an armed enemy, the revolutionary movement has to structure, organize, and routinize its physical force, and its army unavoidably diverges from an instrument of mass liberation toward a bureaucracy of an uncommonly dangerous type. From 1945 until 1949 and from 1950 until 1953, Mao believed he had no choice but to rely upon conventional military power; at all other times, he has tried to keep "professionalism" in the PLA to a minimum in order both to avoid its bureaucratization and to maintain its supreme usefulness as a tool of liberation.

Like many other utopians, Mao has seen the military style of life as an excellent education in revolutionary consciousness and perhaps even as a preview of the ideal society, and since at least the Yenan period the Communist army has been more a school for the people than an instrument of warfare.[22] Life in the army militates against bourgeois individualism: there is little privacy, responsibility is on a group basis, social differences are leveled down, communication is by means of simple slogans, and comradeship develops among people without natural ties to one another. In short, the physical and psychological pressures of barracks life and military routine facilitate the creation of a true and comprehensive community.[23] Service in the PLA has been a pretty thorough education in Maoism, and PLA graduates have usually been among the leaders of the revolutionary campaigns directed at the civilian population.

The education of the masses in revolution and the provision of organized physical protection for the People's Republic are basically incompatible tasks. The PLA, as a consequence, has become a classic instance of the unavoidable tension between ideology and normalcy under a revolutionary regime. Its operative units have been inefficient to the point of necessitating a defensive military strategy,[24] and its administration of internal affairs following the Cultural Revolution has brought it in direct conflict with important sectors of the population that it is supposed to educate.

Before 1945 the Chinese Communist armies operated as a military force only sparingly, but from 1945 until 1949 the Civil War required them to rely rather heavily upon military professionalism, especially since so many of their troops were defectors from the Kuomintang. After the conquest of the mainland, there was little time to reemphasize the educational function of the army before it was sent to Korea, an action that must have been very painful for Mao but one he felt obliged to take to defend Manchuria.[25] In Korea the Chinese soon learned that their usual reliance upon loose structure, political training, small-group controls, and hand weapons was inappropriate against an enemy with conventional discipline and organization and great firepower. Nonetheless, they retained a system of social interaction that did not recognize individual accomplishments, that produced anxiety in combat because of its pattern of surveillance, that humiliated soldiers by the devices of criticism and self-criticism, and that allowed no opportunities for the expression of discontent, with the result that their fighting efficiency was impeded through a loss of morale. Conversely, the need to follow professional military practices "made a shambles of political work in the companies."[26]

At the end of the Korean War, the PLA was probably more professional than ever before or since. After some hesitation, the party organizations in the army were completely overhauled in 1956. In the spring of 1957, the PLA Rectification Movement was initiated, to last throughout the Great Leap Forward. During this movement, professionalism in the army was subject to intensive criticism, and the special military "send down" *(hsia fang),* the "officers to the ranks," counteracted elitism and bourgeois military thinking. The army also was gradually relieved of its tasks in economic production, which had exposed it to too many bureaucratic influences. With the purge of P'eng Teh-huai in 1959, Lin Piao became minister of defense and moved the PLA sharply in the Maoist ideological, nonprofessional direction.[27] In June 1965, the abolition of ranks within the PLA was the final step in its "democratization" and thus deprofessionalization, precisely when United States military action in Vietnam was significantly intensified. This entire process was accompanied by the gradual dismissal of almost all the highest officers who ever had directed the PLA in its purely military capacity. None of these men actively opposed Mao's vision of a new society,[28] but their previous professional experience and responsibilities had made them ineligible to lead the PLA during the purely cultural stage of the revolution. To emphasize the military deficiencies of the Chinese army and the potential military threat of foreign countries, especially of the Soviet Union, indicated a severe deficiency of revolutionary logic.

Although by 1964 the PLA had been reformed to the point where the entire country could be exhorted to "learn from the PLA," it still contained remnants of military professionalism, including a tendency to favor "law and order." These impurities were attacked in the early days of the Cultural Revolution, when a call to "drag out the capitalist roaders in the army" was issued from revolutionary headquarters, and Red Guards and other activists attacked military stores, offices, and bases. Concurrently, a rather extensive and bitter purge of high-ranking PLA political officers took place.[29]

At the start of the Cultural Revolution, Mao intended to use the army only to guarantee the freedom of action of *ad hoc* groups like the Red Guards and revolutionary rebels, and he expected it to tolerate their attacks upon its own conservatism. This conservatism, however, was stronger than he had anticipated, and PLA local commanders were not especially pleased by the attacks upon themselves and by the "seizures of

power from below."[30] Things got even worse because, when a spontaneous revolutionary structure of power failed to materialize and the degree of confusion became unacceptable, the army had to be activated for
the daily business of running the country. In this situation, the army's "law
and order" orientation usually prevailed over its commitment to the mass
line, and apparently there was little that Mao and Lin Piao could do about
it.[31] Mao's success in smashing bureaucracy contained, as the saying goes,
its own contradiction, but it was only a nonantagonistic one.

During the chaotic height of the Cultural Revolution, as well as
during relatively relaxed times, the PLA's nonprofessionalism has prevented it from acting as an independent cohesive force in domestic politics. (Not even P'eng Teh-huai denied that the PLA was a weapon of
revolution.) The army has never been a threat to "take over" the country,
nor has it "taken sides" in the conflicts arising from the great campaigns.
Indeed, during these campaigns, including the Cultural Revolution,
there have been no "sides" but only severe tension between the Maoist
revolutionary thrust and the inertia of the regime's functionaries and
people, and the PLA itself has been highly susceptible to this tension.

Since the PLA, as an instrument of revolutionary education, has
never considered itself a potential agency of government or of "modernization," Mao has been able to use it to counteract other sources of power
such as the former Party apparatus. Furthermore, the soldiers of the
PLA, like everyone else in Communist China, have never been allowed
to forget their own counterrevolutionary impurities.

The driving force behind the most radical phase of the Cultural Revolution was an *ad hoc* body, the Central Cultural Revolution Group. The
power of the Central Group came principally from Mao's informal support, but the Group also benefited from the cooperation of Lin Piao, at
this time Mao's "closest comrade-in-arms" and heir apparent. When the
army had to be used to bring about some degree of social order, Lin was
forced to moderate his revolutionary fervor, a development that the
Cultural Revolution radicals saw as the "reestablishment of bourgeois
rule." The Central Group was soon purged and its leader, Ch'en Po-ta,
was declared an enemy of the people. (Its most famous member, Chiang
Ch'ing, the wife of Chairman Mao, escaped with only a self-criticism to
reemerge as a senior member of the regime's leading group and a prominent force in the anti-Confucius campaigns of the 1970s.)

The Central Cultural Revolution Group no doubt came into some
conflict with the army when the soldiers had to be used as administrators,
but there was a much more fundamental reason for its disappearance: it
had failed to bring about a new revolutionary structure by means of

seizures from below. As usual, the inherent creativity of the masses makes them incapable of error, so all failure is the responsibility of those who have led them. Whether the masses really are helpless without good leadership is a question that Mao has never answered.

To avoid the bureaucratization of the People's Liberation Army in the period following the Cultural Revolution, Mao has begun to build a new Communist Party that is, and is understood to be, no more than an instrument of the Chairman's will. Cadres and leaders purged both before and after the Cultural Revolution have been rehabilitated to staff the new Party, but a high percentage of its positions are still occupied by military personnel. To keep the People's Liberation Army from becoming too bureaucratic, it has been subject to constant criticism and self-criticism and the powerful men who directed its consolidation of the Cultural Revolution were relieved of their positions and possibly also of their lives. Lin Piao, his chief of staff, Huang Yung-sheng, four deputy chiefs of staff, and a substantial number of lesser military figures disappeared from power and from sight during 1971. The posthumous charge against them was "manipulating the army against Mao," and the Chairman has been in no hurry to select their replacements.

In recent years Mao has concentrated political power at the center; the Central Committee and the Secretariat have been eclipsed and the membership of the Politburo has been reduced from twenty-one to ten. The lower ranks of the Party and the army have been kept in constant flux so that outsiders, and no doubt insiders, too, cannot determine who is occupying which office, and even whether the office still exists. Dittmer has suggested that the device of permanent "mass representatives" on the revolutionary committees may have institutionalized the "participation of the masses" and thus the weakness of the apparatus.[32] As the official line put it after the end of Lin Piao, "The most fundamental thing is to obey the commands of our great leader, Chairman Mao. . . ."[33] It appears that the Chairman, far from having lost control in his dotage, eventually will leave China with history's most fluid arrangement of revolutionary power.

In reviewing the commentaries on the first twenty-five years of the People's Republic, one is struck by repeated statements to the effect that "this time Mao really has gone too far" and that the elements of sanity—represented usually (according to the time in question) by those wild old revolutionaries, Liu Shao-ch'i and Chou En-lai—surely now will prevail. Once, however, the Chairman had paused to deal with various unrevolutionary matters such as the food supply and especially to reconstitute and regroup the lower-level cadres, he usually proceeded to go even farther than he had gone before. Despite repeated talk about China's experiencing chaos and being in crisis, Mao and the People's Republic are still there. The Chairman's cult is in tolerable health, normal affairs are attended to, and the various anti-Confucius campaigns proceed on schedule.

Yet following the mass line has inherent limitations. The masses, at least under the circumstances of the world as it now exists, really cannot liberate themselves: leadership is indispensable and leaders (to be distinguished from chairmen) must have power, responsibility, and privilege. The unceasing attack by Mao and the masses upon anything extraordinary may be too much for any cadre to bear. Perhaps Lin Piao himself cracked under this pressure,[34] and Dai Hsiao-ai, the former Red Guard, defected from the People's Republic when he realized that he had been used by the movement to which he had given so much, and that the system required that everyone, from Liu Shao-ch'i to himself, be so used and then cast aside. He saw himself "ten years in the future confronted by a mob of rampaging students." He was repelled by the way that "life contradicted propaganda." He became cynical and interpreted the Cultural Revolution as no more than a struggle for power at the top. He came to believe that the revolution was receiving no firm guidance from the central leadership, especially from Chairman Mao himself, and his former worship of Mao made his disillusionment severe.[35] It appears that Mao's great scheme of bringing out the true nature of his uncounted masses has been impeded not only by the force of habit of his raw material but also by the methods he has adopted to overcome it.

Notes

1. André Malraux, *Anti-Memoirs* (New York: Holt, Rinehart & Winston, 1968), p. 375.
2. See James Pinckney Harrison, *The Long March to Power* (New York: Praeger, 1972), pp. 214, 342; Richard C. Thornton, *China: The Struggle for Power, 1917–1972* (Bloomington: Indiana University Press, 1973), p. 243.
3. Mao, "Talk at the Third Plenum of the Eighth Central Committee" (Oct. 1957), in *Miscellany of Mao Tse-tung Thought (1949–1968)* (Arlington, Va.: National Technical Information Service, 1974), pp. 73–74.
4. See the essays by Ying-mao Kuo, R. J. Birrell, and Thomas P. Bernstein, in A. Doak Barnett, ed., *Chinese Communist Politics in Action* (Seattle: University of Washington Press, 1969), pp. 222–223, 261, 432, 433, 397; and Yuan-li Wu, *An Economic Survey of Communist China* (New York: Bookman Associates, 1956), p. 501.

5. See Franz Schurmann, *Ideology and Organization in Communist China*, 2d ed. (Berkeley: University of California Press, 1968), pp. 191–92.
6. Ezra F. Vogel, *Canton under Communism* (Cambridge, Mass.: Harvard University Press, 1969), pp. 302–5, 322.
7. John Wilson Lewis, in Lewis, ed., *Party Leadership and Revolutionary Power in China* (Cambridge: Cambridge University Press, 1970), p. 1.
8. J. M. H. Lindbeck, "Transformations in the Chinese Communist Party," and Vogel, "Voluntarism and Social Control," in Donald W. Treadgold, ed., *Soviet and Chinese Communism: Similarities and Differences* (Seattle: University of Washington Press, 1967), pp. 85, 174; Barnett, *Cadres, Bureaucracy, and Political Power in Communist China* (New York: Columbia University Press, 1967), p. 442; Vogel, *Canton under Communism*, pp. 302, 322.
9. *The Case of Peng Teh-huai, 1959–1968* (Hong Kong: Union Research Institute, 1968), pp. 9–12; Jürgen Domes, *The Internal Politics of China, 1949–1972* (New York: Praeger, 1973), pp. 107, 112.
10. See William F. Dorrill, "Power, Policy, and Ideology in the Making of the Chinese Cultural Revolution," in Thomas W. Robinson, ed., *The Cultural Revolution in China* (Berkeley: University of California Press, 1971), pp. 30–32.
11. Merle Goldman, "Party Policies toward the Intellectuals: The Unique Blooming and Contending of 1961–62," in Lewis, pp. 268–303; Vogel, *Canton under Communism*, p. 290.
12. Dorrill, "Transfer of Legitimacy in the Chinese Communist Party: Origins of the Maoist Myth," in Lewis, pp. 69–113.
13. Arthur A. Cohen, *The Communism of Mao Tse-tung* (Chicago: University of Chicago Press, 1964), p. 202; Robert Jay Lifton, *Revolutionary Immortality: Mao Tse-tung and the Chinese Cultural Revolution* (New York: Random House, 1968), p. 91.
14. Gordon A. Bennett and Ronald N. Montaperto, *Red Guard: The Political Biography of Dai Hsiao-ai* (Garden City, N.Y.: Doubleday, 1971), pp. 24, 146; Victor Nee, *The Cultural Revolution at Peking University* (New York: Monthly Review Press, 1969), pp. 67–69, 74.
15. Louis Barcata, *China in the Throes of the Cultural Revolution* (New York: Hart Publishing Co., 1968), p. 106.
16. Lowell Dittmer, *Liu Shao-ch'i and the Chinese Cultural Revolution* (Berkeley: University of California Press, 1974), p. 114.
17. Dittmer, pp. 26, 39; Schurmann, pp. 537–40.
18. *Collected Works of Liu Shao-ch'i, 1958–1967* (Hong Kong: Union Research Institute, 1968), pp. 358, 363.
19. See Dittmer, pp. 54, 65.
20. See Jean Daubier, *A History of the Chinese Cultural Revolution* (New York: Random House, 1974), pp. 56, 121.
21. This paragraph follows Dittmer, especially pp. 155, 160, 170, 313, 320, 322.
22. James D. Jordan, "The Maoist vs. the Professional Vision of a People's Army," in William W. Whitson, ed., *The Military and Political Power in China in the 1970's* (New York: Praeger, 1972), pp. 26–27; Samuel B. Griffith, *The Chinese People's Liberation Army* (New York: McGraw-Hill, 1967), p. 76. See Mao, "On Correcting Mistaken Ideas in the Party" (1929), in *Selected Works of Mao Tse-tung* (Peking: Foreign Languages Press, 1965), 1:106.

23. Alexander L. George, *The Chinese Communist Army in Action* (New York: Columbia University Press, 1967), pp. 34, 61, 90; John Gittings, *The Role of the Chinese Army* (London: Oxford University Press, 1967), pp. 252–53.
24. Gittings, p. 262.
25. Allen S. Whiting, *China Crosses the Yalu* (New York: Macmillan, 1960), pp. 150–59.
26. George, pp. 71–76, 94, 101, 107, 211.
27. Dorrill, "Power, Policy, and Ideology," pp. 54–55; Jordan, pp. 32, 33.
28. Gittings, pp. 227, 233.
29. Domes, "The Cultural Revolution and the Army," *Asian Survey* 8 (1968):362–63.
30. Domes, "The Cultural Revolution and the Army," p. 356. Domes estimates that in six provinces the PLA actively supported power seizures, in five it was benevolently neutral, in nine it was strictly neutral, and in nine it gave no support whatever.
31. Dittmer, p. 149.
32. Dittmer, p. 355.
33. Quoted in Thornton, p. 339.
34. Dittmer, p. 358.
35. Bennett and Montaperto, pp. 216, 217, 224, 227, 147, 221.

V
Conclusion

*The world of immediate experience—
the world in which we find ourselves
living—must be comprehended, transformed, even subverted in order to
become that which it really is.*
HERBERT MARCUSE

14
Total Revolution

$\mathbf{A}$lthough the revolutionary regimes of Hitler, Stalin, and Mao have been far from identical in policy and structure, they have exhibited a basic likeness in their complete rejection of the scientific and social principles of what they call "bourgeois civilization" and in their determination to engender a higher and unprecedented kind of human existence. This shared revolutionary stance has been accompanied by a common set of fundamental principles of metaphysics, epistemology, psychology, history, and social analysis. In other words, National Socialism and the two Communisms have been based upon a very similar view of reality and existence, a view that has been an indispensable condition for their belief in the possibility and the necessity of total change. Each of the three revolutionary regimes, moreover, has sought the establishment of a "mass society," a solid and comprehensive community with a high degree of social equality or (better) similarity, and each has tried to implement its goal by an arrangement of power that stresses flexibility and fluidity, condemns administrative organization and other social systems, and involves the absolute preeminence of a single leader.

The total revolutionary has derived his rejection of the past and present, his commitment to a brand-new society, and even the basic outlines of his new society from certain beliefs and practices of bourgeois society that he has failed to understand completely, and therefore his derivations, although accomplished with consummate logic, have become tragic caricatures of the social order he has aspired to transcend. During certain critical periods of the twentieth century, this peculiar distortion of standard bourgeois ideas and institutions has been combined with vast political power, and currently, although no new combinations of this type are in sight, the ideology of the total revolutionary has an undeniable appeal to many social activists faced with an unpredictable future or an unacceptable present.

There is an impressive list of the common elements in the ideologies of Hitler, Stalin, and Mao: the tenets that history is determined and that progress is inevitable; the beliefs that the human psyche can be molded according to plan by the control of overt behavior and that "matters of the spirit" are meaningless abstractions (so-called materialism); the contentions that human history is in essence a history of conflict and struggle and that progress occurs only as the result of struggle; the theory that true understanding comes only by means of action and thus that to understand the world is to change it; the view that everything worth knowing can be known; the conception that each society is a tightly integrated whole of ideas and institutions vulnerable only to a force external to it; the persuasion that human nature is indefinitely plastic; and the conviction that, by an act of willpower, people who have comprehended the preceding simple truths about man and society can bring into being a new and higher stage of human development. In conjunction these beliefs form a logical and integrated worldview, a deformed but quite comprehensible version of the basic belief system of the age of science and representative democracy.

The prevailing belief of this age has been that human progress can be measured by the degree of humankind's ability to control its natural, social, and even psychological environment. Although such control is not presumed to have increased with perfect regularity in the past nor inevitably to increase in the future, the traditional cyclical view of history has been abandoned and the assumption is that, given appropriate motivation and proper care, science can steadily reduce those areas of human experience not subject to human control. The total revolutionary has reduced this view to the proposition that the past has been a straight-line development from lower to higher social and human forms and thus that "history" demonstrates that progress has been and will continue to be regular and inexorable. The "necessity" or "determinism" of his ideology comes from his transformation into an axiom of the empirical generalization that change and even progress have occurred, and it follows that anyone who obeys history's axioms cannot fail to meet with success. Although taking its departure from the science that has made the modern concept of progress meaningful, the revolutionary's determinism has risen grandly above its nonevaluative and tentative nature.

Materialism—the revolutionaries' claim that only overt behavior and the simple motives behind it are real, and their attack upon religion, theoretical physics, nonrepresentational art, and "idealism" in general—is a vulgarization of another aspect of the scientific approach to knowledge and reality. The control of the environment that so impressed Hitler and the Marxists has been in large part a result of the modern scientific method, and since this method usually has been considered applicable only to "material" things, the revolutionaries have inferred that only these things are real. If, moreover, all aspects of human life are reducible to the "material," no aspect is immune to deliberate efforts to control it and thus materialism supports determinism in persuading the total revolutionary of the ultimate success of his efforts.

Rejecting the fatalism of traditional society, the scientifically oriented human being has come to believe he can break free of the restraints of his physical and social environment and change his life for the better. This liberation depends ultimately upon an act of will, and the total revolutionaries, with their typical exaggeration, have concluded that nothing can resist their fanatical determination to move humankind to a higher stage of life. Unlike the normal bourgeois view, revolutionary "voluntarism" assumes that the revolutionary activist can break completely with the past and attain complete independence of the environment in which total change is to occur. Nothing can impede a will of iron, and voluntarism neatly complements materialism and determinism.

The optimism of bourgeois society has been transformed by the total revolutionary into the conviction that everything worth knowing can be known, and known "directly, immediately, and face-to-face"; in other words, man can unambiguously get at the "world of living essence." This conviction, which is both voluntarist and materialist, is not concerned with a higher kind of knowledge far divorced from mundane affairs; it involves a special approach to quite practical problems, if not of daily life at least of human society. In its most elegant form, this concept of total knowledge becomes the theory of the unity of theory and practice, that there is no understanding apart from action. The theory's implication that "to know the world is to change it" indeed attributes to humanity characteristics hitherto reserved for divinity, but, as Hitler put it with the unabashed arrogance of the total revolutionary, "man is becoming God."

The total revolutionary's concepts of society and of human nature similarly are outgrowths of bourgeois social science. Following its lead, he has abandoned the traditional model of society as divided into a ruling class and a ruled class, but he has doggedly retained the traditional idea that somehow society involves the exploitation of the larger part of its members. In accord with modern social science, the total revolutionary has seen society as a tightly integrated whole of social systems, beliefs, and values, and virtually every member of any society as unavoidably committed to its preservation. Such an integrated organism can be destroyed only from without, and the true revolutionary must therefore avoid all commitments to society. He can be perfectly asocial only by having no role in the society he is to destroy; he cannot rely upon social position in any sense but only upon his own insight and willpower. Following the so-called sociology of knowledge, the total revolutionary realizes that he must reject what his society accepts as knowledge, history, beauty, and the meaning of human life, because these serve only to reinforce that which he must transcend.

On the other hand, the total revolutionary believes that this social solidarity hides a basic antagonism between something he often loosely calls the "ruling class"—or the "bourgeoisie" or the "imperialists"—and the average honest member of the people. Again following modern social science, this ruling class, which will never voluntarily "give up its power," has no determinate membership identifiable through standard sociological analysis. It is rather an attitude that dominates society, and the current term, "the establishment," fits the concept very well. The basic antagonism thus turns out to be between all people, but especially those who have not got their share of the existing culture, and society itself. Society, despite its hold upon everyone, has been only a thin and artificial imposition upon human life.

The sociological theory that every idea is invariably a reflection of a total social situation has led the revolutionary to the position that no idea is politically neutral and to the concept of the objective enemy. It follows for him that the nonrevolutionary world cannot avoid actively seeking the destruction of his movement, for the very existence of revolution challenges the entire ideological and institutional edifice of the normal world. Representatives of the old order inherited by the revolutionary regime from its predecessor—such as Jews, capitalists, kulaks, and landlords—must be liquidated. When taken completely seriously, cultural relativism, another prominent strand of modern thought, unsurprisingly has terminated in absolute intolerance.

Since each society is a tightly integrated unity of institutions, practices, and attitudes, the individual person is in essence a reflection of his society and hence "human nature" can be defined only by reference to a specific social context. The historical progression of society from one type to another, moreover, has meant that upon the triumph of each social revolution a fundamental change has occurred in the nature of the human being. The total revolutionary has deduced from this interpretation of the past that human beings are indefinitely plastic and that their "psychologies" can be remolded by those who have correctly understood the past. He thus has neatly turned the basic liberal faith in the power of education against liberalism itself. Rather than representing the highest potential of human nature, the ideal citizen of bourgeois democracy, who has been "liberated" from preconceptions and prejudices, only exemplifies one of many possible psychologies and one, moreover, doomed to become extinct.

Since, according to the total revolutionary, each society has powerful forces of internal cohesion, he has difficulty accounting for change and thus for progress. To provide this account, he has stressed conflict and struggle, either real or invented, among societies or has seen latent contradictions within single societies that periodically become manifest and lead "dialectically" to conflict and to change. (Often the revolutionary, and especially the Marxist, uses a pseudo–social scientific approach to supplement his thesis of "latent contradictions," but the thesis is really a postulate and therefore only the revolutionary himself can correctly establish it.) The revolutionary's commitment to and his affection for conflict and struggle come in part from his realizing just how persistent the old social order can be, but they also derive from a misreading of the modern concept of competition. Clearly, he has failed to understand that the "struggle" involved in, for example, economic rationality and scientific probability rests upon a stabilizing consensus regarding the grounds of economic and scientific competition.

The total revolutionary believes he has discovered a principle of social cohesion vastly superior to that relied upon by normal societies, both traditional and bourgeois. Structuring human behavior by means of hierarchical social systems with their differentiations of roles and functions creates only a specious unity and results in the institutionalization of inequality and of the exploitation of man by man. Community sentiment, on the other hand, the unqualified identification of every individual with every other member of the society, has none of these defects, and it will hold the new revolutionary society together. There is implicit in this view more than a little reliance upon a true "human nature" shared by at least everyone eligible for membership in the "people" or the "masses."

The utopias of total revolution have been more or less extreme versions of mass society: they are devoid of social systems and they approach the structurelessness required by perfect similarity and true community. The spirit of community will hold them together, and they will be pervaded by a vast sense of togetherness. This sense will guide social and political participation. All standards for interpersonal relations will be determined by the spirit of community, and thus morality will become concrete.

This emphasis on community to the virtual exclusion of formal structure and hierarchy has some connection with a nostalgia for a golden age, but it also has some grounding in the total revolutionaries' recognition of the importance of community to the strength of bourgeois society. Despite some opinion to the contrary, representative democracies have developed the strongest sense of community ever to have existed in large groups, an awareness of shared common interest that, in its ability to support sophisticated political systems, has far surpassed the cultural, religious, and tribal senses of community that have preceded it. Hitler and the Bolsheviks did not commit the error of some recent would-be revolutionaries of underestimating the power of "nationalism." Indeed, they typically followed their logic too far by exaggerating the contribution of community solidarity to the strength of bourgeois society and interpreting this kind of solidarity as complete conformity. They thus failed to understand that the truly cohesive community can tolerate a high degree of individualism and that the diversity of bourgeois society is a measure of the strength rather than of the weakness of its community. Although the national community can live in harmony with other national communities because it does not expect an internal solidarity that forbids variety, the racial or class society cannot tolerate deviations and hence must see all outsiders as objective enemies. Again, total revolution overtly denies the existence of a universal human nature, and it considers the rights of man, which bourgeois society finds fully compatible with the rights of the citizen, to be logical absurdities.

The new and higher society will be a true mass society because once all normal social structures and differentiations are destroyed—once the establishment has been eliminated—only the masses (by definition) can remain. When the facade of normal social regularity, which is no more than exploitation, has been removed, the honest, pure, and elemental force of the masses will prevail. Here, as usually recognized, the total revolutionary is extending the earlier bourgeois challenge to traditional special privilege and the traditional autocratic ordering of society. As the bourgeoisie once condemned the social roles of the nobility as useless and obsolescent, so the total revolutionary condemns the roles of the bourgeoisie, from that of parliamentarian to those of physician and art critic. The bourgeois demand that low social status must not prevent the development of talent has been corrupted to the contention that talent is no more than a result of social differentiation and will become meaningless upon the disappearance of the stratified society. The demand for social mobility has been changed into the insistence that the conditions requiring social mobility be abolished.

The total revolutionary's true community is perfectly comprehensive and consequently thoroughly egalitarian: no social differences will remain; even authority and expertise, from the scientific to the artistic, cannot be tolerated. Such a radical egalitarianism must necessarily reject all individualism. The rights of the individual against the collectivity disappear, and normal constitutional rights are reinterpreted as rights to conform to the group. Claims against the group—to material goods, to restricted human relationships such as love, and to privacy—are condemned as divisive. In the name of equality, there is postulated a community of such solidarity that it can be said to have a consciousness of its own, and individual consciousness becomes at best an antisocial deviation.

This kind of community, the "we" that is to replace the multitude of "I's," may appear to be a simple paleolithic reaction against the painful and slow historic process of removing impediments from the individual's freedom to develop his own personality, an impression reinforced by the revolutionary's antiscientific stance and reliance on willpower. Yet the attack upon individualism in the name of equality has long been recognized as a reduction to absurdity of certain premises of liberal-bourgeois society. The political democracy of bourgeois society implies the equality of every citizen regarding a limited number of interests considered relevant to the maintenance of political society. This kind of equality, and of course the community underlying it, have been essential to bourgeois individualism, which, unlike the withdrawn and isolated individualism of traditional society, depends upon a high degree of human cooperation. The total revolutionary's misunderstanding, ignorance, and dislike of bourgeois society have led him to mistake the means for the end and to see individualism as an obstruction to complete "equality." Hence, not just a few common interests but every aspect of everyone's life becomes relevant to the maintenance of society, and the truly egalitarian mass culture becomes mandatory.

It is not easy, however, to be completely selfless and thus indistinguishable from everyone else. Although the total revolutionary believes people to be capable of absolute selflessness, and even (unconsciously) to desire it, no person is ever entirely free from attitudes derived from the era of individualism and exploitation. The requirement of absolute similarity can tolerate no deviations; membership in the "people" is strictly defined and therefore difficult to attain. No previous political theory has matched the purity of the theory of mass society, with its austere concept of "enemies of the people." Under total revolution, the intolerance implied by unqualified egalitarianism has come to full fruition.

The total revolutionaries claim that the true community they have envisioned is in some sense willed by the people who will eventually become its members. These "masses" have only tenuous connections with the establishment; they are people who, no matter what their objective socioeconomic status, have little real commitment to the old society whose forms they only automatically and unenthusiastically abide by.

The new society cannot appeal to the masses' normal desires for peace, prosperity, and happiness, since these values are determined by the old exploitative order and thus serve as opiates of the masses. The new society's values will be those of strict egalitarianism and selflessness, and because the masses, like everyone else, have never experienced such a society they cannot wish for or even understand its values. Nonetheless, the advent of the total revolutionary's utopia is willed by the masses because it corresponds exactly to their own true nature. In short, the famous desire of the masses for revolution is only a deduction from an *a priori* definition of human nature. When the revolutionary "follows the vital laws of the masses," he merely draws logical conclusions from his concept of the human being as a thoroughly communal animal.

Virtually all the evidence supports the statement that whatever widespread support the three great revolutionary movements received prior to their capture of state power occurred for reasons having little to do with the movements' ultimate goals. After the revolutionary regimes had been established, moreover, their most radical programs met with little popular enthusiasm and much popular opposition. Hitler accounted for this resistance by describing the masses as passive and without spirit and thus incapable of understanding revolutionary necessity. Lenin was more theoretical in his conclusion that the masses can never transcend the perspectives of existing society, and Stalin agreed that if left to their own devices the masses would form trade unions and engage in capitalist production. Neither of the Bolshevik leaders had the slightest illusion about the popularity of Soviet Communism's great economic programs, and Himmler took for granted the social isolation of the SS.

Mao, in contrast, has insisted that the masses desire and will the means to his Communism as well as its goals, and he has accounted for the resistance, for example, of the peasants to collectivization and communization in terms of the cadres' failure to follow the mass line. By introducing the principle of bureaucracy to explain away awkward facts, Mao has avoided, as Hitler and Stalin did not, a considerable ideological impurity. Perhaps his reasoning has been that the Chinese masses' exposure to both traditionalism and imperialism has been so superficial that they are capable of more than mere sympathy with his efforts to move them in a direction that accords with their own nature. In any event, he has properly avoided taking a stand on the celebrated basis of facts.

Many ordinary people may well have been attracted by the complete security that would result from the loss of individual identity in the perfect community, but there is no reason to believe that most of them have been unaware of the cost of such an escape from responsibility. The subjects of the revolutionary regimes we have examined have demonstrated a remarkable ability to adjust to their policies of homogenization, but it does not follow that, given a choice, they would prefer these policies. The total revolutionary, however, is constrained by his logic to claim that he is doing only what the *Volksgeist* demands. As has often been pointed out, the bourgeois-democratic principle that the legitimacy of political society depends upon an almost unanimous popular acceptance of its general principles (or constitution) has prompted the invention of a "general will" that accepts all specific actions of the society's agents, no matter how the individual members of the society appear to feel about them. This general will—or, in revolutionary parlance, the vital laws of the masses—can be deduced by those who understand the essence of human nature. Since the total revolutionary is only striving for the goal that the masses really desire and only using the methods absolutely required by this goal, the masses ought to be dancing for joy at his policies and thus, in contrast to the bourgeois order that rests upon a superficial and nonvital popular consensus, his regime has genuine legitimacy. Once again, iron logic and true simplicity have taken the bourgeois political tradition in an unanticipated direction.

The Communists and National Socialists have not been alone in ignoring the facts of modern political life and relying upon deductions from a definition of human nature in terms of a fundamental desire for complete social homogeneity. The self-styled "new democrats" of the Western world confidently predict that the common man will eventually realize that bourgeois democracy is no more than a mask for traditional privilege, and the more genuine traditionalists have despondently seen bourgeois democracy as the prelude to a complete and thorough social, intellectual, and cultural leveling. By committing themselves to the same premises, those of the Ortegian "revolt of the masses," both have refused to acknowledge that the behavior of the ordinary person in bourgeois society demonstrates his rather sophisticated appreciation of the need for both social similarity and social differentiation.

The consummate solidarity and homogeneity of the mass society prohibit specialization, expertise, professionalism, and administrative hierarchy. Strictly speaking, every social action should be action by the whole society, it should be popular action in the sense that no one "participates" any more or any less in it than anyone else. The all-embracing phenomenon of culture will be created by the masses themselves, or at least drawn directly from their experiences and sentiments. Ideally, the masses will become their own artists and their own physicians, as well as their own employers and their own governors. Since they will be expressing their own feelings, diagnosing their own illnesses, determining their own jobs, and ordering their own behavior, breakdowns in "communication" will be impossible. No longer will anyone be presented with a painting or a prescription or an assignment or a policy that he cannot understand. This state of affairs not only will mirror the true desires of the masses, but its correspondence to the elements of human nature will enable it to transcend in power, effectiveness, and efficiency any social arrangement hitherto known. Its very lack of structure, however, means that the new society's methods of operation cannot be anticipated in any detail. It will not proceed according to a plan, but spontaneously and voluntaristically.

This notion of full participation is obviously an extension of the liberal concept of the participation of all citizens in certain phases of the bourgeois-democratic political system. The possibility that representative government might degenerate into rule by plebiscite has long been recognized, but total revolution has carried this possibility one step farther. During the period of transition to the ideal society under the great revolutionary regimes, the act of asking for an overt popular response has been eliminated, and the masses "rule themselves" by providing the spirit or consciousness that is manifested in all policy. As a result, the goals of revolutionary policy are blended in both theory and practice with the methods used to accomplish them.

Although no totally revolutionary regime has been able to free itself completely of administrative organization, all have been remarkably successful in minimizing their reliance on it. The references of outside observers to the "politics" of these regimes are inappropriate, for the shifting patterns of power within them have little resemblance to the politics of the normal world. The activities of those who have social power take place within no defined area; the use of social systems has been reduced to a bare minimum, and even the concept of the state has been abandoned. Bargaining, compromise, and the other practices of ordinary politics are of only secondary importance in an arrangement that operates by command from above. And, although struggles for power certainly occur among the regime's functionaries, the classic revolutionary purge is designed not to eliminate opposition and rivals but to attack in one way or another the very principle of organizational power that creates the functionaries.

The attempt to put into practice the theories of mass participation and antibureaucracy has led the revolutionary regime to both the concept and the fact of the single omnipotent and omniscient leader. If leadership is needed during the transition to utopia, clearly the only way to avoid bureaucracy is to vest complete power in a single person who cannot possibly exhibit bureaucratic characteristics, who is antibureaucratic by definition. The view is the same from the bottom up: if participation is to be equal and universal and precisely express the true nature of the masses, a unanimity is required that, again, at least during the transitional period, can be had only when a single person is the sole interpreter of the spirit of the masses. Thus the leader becomes a substitute for the masses, and the continuous plebiscite of "participatory democracy" becomes a series of the leader's autonomous decisions. Total revolution has brought to full fruition the recognized tendency of complete participation to develop into complete autocracy. In the most advanced form of the leadership principle, the leader and the masses become as one; in all forms, the adulation the people accord to the leader is in essence a praise of themselves.

During the transition to the true mass society, the full identification of the leader and the masses is not possible because the normal world requires the interposing of functionaries, cadres, and generally bureaucrats. The combination of at least semirational administration with the leadership principle leads to enormous confusion and inefficiency in conducting the nonrevolutionary normal business of society that the regime cannot ignore, but the revolutionary program itself can still be pursued with determination, proficiency, and remarkable success. The fluidity of power in the totally revolutionary regime provides its leader with a degree of autocracy only dreamed about by traditional despots concerned solely with the perfection of existing society. Once the leadership principle is established, it is almost impossible for anyone to escape its logic.

Those who are to be members of the new society must be drawn from a limited group of ordinary people, for in practice the revolution cannot include all of humankind and some people may be more amenable than others to incorporation into the specific collectivity to be constructed. One of the vital laws of the masses, moreover, is that in his heart the average person cannot accept the bourgeois humanist concept of a universal human nature, or the principle of human brotherhood of the

traditional world religions. Each of our three great revolutionary movements has brought a specific concept of the future community to a
specific preexisting demographic situation and thus has had to select the
raw human material for its social experiment in its own way.

For Hitler, the problem was to create the Aryans, whose sense of
racial identity would enable them to attain the bliss of complete solidarity. Although all people are aware of racial differences and thus capable
of racial consciousness, the concrete problem was to make this potential
an actuality in Germans and other "Germanics" under the influence of
the bourgeois national community. These people had a number of common physical and cultural characteristics that would facilitate their acquisition of a sense of race, but their principal appeal to Hitler was that they
were both temporally and physically available. Although he often
thought in terms of Europe, it was to him only a vague cultural entity the
Aryans were to take to its next stage of development and a geographical
area the Third Reich was to occupy for solely practical reasons. The
military policy that was such a large part of his revolutionary scheme was
designed both to destroy national consciousness in Europe and to obtain
living room for his new order.

Stalin's problem was to create a population of working peasants,
intelligentsia, and laborers by means of massive changes in the forces and
relations of production. Once the Bolshevik coup and the Civil War had
proved that the Russian Empire was ready for revolution, Stalin had at
his disposal enough human and other resources, including relative isolation from the rest of the world, to begin to construct socialism "in one
country." The country itself, its people and its territory, had no special
connection with the pursuit of the revolution. The Russian or the
Ukrainian was no more responsive to the appropriate conditions of
production than anyone else—he had nothing resembling the Germanic's potential for Aryan racial consciousness—but he was available
and there was no point in not using him. Workers and peasants of other
countries were equally good raw material; when they became available
through Leninist coups or Soviet military occupation, the revolution
could be applied to them as well.

Mao, on the other hand, could select the subjects for his experiment
in mass society from a group that already possessed its own latent principle of cohesion. He did not have to do anything comparable to making
Germans into Aryans or Russians into workers, for his Chinese, with
their common "racial instinct," already had a natural feeling of identity
upon which his new society could be based. He thus could proceed
directly to the education of his subjects in community consciousness; he
required no policy comparable to the Final Solution and the First
Five-Year Plan. His Great Leap Forward was designed not to create

sympathetic workers but to remove structural obstacles to the full "to-getherness" of the already sympathetic Chinese. Like Lenin before him, Mao's initial problem was to capture control of an internationally recognized entity, but unlike Lenin, once he had succeeded, he had a naturally revolutionary demographic entity. As a consequence, he has had no interest in adding new people to his new society.

The total revolutionary's efforts to bring about the next, inevitable stage of human history unavoidably occur during the present, necessarily obsolescent stage. Although he demonstrates his understanding of this present stage by acting to eliminate it, this action comes up against a number of specific environmental restraints; although he indeed may ignore what lesser men consider to be facts, these facts do not, so to speak, ignore him. As a consequence, his revolutionary drive has been compromised and corrupted.

Total revolution is not dependent upon advanced technology to gain and maintain control over its own people. Devices for rapid communication have been the only necessities, and radios, telephones, and aircraft can be imported by very "undeveloped" countries. Technological sophistication is also not required to bring rudimentary literacy to a large population, in case revolutionary education is to depend on the written word. The revolutionary regimes, nonetheless, unavoidably have had to compromise with the bourgeois principles of technology and expertise.

Some of this compromising of revolutionary drive has occurred because not even the leadership principle can eliminate the need for normal social systems, especially the economic system. This limitation must not be overemphasized, however, since total revolution has demonstrated a remarkable ability to resist the demands of technology in these areas. The principal technical constraint upon the regimes here examined has come from the presence of a world outside the sphere of their methods of control—from, that is, international and regional political systems. Their inability to avoid eventual entanglement in the normal power relations of interstate politics has obliged them to utilize the methods of bourgeois expertise in military, economic, and diplomatic affairs. Each regime became established during a period when the interstate system in its area was in dilapidation, but this advantage eventually dissipated. After World War II, the Soviet Union experienced another brief period of isolation when the construction of a nuclear arsenal, an activity having only a minimal impact upon socialist culture, appeared to be the only required response to the international situation. The nuclear stalemate, however, meant that technical rationality could no longer be restricted to the nuclear laboratories and the missile sites. Although the fulminations against "capitalist encirclement" and "cultural imperialism" are thus quite justified, the remarkable thing again is how well bourgeois expertise has been resisted in matters such as international economics.

Compromises with bureaucracy also are unavoidable. When "bureaucracy" refers to the rational allocation of functions and responsibilities in order to accomplish some large but specialized task, the problem is one of expertise. In another sense, however, "bureaucracy" refers to a very untechnical desire for some kind of stability in human relationships. The Soviet family circle best exemplifies the ubiquitous human predilection for an understood position and an acknowledged status, a bit of individualism that not even the artifices of Chairman Mao seem sufficient to overcome.

The principal goal of the total revolutionary has been precisely to educate his subjects away from the normal preference of both modern and traditional people for individual identity in a structured society and to remold the human psyche into a fully synthesized part of the social collectivity. Although on a number of occasions in the past, as when bourgeois society replaced traditional society in Europe, some significant changes have occurred in the basic belief systems of certain portions of humankind, it does not follow that the specific changes the total revolutionary has in mind and his effort to effect them deliberately and "from above" will prove feasible.

The total revolutionary's educational program is hampered, on one level, by the ideological difficulty that he cannot precisely anticipate the kind of human nature he wishes to engineer into being. On the more important practical level, his program must be applied to vast numbers of people who have matured within the old society and whose daily lives even under the revolutionary regime are constantly shaped by the normal social systems, such as the family and the economy, the regime has been unable to dispense with.

The revolutionary may try to avoid these practical problems by withdrawing a small segment of the population from normal life in order to transform it into an embryonic new society. This method had limited success under National Socialism, but the SS was, to say the least, not appreciated by the nonelite peoples of the Third Reich and many SS men, including Himmler himself, were willing to come to terms with the old order as the military situation deteriorated. Under Stalin, the political police and others most responsible for the maintenance of the revolutionary drive tended to become cynical and amoral.

When the total revolutionary concentrates on remolding the entire population under his control, his success appears to be at best negative. Stalin's use of revolutionary terror seems to have resulted in the perhaps fatal weakening of traditional and bourgeois attitudes, but it probably has failed to replace them with true socialist morality. Mao's comprehensive thought reform has been efficient enough, but there is little reason to suppose that it will have a lasting effect. It is virtually impossible to imagine his successors sustaining his educational program at the level of intensity necessary to prevent the habits of hundreds of millions of people from reasserting themselves.

The efforts of the total revolutionary are limited by normal attitudes in another, rather ironical way. Frequently enough, he receives support from his own population for reasons that work directly counter to the thrust of his education: some may acknowledge his regime because, like good traditionals, they defer to all sources of political power; others may see him as a nationalist or a modernizer; and still others may follow him to improve their own personal prospects or because they appreciate his efforts to improve general living standards. In all such cases, these people are inadvertently resisting the revolutionary's efforts to move them to a new level of consciousness. To a lesser extent, the tolerance he receives from outside fellow travelers, who tend to interpret his actions in bourgeois terms, and his acceptance into various international social systems blunt his revolutionary action or dilute his revolutionary message.

In all the above circumstances, the total revolutionary's attempt to remold humankind is impeded by social factors. Another impediment may be the possession by the individual human personality of an element that resists the destruction of its uniqueness. Perhaps, under carefully controlled conditions, the "I" can be totally absorbed into the "we," but whenever people have had a choice in the matter they appear to have seen the "we" only as a means of augmenting the "I." One need not be committed to a rigid concept of "true human nature" to conclude that the total revolutionary is trying to change something very basic in what used to be called civilized humanity.

The revolutionary regime depends for its force and stamina solely upon its own internal resources, and revolutionary change can tolerate no relaxation. Since the regime's great strength, and thus the meaningfulness of its ideology, depend upon the leadership principle, there is real doubt about its ability to survive beyond the lifetime of the single person who created it.

At the present time, only the Soviet experience has been relevant to this question, and although it obviously can support few firm generalizations, some reasoned speculation is not out of the question. Upon Stalin's death, there disappeared not only the revolutionary leadership principle but also the power to hold the Soviet Union together as a normal domestic and international political entity. In responding to this situation, Khrushchev—a far from negligible ideologue, as his *agrogorod* and virgin-lands policies attest—achieved his personal predominance by concentrating an unprecedented amount of power in the apparatus of the Soviet Communist Party. As the Chinese Communists were quick to recognize, this arrangement of power did not reestablish the leadership principle in order to carry on the revolution but established bureaucracy and consequently could lead only to revisionism. The exigencies of the international political system, and recently the international economic system as well, have reinforced revisionism, and the Soviet Union has become an unimaginative dictatorship that can only repress its own population and play power politics in the world arena. Throughout the post-Stalinist period, the Soviet leaders have been unable to come to terms with the inconsistency of their revolutionary Stalinist heritage and their constantly increasing concessions to the normal world.

The foremost theoretical question regarding the succession is whether Khrushchev, or anyone else, could have avoided introducing the fatal germ of bureaucracy as a response to the power vacuum created by Stalin's demise. Although this question cannot be answered with much confidence, Khrushchev's arrangement of power, retained by his successors, may have been necessitated by his inability to destroy everything that Stalin had built without seriously jeopardizing the position of the Soviet regime in the world political system, its dominance of its satellites, and some of its own normal but essential domestic social systems. To reinstitute the unity of theory and practice, a complete reconstitution of "Soviet power" was required; everyone who was to possess any kind of power had to become dependent upon a new leader. Stalin himself did not have this problem when he moved to succeed Lenin, for Lenin had just begun the construction of "Soviet power" and, moreover, had only rudimentary commitments to normal foreign and domestic social systems. Stalin's method of quasi hierarchies, however, may have created too much solidified power to enable one of his successors to become leader in his own right. Without a true leader monopolizing power, revolutionary ideology was bound to decay.

Although the more fluid power arrangement devised by Mao may have avoided such a potential for bureaucratization, it may make, in another way, his revolution's continuance dependent upon his own existence. Mao's ideological preeminence, his claim to a perfect understanding of history and the masses, depends not only upon his superb ability to simplify and to follow iron logic, but also upon the absence of all impediments to his exercise of this ability. Among the most important impediments are potential ideological rivals; if Lenin had had time to perfect "Soviet power," Stalin certainly would not have been available as his successor. In other words, Mao's brilliant handling of the problem of bureaucracy necessarily has involved the most thorough turnover in personnel of the three revolutionary regimes. His superior unification of theory and practice may well mean that his revolution will not outlive him. At the moment, the most reasonable expectation is that, assuming China does not once again disintegrate after the Chairman's death, a revived Party apparatus or the People's Liberation Army before long will follow the bureaucratic, revisionist path of Khrushchev and Brezhnev.

State power has been captured by the total revolutionary when his society has been suffering from an incongruence between its beliefs and its institutions. Certain social systems have lacked corresponding beliefs to make them meaningful, and certain beliefs have had no social systems to make them effective. Before harmony could be restored by the creation of new values or new methods, the total revolutionary—recognizing, as no social scientist could, the potentialities of the situation—had intervened and deflected, at least temporarily, events from their normal course.

During such a tinsel-free period, the total revolutionary may gain a rather large popular following, but the evidence indicates that his typical supporter does not even know what the ultimate goals of the movement are. Since the total revolutionary is offering something different from both the traditional and the bourgeois-democratic, the social experiences of normal people cannot give rise to anything resembling "social classes" predisposed to the new order he has in mind. There is, moreover, no justification whatever for proclaiming that the masses appreciate the revolutionary's "logical and comprehensive world view" just because they are temporarily without one of their own. They have no capacity to recognize a new world view; the best they can do, until they have experienced the thorough education of the revolutionary movement in power, is to try to interpret the ideology and the promises in terms of their own, most normal aspirations. Their uncertainties, indeed, may strongly incline them to attempt such interpretations, but, as most revolutionaries recognize, this response is at best an expression of sympathy.

The revolutionary's conviction that beneath this sympathy, deep in the masses' subconscious, exists a commitment to the perfect social collectivity cannot in this context be dismissed as fantasy. The average person's response to the drift of a tinsel-free period may be based in part upon his desire to gain the certainty of a merging with the collectivity. On the other hand, once the total revolutionary gains power, he must wage a constant and probably losing war against the normal traditional and bourgeois forces of individualism. If the vital laws of the masses do imply the perfect community, the masses prove unwilling to pay the costs of realizing this implication, and they use their great powers of inertia to resist its consummation.

In recent years, ideas and organizations reminiscent of the great European revolutionary movements of the 1920s and 1930s have appeared in North America and Western Europe. Ideology, pronounced dead a decade ago on the grounds that advanced societies had only to decide upon the means of arriving at generally agreed upon goals, has experienced a rather significant revival. Those who wrote that epitaph did not see that the very success of technology would initiate a transitional period not unlike those that gave Bolshevism and National Socialism their opportunities to seize power. As the problems of material existence have come to appear solvable, the goals of social effort and indeed the meaning of human life have required redefinition or at least refinement.

In responding to this basic social and human uncertainty, the contemporary ideologues of the Western world have followed the great revolutionaries of a generation ago in seeing science, art, education, and all other aspects of contemporary capitalist democracy as purely relative to this society, and in rejecting them in the name of an imminent revolution vague in its details but certain to usher in a mass society under the label of "participatory democracy." Politics has made a sustained effort to take command of expertise, especially in the academic world, where the "new democratic theory" is not an effort to understand contemporary society but a blanket condemnation of its commitment to structure through social systems.

Despite the vigor of this ideological movement, the experience of total revolution strongly indicates that ideology has no force of its own, that an effective rejection of the past is conditional upon the unity of theory and practice, that, in short, revolution depends upon the utilization of the power of the contemporary state, a power that average people consider normal and appropriate for both domestic and international life. Experience further indicates that, prior to its seizure by the revolutionaries, the state power available to them was badly organized and ineptly used. Since the current Western world seems to contain nothing approaching the futility of the Weimar Republic or the Russian Provisional Government, the chances are very good that the institutions of the "industrial" era will be able to adjust themselves gradually, during a generation or two, to the conditions and expectations of "postindustrial" society. Contemporary revolutionaries in so-called developed societies have been forced to adopt measures that are opportunistic when they are not desperate, measures that would have horrified Lenin and Hitler. The ideology of the 1960s and 1970s appears destined to serve only as an inadvertently constructive challenge to the rationality and individualism of bourgeois thought.

The prospects for the less developed areas of the world are probably not quite so favorable, since most of them lack stable institutions and experienced personnel to direct their transition into the modern era. This institutional instability has enabled men, including many professional soldiers, who like Chairman Mao reject both tradition and bourgeois democracy, to obtain state power. Yet most of these sometimes rather impressive ideologues thus far have brought about only relatively superficial and possibly transitory changes because they have been unable to control areas and populations large enough to support the cost of making total revolution in a nonrevolutionary world. Their power has been restricted, in the final analysis, because they have had nothing comparable to the Chinese "racial instinct" and the Chinese "Empire" that were essential to the success of Maoism.

Although the total revolutionary is correct when he states that in the past the forms of human society have undergone fundamental change and that contemporary society in its turn will some day be transcended, both the higher new society he has envisioned and the methods he has used to approach it can be condemned without hesitation. According to the estimates previously given, about 110 million people have died in the name of the three revolutions, and the amount of additional physical and mental suffering they have caused defies the imagination. A full evaluation of this cost depends upon a careful comparison with the costs of other great social changes, such as the bourgeois and industrial revolutions, and this comparison cannot be made here. Nonetheless, a partial evaluation can be based on the consideration that this cost has been willfully and premeditatively incurred by groups of self-appointed visionaries who have scorned the methods of experimentation and adjustment and who have openly believed that they act on a historical level beyond the conscious comprehension of the ordinary person. The total revolutionary thus has been unable to justify his goals to those whom he controls, and he has spurned the kind of popular support sought by normal politicians. He has claimed that he only pursues what the masses desire in their hearts, but he alone can interpret this subconscious urge. The only promise he can make, as he expends, perhaps reluctantly but with the professional dispassion of a general of the army, dozens of millions of lives, is that the normal standards of happiness and well-being are obsolescent and their replacement inevitable. His contempt for the discoverable opinion, interests, and values of humankind is confirmed in its arrogance by his pretensions to an infallible insight into historical necessity. It follows that those who do not share his vision are not merely mistaken but outside the pale of humanity.

The methods of the total revolutionary can be faulted even on his own terms, for his failure to usher in the new society seems patent. The most lasting effect of Hitlerism seems to have been the strengthening of bourgeois democracy not only in Germany but in all of Western Europe. Lenin and Stalin are hardly justified by a contemporary Soviet regime and its satellite countries and parties that aspire only to an enforced and dull conformity, and there is not much evidence that, upon his ultimate departure, Chairman Mao will leave the Chinese people any closer to the true mass society than they were when he began to reform them more than a generation ago.

Although most normal people probably are repelled more by the total revolutionary's arrogant presumption than by the nature of the new humanity to which he has called them, the perfectly homogeneous mass society, as many of our best writers of fiction have insisted, is repressive, retrogressive, and repulsive. The total revolutionary, although a product of the twentieth century, has missed much of the significance of the twentieth century. He has not understood the characteristic modern blend of the individual and the community and, by seeing them instead as incompatible, has opted for a collectivist utopia in which everyone is to do nothing but maintain a meaningless preoccupation with the similarly purposeless affairs of everyone else. This lack of a real goal of human life gives the utopias of the total revolutionary a distinctly archaic flavor.

The isolation and parochialism of traditional individualism are unquestionably impediments to the proper human condition, but the community must supplement rather than replace the individual. The total revolutionary has failed completely to understand the impersonal trust that the institutions and social systems, such as courts and savings banks, of the detested bourgeois society have provided. He has not realized that principles of morality are not mysteries explaining the unknown or rationalizations of exploitation but understandable and usually understood principles of interpersonal behavior. It is tempting to go farther and see him as a personal misfit who has never been able to experience the support that well-ordered societies can give to the individual personality. He has felt alone, and his loneliness has led him to see with crystal clarity that all institutions and social systems are only liberal-democratic devices to keep human beings apart. Not all the contemporary Western admirers of Chairman Mao, nor their ideological fathers who admired the *Führer* and Comrade Stalin, have possessed the logic of these great revolutionaries. Too many have thought that freedom can be had once oppressive social systems have been destroyed; too few have realized that in the perfect community the idea of freedom will no longer be meaningful.

Index

247

Total Revolution was edited by Lloyd W. Garrison;
copy editing by Judyl Mudfoot; proofing and entire production
supervision by Paulette Wamego.
Text design: Shelly Lowenkopf,
Cover design: Valerie Huston.
Composition: Variable Input Phototypesetter using Garamond
for text and display, set by Holmes Composition Service, San Jose, Calif.

Offset by Edwards Brothers, Inc., Ann Arbor, Michigan, on 55 pound book
natural stock, opacity 92, bulking at 390 PPI.

Binding, also by Edwards Brothers, uses Kivar 6 over boards for the casebound
edition, 10-point Carolina C1S for the paperbound edition.

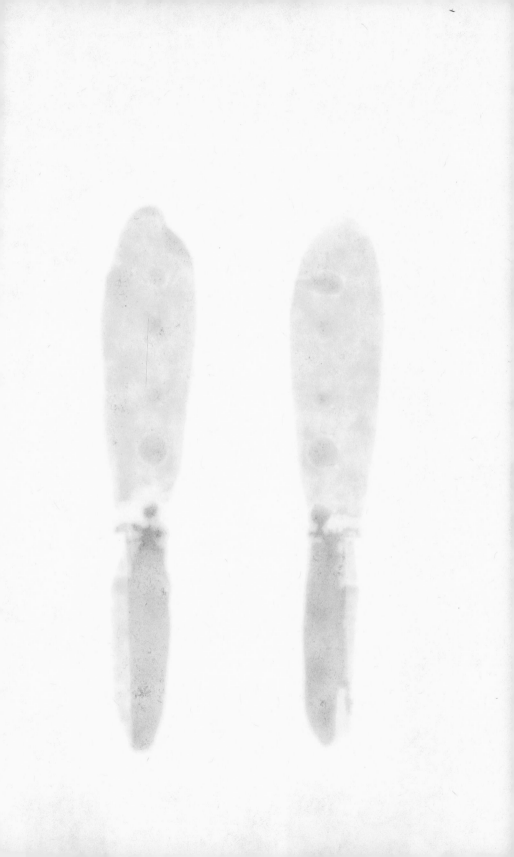